P9-AQQ-628

PENGUIN AFRICAN LIBRARY

Rhodesia: White Racism and Imperial Response

Martin Loney was born in 1944 and grew up in Bradford.
He studied politics and economics at Durham University
and later took an MA in political science at Simon Fraser
University, Vancouver. He has been vice-president of the
National Association of Labour Student Organisations,
President of the Canadian Union of Students, Director of
Research for an international voluntary organization and
General Secretary of the National Council for Civil
Liberties. He has contributed to many journals including
the *New Statesman*, *Race Today*, *The Times Higher
Educational Supplement* and *Race*.

MARTIN LONEY

Rhodesia: White Racism and Imperial Response

Penguin Books

Penguin Books Ltd, Harmondsworth,
Middlesex, England
Penguin Books Inc., 7110 Ambassador Road,
Baltimore, Maryland 21207, U.S.A.
Penguin Books Australia Ltd, Ringwood,
Victoria, Australia
Penguin Books Canada Ltd,
41 Steelcase Road West, Markham, Ontario, Canada

First published 1975
Copyright © Martin Loney, 1975

Made and printed in Great Britain by
C. Nicholls & Company Ltd
The Philips Park Press, Manchester
Set in Monotype Plantin

To the living

It is not seemly for you to
Mourn,
It is not seemly for you to
Delay;
You have received a legacy
Soaked
In the heart's blood of your brothers.
The pregnant deed
Waits
For you.

The time,
Burdensome,
Presses upon your necks.
Wide burst
The gates
Of bright morning!

ERNST TOLLER

Contents

Contents

Chronology of selected events

1888 Matabeleland and Mashonaland were declared British spheres of influence. Rhodes secured a concession from Lobengula granting exclusive mineral rights in Matabeleland and Mashonaland.

1890 The British South Africa Company (BSAC) occupied Mashonaland.

1893 The BSAC defeated the Ndebele and occupied Matabeleland.

1896 The Shona and the Ndebele revolted against rule by the BSAC.

1898 The BSAC finally broke the revolt. The Southern Rhodesia Order in Council established a Legislative Council to govern the territory. The BSAC continued to occupy the dominant position.

1923 In a referendum, Southern Rhodesia rejected union with the Republic of South Africa but opted for self-government.

1924 Coghlan, who had led the campaign for responsible government, became the first Prime Minister elected under the 1923 Southern Rhodesian Constitution Letters Patent.

1933 Huggins became Prime Minister of the Reform Party government which laid the basis for a ruling inter-class coalition which survived until 1962.

1953 The Federation of Rhodesia and Nyasaland was formed.

1955 The formation of the City Youth League
        marked the birth of mass nationalist politics.

1957 The African National Congress (ANC),
        headed by Joshua Nkomo, became the major
        nationalist movement.

1958 Prime Minister Garfield Todd was forced to
        resign by his own party because of his
        'liberal' approach.

1959 In February, a state of emergency was
        proclaimed and the ANC banned.

1960 The National Democratic Party (NDP),
        successor to the ANC, was founded on
        1 January.

1961 A Constitutional Review Conference to
        determine Southern Rhodesia's future was held
        in London. Under the new constitution there
        were two electoral rolls which ensured the
        election of Africans to the Legislative
        Assembly. The proposals were rejected by the
        NDP who said they paved the way for
        independence without majority rule. In
        December the NDP was banned and the
        Zimbabwe African Peoples' Union (ZAPU)
        was formed.

1962 In September, ZAPU was banned. The
        Rhodesian Front led by Winston Field won
        the Southern Rhodesian elections.

1963 The nationalist movement split, and ZAPU
        dissidents formed the Zimbabwe African
        National Union (ZANU). ZAPU loyalists
        responded by forming the People's Caretaker
        Council (PCC).

1964 Winston Field was replaced as Prime Minister
        by Ian Smith who, Rhodesian Front members
        felt, would take a firmer line on the demand for
        independence from Britain. ZANU and the
        PCC were banned.

1965 On 11 November, the Rhodesian government

made a Unilateral Declaration of Independence (U D I). The British government invoked selective sanctions.

1966 British Prime Minister Wilson and Rhodesian Prime Minister Smith discussed terms for the restoration of 'legality' on H M S *Tiger*. The United Nations imposed mandatory sanctions against Rhodesia.

1968 On board H M S *Fearless*, British Prime Minister Wilson and Rhodesian Prime Minister Smith again discussed terms for the restoration of 'legality'.

1971 British Prime Minister Alec Douglas Home presented new proposals for a 'settlement'.

1972 The Rhodesian Pearce Commission found the proposals for a settlement unacceptable to Africans. In December, the Rhodesian liberation movements undertook significant attacks in the border areas. Rhodesia's export trade exceeded pre-U D I levels.

Acknowledgements

I would like to thank a number of friends who assisted in the preparation of this book, in particular: Mark Amen, Carol Moran, Denyse Glasscock, David Macgregor, Peter Findlay, Barbel Helwig, Dorothea King, Bill Kaye, Paul Walton, Roger Egglestone, Ian Taylor, René Lampsas, James Beckett and Henrietta Resler. In addition, I would like to thank friends in Southern Africa who must be nameless.

Introduction

The late 1950s and early 1960s saw the rapid decolonization of Africa. Generally the transition was peaceful; uniquely in Algeria it came as a result of a prolonged military confrontation with the colonial power. Ten years later Rhodesia remains colonized, no longer controlled by the imperial power but still governed by white settlers.

It is the argument of this book that the continuance of white domination in Rhodesia can only be understood in a historical context. The colonization of Rhodesia and its subsequent development were in crucial respects different from the pattern in other British colonies. The massive presence of white settlers was not unique to Southern Rhodesia; nor was the method of colonization – the granting of a charter to a private company. But Southern Rhodesia was unique in that as early as 1923 it became a self-governing colony, with its own parliament and its own police force and army.

The political power wielded by the white settlers enabled them to establish a pattern of race relations which ensured that in every respect the Africans served white interests. Colonization in any form is undertaken in the interest of the colonizing power; but the presence of a large number of settlers, intent on establishing themselves in the country, produces dynamics substantially different from those inherent in the process of extending imperial trade and investment. These dynamics led in the Americas to a successful revolt against the British and Spanish colonizing powers, and in Rhodesia to a unilateral declaration of independence in 1965. The Rhodesian state has reflected the development of a relatively independent, stratified white society, based on the exploitation of the indigenous population, with a legitimating ideology of white superiority.

The purposes of trade and investment can be served by any form of rule, black or white, which is able to maintain stability and is favourable to free enterprise. In the nineteenth century direct rule was important as a protection for the interests of one imperial power against another, while the existing political structures of the colonized state did not generally lend themselves to formal control. Today the pre-eminence of the United States, and the growth of multinational corporations, has fundamentally transformed the nature of imperialist rivalry. The creation by the colonial powers of 'nations' in Africa and Asia, with centralized administration and the infrastructure necessary for trade and investment, has obviated the need for direct imperial control. Formal political power has passed from the imperial metropolis to the former colony; and economic power has shifted too, with domination by the former major imperial powers challenged by others, such as the United States, Japan and even, on occasion, the Soviet Union.

This process has taken place without any major dislocation of the international economy or any set-back to corporations with substantial trading and investment interests in the Third World. The instability in the latter years of colonial rule has given place to the relative stability of independent governments, governments which, whatever their nationalist protestations, show remarkably little inclination to challenge the hegemony of foreign capital. Frantz Fanon has described this colonial bourgeoisie well:

In its beginnings, the national bourgeoisie of the colonial country identifies itself with the decadence of the bourgeoisie of the West. We need not think that it is jumping ahead; it is in fact beginning at the end. It is already senile before it has come to know the petulance, the fearlessness, or the will to succeed of youth.

This bourgeoisie is too weak to stand and administer its own state. Instead, it hides behind the moral authority of the great leader 'in whose shelter the thin and poverty-stricken bourgeoisie of the young nation decides to get rich'. Nationalism and anti-colonialism become the rallying-cry of an aspirant ruling class which 'waves aloft the notion of the nationalization and

Africanization of the ruling classes ... until the bourgeoisie bluntly puts the problem to the government by saying "We must have these posts!! ..." From nationalism we have passed to ultra-nationalism, to chauvinism, and finally to racism.'[1]

Uganda's President Idi Amin is among the clearest examples of this phenomenon. His military coup against the somewhat more radical Milton Obote was swiftly recognized by the British government and rewarded with a substantial increase in aid. Amin is able in the same speech to suggest the liberation of Rhodesia by the joint forces of Kenya, Uganda and Tanzania; to threaten Tanzania with invasion, if certain demands are not met; and to accuse Tanzania and Zambia of being penetrated by communists. The rhetorical flourishes exist alongside a policy ensuring that the exploiter's face in Uganda is black and not brown.[2]

There was one group, however, for which the development of a black government favourable to private enterprise could not be the major criterion in determining the political future. For white settlers, the maintenance of white control was synonymous with their own survival. Where the settlers were a relatively small group composed of professional large-scale farmers and businessmen, the threat posed by decolonization was not fatal. But to those whites whose economic well-being rested on a basis of laws and administrative practices discriminating against African competition, decolonization sounded their death-knell. Where the white farmer is protected by laws which deny Africans access to large areas of farm land and by policies which favour white rather than African agricultural produce, African rule is an immediate threat. The same policies which favour the white farmer create a large class of Africans whose only recourse is to work for low wages on white farms. The repeal of discriminatory legislation would not only terminate the white farmers' monopoly of the best land but also enable more Africans to farm independently and in consequence put up the wages necessary to attract farm-workers.

For the white working class in clerical or blue-collar jobs, majority rule means the end of racial job restrictions which protect the high living standards of European artisans. The larger the European group involved, the less skilled its members, and the greater the degree of segregation in land and labour, the more calamitous appears the prospect of a black government. For the white doctor or university lecturer, independence in itself would not create competitors for his job; and if competition did arise, then jobs with similar salaries are available elsewhere. For the white bricklayer or train-driver, with the prime marketable asset of his 'whiteness', there seems no future but degradation under majority rule.

In 1923 self-government gave the European settlers in Rhodesia political control. Henceforth, Rhodesia's racial policy would not be decided by civil servants and politicians in London, but by the local white electorate. This electorate was quick to make racial policy the key issue. The government reflected a coalition of white class interests excluding those who consistently espoused complete racial segregation. This coalition, which gave the 1950s a retrospectively 'liberal' image, was finally broken in 1962 with the election of the Rhodesian Front, which today holds all but one of the European seats in Parliament. Where once a very gradual transition to majority rule, led by the white bourgeoisie in coalition with the African middle class, appeared as a strategy, today the permanent institutionalization of white supremacy is the dominant movement, with the white working class in the vanguard. The multinational corporations have lost much of their influence. The white bourgeoisie is no longer able to set the pace. The stage is set by the Rhodesian Front, and the bourgeoisie is restricted to urging the kind of policies which would be acceptable to the white electorate and yet allow Britain sufficient cover to recognize the legality of independence and end sanctions.

The international perspective has also changed since the 1950s. Where once South Africa was seen as a temporary aberration in a continent soon to gain its independence, it now stands at the centre of an imperial white supremacy encompassing Rhodesia, Mozambique and Angola, dominating the political life of Lesotho, Botswana, Swaziland and Malawi, in triumphant occupation of Namibia, and extending a well-greased palm to any other African country prepared to take it. With avowedly revolutionary movements fighting in Mozambique, Angola and Guinea-Bissau, and with the nationalist movements of Namibia, Rhodesia and South Africa itself well to the left of those which came to power in the recently independent African states, the strategy of international capital is further complicated. The determination of the white supremacists to retain power is clear. For them there can be no peaceful transition to a loyal black bourgeoisie. Now the political initiative has passed from the hands of bourgeois nationalists to those who have learnt in the struggle that political independence without a revolutionary transformation is an empty victory.

For both the Labour Party in power and the Conservative Party in power, British interests have seemed remarkably similar. Briefly, in Southern Africa, these interests have been synonymous with the interests of the many British corporations investing and trading there. British governments waged an eight-year war to prevent communists from coming to power in Malaya. They were not prepared to send a single British soldier to Rhodesia to prevent the illegal seizure of power by a white minority government. The reason, I will argue, is that while in Malaya the interests of British capitalism could never be served by a communist government, in Rhodesia, and inevitably in Southern Africa as a whole, there is no fundamental threat to the interest of capital from white power, even though British capital might well prefer an alternative, more stable, political and economic system.

Western governments have had to come to terms with the white supremacist governments. Arms are sold to Southern Africa, Western credit and military equipment enable the Portuguese to continue their fight in Africa, the United States purchases chrome from Rhodesia, Western trade and investment in the white-dominated countries increases. Rhodesia remains the disorderly element, its government exercises effective control of the country but it is officially recognized by no other nation; exports have surpassed the pre-U D I level but the United Nations mandatory sanctions remain. Western politicians, conscious of public opinion at home and in the Third World abroad, have pursued a strategy of cooperation with the white supremacist governments hand in hand with ritual denunciations of racism and apartheid. The recognition of Rhodesia threatens dangerously to expose the hypocrisy and so the search for some face-saving formula continues. It has been a search so far frustrated by those same factors which have proved so decisive in Rhodesia's history: the power of the white settlers, and their intransigent hostility to any move which threatens to undermine the permanence of their position.

This book is about the historical development of that power, the systematic use which has been made of it to build a prosperous white society in Africa, and the consequent impoverishment of the African population. It is also about the complicity of British governments, Labour and Conservative, in this process. The record, it is hoped, will give cause for second thoughts to those who have faith in the underlying justice of Britain's parliamentary system and the wisdom of British parliamentarians.

1 Conquest

History will have its say one day – not the history they teach in Brussels, Paris, Washington or the U N, but the history taught in the countries set free from colonialism and its puppet rulers – Patrice Lumumba

Studying the colonization of Southern Rhodesia is a tortuous process, for it involves a careful unravelling of several myths created, accepted and propagated by the conquering whites and reflected in subsequent histories. One recent historian, for example, writing on the first war against the Matabele in 1893, fully endorses the description of Lobengula, King of the Ndebele, provided by a contemporary colonialist: 'He was a savage in the fullest sense of the word.'[1] It is a description which tells us much about the writer and nothing about Lobengula.

Even sympathetic writers are apt to fall into the trap and accept the historical myths. Philip Mason commented that 'every Mashona held his life from the Matabele under a suspended sentence of death'.[2] In fact, many Shona had no contact with the Ndebele. But it was in the interests of the early white settlers to claim that Lobengula had control over the territory in Mashonaland which they occupied on the basis of the dubious Rudd and Lippert concessions, just as it was in their interest, having occupied these territories, to present themselves to the world as protectors of the peaceful Shona against the warlike Ndebele.

It is important to summarize the early history, for it clearly reveals the moral basis of the white man's current control.

African society before the British invasion

The African population of Rhodesia, at the time of colonization, can be roughly divided into two groups: the Ndebele and the

Shona. The Ndebele, who were otherwise known as the Matabele or the Amndebele, were a breakaway Zulu group, given their name by Basuto clans ('those who disappear, disappear behind their shields'). They had arrived in what is now known as Matabeleland around 1840. The Shona were a more diverse group and included all those who spoke a dialect of Shona. They were resident in both Matabeleland (some of them in fact becoming incorporated into the Ndebele state), and also in what is now called Mashonaland. The Shona-speaking peoples appear to have been resident in Southern Rhodesia for more than 1,000 years prior to colonization, occupying the area between the Zambesi and the Limpopo rivers, stretching eastwards to the sea.

In the fifteenth century, the Mwene Mutapa dynasty was established in what is now north-east Mashonaland and held sway over neighbouring tribes. The Mutapas were to become the first victims of European imperialism. By the seventeenth century, they had become Portuguese puppets; and by the eighteenth century, there was little trace of their former empire.

The Portuguese were driven out by a second major Shona empire, that of the Rowzi Mambos. The Mambos developed a complex and stable political and economic system which left permanent evidence of its sophistication in the famous Zimbabwe ruins. The society which they organized was hierarchical and no doubt contained great distinctions of wealth and status; but it also appears, at least until 1830, to have been generally peaceful and prosperous. Certainly the Rowzi empire was based on a level of social organization which subsequent white settlers preferred to believe was beyond African capabilities.

The stability of the Rowzi empire was disrupted by the attack on the Rowzi Centres or Zimbabwes by a breakaway faction from the Zulu state. The actual destruction of Rowzi power was accomplished by a faction under the leadership of Zwangdaba, who killed the ruling Mambo and destroyed the Zimbabwes. This faction did not settle in the area but was soon followed by another under Mzilikazi who, in the early 1830s, established a state modelled on Zulu lines, in what became known as Matabeleland.

Mzilikazi, who had moved north after conflict with the advancing Boer trekkers, exacted from the neighbouring peoples tribute which, when necessary, was collected by raiding. Contrary to the views put forward by some historians,[3] raiding was not carried out indiscriminately against neighbouring tribes but largely against those who refused to acknowledge Ndebele sovereignty and to pay tribute.[4] There were in fact many Shona-speaking areas which rarely came into contact with the Ndebele and where the traditional Shona paramounts continued to reign unchallenged. The picture presented by Glass of the 'degenerate' Mashona, subject to constant Matabele raids which 'became mere expeditions of robbers, seizing cattle, tribute and youths', with fighting 'limited to the slaughter of women and old men' provides a typical justification for colonization. It certainly does no justice to the historical evidence.[5]

The situation, then, which existed at the time of the occupation of Mashonaland by Rhodes and the pioneers was one where a strong Matabele state, based on a mixture of pastoral farming and agriculture, tribute and the proceeds from raiding, occupied the southern part of Rhodesia centred in Bulawayo. In the northern areas, various Shona paramounts held sway over a society in which agriculture was much further advanced and where raiding played a relatively small part in the life of the tribes. An attempt by the Ndebele to gain control over, or at least to exact tribute from, central Mashonaland had been successfully repulsed. The Ndebele state was not strong enough to dominate areas far from its centre.[6]

The Ndebele state was much more centralized than the empire of the Rowzi Mambos. This centralization was based on the king's control over the military regiments, which in turn were the basis of the different Ndebele towns. While the Shona chiefs held ritual and hereditary claims to their offices, the Ndebele indunas owed their position to the king's appointment. The Ndebele nation was organized on a caste rather than on a tribal or clan basis, with the original Nguni element forming the higher caste, captives who had been integrated into the structure prior to settlement in Matabeleland, in the middle, and recent captives at the bottom. An important aspect of the king's economic power was his control over the cattle of the Ndebele nation, which could be entrusted by the king to different kraals or families for care, but the control of which remained ultimately in his hands. Terence Ranger writes that the king's authority 'depended upon control of cattle and captives rather than on control of the land; the basis of Ndebele political organization was military rather than territorial'.[7] This military basis of the Ndebele state was to be important in the developing conflict with the whites:

> Raiding was still an integral part of the Matabele system at the time the challenge came. The economy relied heavily on cattle captured in war ... The subordinate leaders, especially the younger men with a position still to win, sought captives as a means of building up their power and prestige while the rule, apparently somewhat relaxed during Lobengula's reign, that regiments had first to win their spurs in battle before being allowed to marry also helped to make raiding self-perpetuating.[8]

The importance of the martial spirit and raiding resulted in two particular problems for the Ndebele king Lobengula. The young Ndebele had to be prevented from attacking the whites, while the continuance of raiding, which Lobengula regarded as 'indispensably necessary to the preservation of his power and the political existence of his people', ultimately provided the British South Africa Company (BSAC), who colonized Mashonaland with an excuse to destroy the Ndebele kingdom.[9]

Lobengula exercised a great deal of arbitrary power, often in a very brutal fashion – though arguably no more brutal than some of the methods which have been used at various times for dealing with social deviants in Europe, and certainly less brutal in scale than the methods which were subsequently employed by white imperial powers. Philip Mason argues that the cruelty of Lobengula was most often put forward by early white visitors to his court as the major barrier to closer relations between the Africans and the whites.[10] If this was indeed the case, one can only wonder at the hypocrisy of those who in a few years, with an apparently untroubled conscience, would be mowing down the Ndebele and Shona with machineguns, and dynamiting the caves where they had hidden, young and old, women and children.

In contrast to the Ndebele kingdom, the Shona paramountcies

appear to have been more peaceful and more egalitarian. A recent writer, drawing largely on the oral tradition, has given us an account of the Vashawasha people who lived in an area near Salisbury. Popular memory may have embellished the 'good old days', but there seems no doubt that the Vashawasha people were peacefully settled in a prosperous area of the country. The governing system was based on a considerable degree of popular discussion and consent. There was only one raid by the Ndebele, and the outcome of that appears to have persuaded the Ndebele themselves that any attempt to advance their sovereignty into the area would prove a dangerous undertaking. There were rivalries between different Shona paramounts which frequently erupted into raiding and skirmishes, but these were the exception rather than the rule.[11]

Religion was of great importance in the life of both the Shona and the Ndebele (who appear to have adopted much of the Shona religious system). The supreme god was known as Mwari or, in Matabeleland, the Mlimo. In north-east, central and parts of western Mashonaland, a system of spirit mediums served as a connection with dead ancestors and, on occasion, as nature spirits or manifestations of Mwari. The paramounts and tribal elders would frequently visit the local spirit mediums bearing gifts and seeking advice on important tribal affairs. Indeed, this was an important part of their responsibilities and a source of their legitimacy, for the mediums spoke for important royal ancestors and other dead tribal figures like Dzivagura, a famous rainmaker. As subsequent events amply demonstrated, the role of the spirit mediums was not purely limited to religious affairs; in many ways they acted as a link between the different tribal groupings and were, on occasion, called on to settle differences between them. Certainly, they were in an excellent position to comprehend the developments and problems of the different Shona communities.

Given the role of the spirit mediums in providing what has been called '"the tender bridge" between the living and the dead',[12] it was to be expected that they would play a major role in seeking to rebut the assault on ancestoral integrity which the European settlement constituted.

The religious system predominant in Matabeleland was based upon the idea that God took a close and personal interest in the welfare of the tribe which he expressed through the officers of the cult. 'Mwari speaks through or inspires the utterances of the chief officer of the cult, the Mouth; he receives petitions from another high officer, the Ear, and information from a less important officer, the Eye.'[13]

The dead played a very important role in Shona life, watching over and rewarding or punishing the living. In turn, the land which the Shona occupied, being the land of their ancestors, had a sacred quality. Thus the invading Europeans were not only robbing the living but also offending the dead. When the Europeans first arrived in Mashonaland, they were welcomed as temporary visitors. As an African historian writes: 'It never occured to them that their land could be taken ... this was due to the Mashona concept of land as being something very sacred – *cinon yera* – belonging to the whole tribe and to be held in trust by the chief and elders whose duty it was to allot it to those who needed it.' Those who took the land outraged the spirits of the ancestors, who would rise to meet the challenge. As the Shona said: '*Rejayi vatore zwinonyera* – let them take away that which is so sanctified that it cannot be taken away.'[14]

The white man in the Zambesi – the Portuguese

The nineteenth-century colonialists were not the first white men who had had designs on central Africa. In 1415 the Portuguese had captured Ceuta, and established a base on the African continent. In 1505 they had secured a foothold in Mozambique, and by 1507 had gained control over large areas, hoping to secure the gold trade previously in the hands of Arab merchants.

Eager to by-pass the Arab traders and find out more about the potential wealth to be gained from the Mwene Mutapa dynasty, the Portuguese dispatched Antonio Fernandez, the first white explorer of Southern Rhodesia. Some years later, his expedition was followed by a Jesuit priest, Goncalo da Silveria. After an initial success, Silveria was strangled at the court of the Mutapa, apparently at the instigation of Arab traders who feared Portuguese competition. Eight years later, in 1569, the Portuguese sent out an expedition to take reprisals – an expedition rich in examples of what Christianity's civilizing mission in Africa would be like. A number of Arab traders were killed, some impaled, and others hacked to pieces. The party was able to reach the Mutapa who, anxious to use Portuguese fire-power to strengthen his disintegrating empire, agreed to cooperate. In 1607, the Mutapa entrusted the expeditionaries with some of his children to be raised as Christians, and gave his mines to the Portuguese in return for military aid. It is an open question as to which of these acts the Portuguese believed more valuable; for though the second promised immediate wealth, the first opened up the prospects of permanent control. By 1629, after thwarting an attempt at rebellion, the Portuguese had successfully installed a puppet Mutapa, at whose court they appropriately built a church and baptized their acolytes.

Despite a number of reversals, the Portuguese maintained a tenuous hold in the area until the last decade of the century, when the expanding Shona empire of the Rowzi Mambos drove the Portuguese towards the coast, breaking the back of the Mwene Mutapa empire. Though the Portuguese continued to trade in the area, they were never to regain their former position. And, indeed, Portugal left little to show for its abortive colonial venture. Africans look back with pride on their resistance: 'The success and determination of Shona resistance should be rated as an epic struggle against European power . . . Shona resistance can only underline a very high level of political, social and military organization.'[15]

The role of British missionaries

Like the Portuguese, the next aspirant colonialists also claimed religious motivation. The British religious revival of the late eighteenth and early nineteenth century was well suited to provide the ideological arm of the colonial process. It was in general led by men less taken with the necessity of confronting the brutality of contemporary industrialization in Europe than with preparing for the kingdom of God. It was a perspective that was to prove as useful to capitalism abroad as at home.

The London Missionary Society had been established in 1795, and it was this society which in 1816 sent Robert Moffat out to Southern Africa. In 1829, Mzilikazi, hearing of Moffat's activities, invited him to his court. But he refused to let Moffat preach, concerned at the destructive effect that Christianity would have on the social fabric of Matabele life.

By 1860, Robert Moffat had established the first white settlement in Matabeleland at Inyati, though Mzilikazi would not allow any missionaries into the tributary Shona areas. In any event, even with a permanent settlement, 'the mission made no head-way until white frontiersmen conquered the country'.[16] This situation encouraged the emergence of the missionary view, expressed by Robert Moffat's son John, that 'there will be no change for the better until there has been a breaking-up of Matabele power and a change in the whole régime'.[17] In 1893, at the start of the Matabele war, the Reverend R. W. Thompson, Foreign Secretary of the London Missionary Society, was moved to oppose the physical annihilation of the Ndebele in these terms: 'Indeed it would be great folly, on economic grounds, to think of such a thing. All that is needed is that the tyranny under which they live should be broken and a different government substituted for it.'[18]

From the beginning of organized white settlement, the missionaries were closely identified with the settlers, whose spiritual needs they cared for. They were grateful to the colonizing efforts of the British South Africa Company for making mission work possible by subjugating the uncooperative indigenous population and they came to depend on the BSAC to provide the land on which the mission stations were built. The view which the African population had of the missionaries and their work is evidenced by the fact that in the African revolts in 1896 'mission stations, alien Christian Africans and indigenous Africans loyal to the missions were made a particular object of attack'.[19]

Early treaties

Missionaries were not the only pre-conquest visitors to the Ndebele kingdom. Hunters, traders and explorers were often active there. In 1834, Dr Andrew Smith, the founder of the Royal Society, made a journey from Cape Town into the interior and was authorized by the government of the Cape Colony to exchange gifts and letters of friendship with the local chiefs. Moffat presented him to Mzilikazi, and on his return to the Cape Smith was accompanied by Mzilikazi's senior councillor, Nnomdata, who, on 3 March 1836, entered into a treaty of friendship with the British government through the Governor of Cape Colony.

The treaty with the British proved of little value when, four years later, the Ndebele were driven north by the Boer trekkers. A subsequent conflict with the Boers took place when an Ndebele *impi* (or military regiment) crossed the Limpopo in 1847. The Ndebele signed treaties with the Boers, though it is extremely doubtful that the Ndebele agreed to the humiliating terms which the Boers presented to the world. In making written treaties, the illiterate Ndebele were inevitably at the mercy of white honesty, a quality which in Africa generally took second place to self-interest. Lobengula was given to remark: 'The white man is, indeed, the father of lies!'[20]

Rhodes and the scramble for Africa

In the 1880s, the Boers and the British were competing to establish a sphere of influence in Lobengula's kingdom. Lobengula looked to the Boers to provide him with assistance against Khama in Bechuanaland, a British ally who was rejecting Ndebele sovereignty. In 1887, a further treaty, the Grobler Treaty, was signed between Lobengula and the Transvaal Republic. This produced some concern in Cape Town; Cecil Rhodes, who had already made his fortune with De Beers Mining Company and was soon to become Prime Minister of the Cape Colony, argued that Britain should declare Matabeleland and Mashonaland protectorates. This would insure that the exploitation of these areas would be undertaken by British enterprise. Rhodes was especially alarmed that the Boers were already claiming the right to mining concessions on the basis of the Grobler Treaty.

The Reverend John Moffat, son of Robert Moffat, was sent to Lobengula to obtain information about the Grobler Treaty and to seek a treaty that would grant Britain sole rights of influence in the area. Moffat was authorized by Sir Sidney Shippard, administrator of British Bechuanaland, to assure Lobengula 'that Her Majesty's Government has no wish either to obtain possession of his country or to interfere with his sovereign rights'. Indeed, Moffat was to argue that a treaty with Britain would secure Lobengula 'against insidious attempts or open aggression' upon his kingdom.[21] Moffat succeeded in securing a repudiation of the Grobler Treaty in favour of a new treaty with Britain. The Transvaal Government ignored this development and sent the treaty's author, P. Grobler, as their first ambassador to Lobengula's court. Grobler never arrived. He was killed by a war-party sent out by Khama, who was acting on information from an assistant of Rhodes to the effect that the Boers were massing for an attack on the Limpopo.[22] The route to British ascendancy was now open.

Rhodes was interested in Matabeleland and Mashonaland for a number of reasons, not the least of which was his general and passionate interest in expanding British imperial control. In a will written at the age of twenty-four, he envisaged the empire covering 'the entire Continent of Africa, the Holy Land, the valley of the Euphrates, the Islands of Cyprus and Candia, the whole of South America, the islands of the Pacific not heretofore possessed by Great Britain, the whole of the Malay Archipelago, the seaboard of China and Japan, and the ultimate recovery of the United States of America'.[23]

In this grandiose vista the taking of Mashonaland was an indispensable element, for, as Rhodes told Sir Sydney Shippard, 'if we get Mashonaland, we shall get the balance of Africa'.[24] On a more worldly level, Rhodes, who had a very clear understanding of the relationship between power and money – using money to buy power and power to make more money – believed that

Mashonaland contained gold resources which would dwarf those of the Transvaal Rand. These resources would both enrich Rhodes, the capitalist, and strengthen Britain's economic base in Southern Africa, where the boom on the Rand threatened to shift the balance of power away from the Cape Colony to the Transvaal Republic.

The British attitude to imperial expansion varied with the government and indeed with the dominant commercial interests in any particular government. British imperial policy has been aptly summarized as 'trade with informal control if possible, trade with rule when necessary'.[25] There were those, like Palmerston, anxious to cut back on the expense of empire, and those, like Colonial Secretary Joseph Chamberlain, eager, with Rhodes, to paint the map red. In many ways, however, the personalities were secondary to the historical moment, for in Southern Africa there were other dynamics which would have forced even a Palmerston to take action. As two writers on British imperial policy have noted, Britain

exhausted all informal expedients to secure regions of British trade in Africa before admitting that further annexations were unavoidable ... The granting of charters to private companies between 1881 and 1889, authorizing them to administer and finance new regions under imperial licence, marked the transition from informal to formal methods of backing British commercial expansion. Despite these attempts at 'imperialism on the cheap', the foreign challenge to British paramountcy in tropical Africa and the comparative absence there of large-scale, strong, indigenous political organizations which had served informal expansion so well elsewhere, eventually dictated the switch to formal rule.[26]

The last decades of the nineteenth century were decisive in the scramble for Africa. The discovery of diamonds in Griqualand West had led to its annexation by Britain in 1870. The gold boom in the Transvaal, which necessarily fortified Boer independence and threatened Britain's long-term paramountcy in Southern Africa, had led to intensified efforts to contain the Republic and deny it access to the sea. The proclamation of a German protectorate in South-West Africa in 1884, and the extension of German interests in East Africa, had brought a new power into the area. The Portuguese, too, were continually eager, if unable, to realize their historic claims.

A further factor in Southern Africa was the strong expansionist pressure from the local settlers, led by Rhodes. The impetus for the colonization of Mashonaland came from the Rhodes group; the war with the Matabele was provoked by the Rhodes group; the invasion of the Transvaal in 1895 was initiated by the Rhodes group; and it was this same group which did so much to make the Boer War inevitable three years later. Rhodes was quick to argue that if Britain did not advance northwards, the Boers, the Portuguese or the Germans would do so, that the reputed mineral wealth of Matabeleland and Mashonaland should be retained in British hands and that the area was of important strategic value in the struggle for the control of the African continent. This last point should not be underestimated, for while Britain may at times have had second thoughts about building an African empire, there had never been any doubts that India, the jewel of the Empire, and one worth £50m. annually to the British balance of payments, must be protected. The Nile Valley, the Indian life-line, had to be secured from foreign influence, and this gave the rest of Africa added significance.

In 1885, in order to prevent German or Boer control of the Cape Colony's road to the interior, the British dispatched an expeditionary force to eradicate the Boer republics of Stellaland and Goshen. The region closest to the Cape was declared a Crown Colony, and the remainder of Bechuanaland a British Protectorate. If either the Portuguese or the Germans had been successful in linking their possessions in the South East and South West – Mozambique with Angola, or Tanganyika with South-West Africa – Britain's position in Africa would have been severely jeopardized. By offering the device of a chartered company, Rhodes could spare the British government the cost of empire while ensuring the paramountcy of British interest. It was a device favoured by Rhodes himself, who did not care for too close an interference from Westminster.

The Moffat Treaty, appropriately witnessed and interpreted to Lobengula by C. D. Helm, a missionary in Rhodes's pay, committed Lobengula to 'refrain from entering into correspondence or treaty with any foreign state or power, to sell, alienate or cede any part of his territory without British approval'.[27] It is doubtful that Lobengula realized that these were the terms he had accepted. But the treaty was sufficient to ward off other foreign powers and to allow Rhodes to move onto his second objective: securing for himself the supposedly vast mineral resources of the region. Rhodes then sent a group headed by C. D. Rudd to Lobengula's court to gain control of mining rights. They were not the first white entrepreneurs who had gone to Lobengula's court with this objective. Indeed, when they arrived they found there a number of hunters, traders, missionaries and concession-seekers waiting for various favours from the King. As early as 1868, a concession had been granted to the London and Limpopo Company for mining rights in the Tati area, over which Khama also claimed authority.

Rudd did not have an easy task in securing the concession, for the rival European factions at the court constantly sought to sabotage his chances. Lotje, one of the King's trusted senior indunas, was promised 300 gold sovereigns for his support, and was also encouraged in a belief that the Matabele would get guns to maintain their pre-eminent position. Sekombo another prominent induna, was also bribed. Rudd was further helped by a visit to the court from Sir Sydney Shippard, who encouraged the King to deal exclusively with the Rudd group. Indeed, Lobengula became convinced that Shippard had a share in the concession. This cooperation between the local officials of the British Crown and Rhodes was to continue proving very valuable.

To this alliance of private enterprise and state, it is only proper that we should add the church. Missionary Helms, resident at Lobengula's court and regarded by Lobengula as a friend of the Matabele, again served as interpreter – a key role, since it was he who told the King what he was signing – and also urged Lobengula to accept. Since Lobengula consistently denied that he had ever agreed to the terms of the concession which Rhodes presented to the world, we may assume that Helms was not above reproach.

Rudd finally persuaded Lobengula to grant an exclusive

concession for all mineral and metal rights in his country, in return for 1,000 rifles, an armed steamboat for the Zambesi river (which could be used against his enemy Khama), and a payment of £100 per month. It is worth noting that Rudd was prepared to offer the militaristic Matabele further weapons to use against their enemies, an offer which Shippard defended to the British government on the grounds that rifles would be less devastating than assegais in native wars! In any event, the steamboat was never delivered, while the rifles were deposited for Lobengula at a local store but never collected. The concession itself was subsequently sold by its holders, the United Concessions Company, to the B S A C for £1m.

Lobengula was placed in a difficult position. The young Ndebele warriors were anxious to turn all the whites out of the kingdom; while the older indunas and Lobengula recognized that war with the heavily armed whites could be disastrous. Lobengula himself was also well aware of the danger of a Boer incursion into his kingdom, and of the unsettling effect which flowed from a large number of whites competing for concessions. The problem was to find an acceptable compromise which would not split the Ndebele kingdom between those who favoured war with the whites and those who saw the need for a settlement. Such a compromise had, above all, to protect the Matabele state from the interests of other foreign powers and white speculators.

Richard Brown, in the most detailed account of the negotiations from the Ndebele viewpoint, has argued that Lobengula believed he had given a concession which would allow only ten whites to come in and mine for gold under his control; this would have protected the kingdom from other concession-seekers, and at the same time would have provided arms for use against any Boer or Portuguese threat.[28] Lobengula's discovery that the written concession allowed much more than this, and that Rhodes's group intended to use it as a basis for an occupation of Mashonaland, resulted in efforts at repudiation. But he was essentially helpless. He could not allow his young warriors to attack the whites, since this would mean a war that the Ndebele were unlikely to win.

Subsequent Shona writers have pointed out that in granting the Rudd concession, Lobengula was in fact conferring rights over areas in Mashonaland where his sovereignty was not only in dispute but effectively nonexistent.[29] After the Moffat Treaty, Lord Knutsford, the British Colonial Secretary, had stated: 'Her Majesty's Government have satisfied themselves that Lobengula ... is undisputed ruler over Matabeleland and Mashonaland.'[30] How the government had satisfied themselves of this is by no means self-evident. The B S A C itself provided adequate testimony to the contrary by entering into separate treaties with local Shona paramounts. However, on the insistence of headquarters, these treaties were allowed to lapse, and the Company made no payments – a fact which promoted the hostility towards the Company that erupted in open revolt in 1896.[31]

Lobengula, hearing that in effect he had sold his country, revoked the treaty and even sent two of his indunas to England to clarify the situation with the British government. But though Lobengula was legally entitled 'to cancel any grants within his territory', Rhodes proceeded to use the treaty as a basis for obtaining a charter from the British government.

This charter ensured British control without any financial commitment. Indeed, the company which was to operate the charter, the British South Africa Company, promptly paid the government £30,000 for the extension of the telegraph line into the Tati area of Matabeleland, and Rhodes even offered to pay the costs incurred by the government in placing an officer in Matabeleland. From the government's point of view, it was indeed 'imperialism on the cheap'. In return the Company was allowed to maintain a police force, levy taxes, promulgate laws, engage in any trade, construct roads and railways, and seek further concessions – all this, it should be noted, in a country to which Britain had no legal claim, and on the basis of a document repudiated by its signatory. Yet further to secure its position against rival foreign powers, and particularly against the expansionary aims of the Boers, Britain proclaimed a protectorate over the area in 1891.

Lobengula's efforts to nullify the concession continued with messages to the Queen repeating his denial that he had granted sovereign rights in his country or, indeed, any rights except for people to 'dig for gold ... as my servants'. In Matabeleland, Lotje, who had urged the concession upon Lobengula, was killed for treachery.[32] Confronted with this situation, Rhodes offered Frank Johnson, subsequently to become the leader of the pioneer column, £150,000 to break the Matabele military power and capture or kill Lobengula. But word of this plan reached the British High Commission, which would not yet countenance an invasion.[33] Rhodes was forced back upon his old strategy. He sent Jameson to Lobengula to obtain permission to dig for gold, so as to be able to claim that Lobengula had recognized the concession and allowed it to be put into operation. Moffat, the Queen's representative, was in Matabeleland and, it may be supposed, helped to secure Lobengula's agreement; certainly he allowed Jameson to rewrite a message from the Queen which was delivered to Lobengula's court.

The British government still had reservations about allowing Rhodes to carry out his plan of occupying Mashonaland without Lobengula's explicit approval. But Rhodes, successfully exploiting rumours of imminent Boer and Portuguese moves into the area, at last gained the authorization. It was an authorization granted after Lobengula's envoys had unequivocally stated to the British High Commissioner in Cape Town the strongest objections to the entry of Rhodes's party.

The occupation of Mashonaland

In September 1890, Rhodes's party entered Mashonaland, halting at Harare Kopje on the outskirts of what was to become Salisbury. Rhodes had still obtained no concession which gave him any entitlement to land. The Rudd concession conferred only mineral rights. Another group of speculators, led by Edouard Lippert, seeing the opportunity to profit from the situation, persuaded Lobengula to grant them the land rights, on the grounds that these would effectively control the BSAC. They then sold the rights conferred in the 'Lippert concession' to the Rhodes group. Lobengula had been tricked again.

The determination of the B S A C to proceed at any cost is evidenced by the comments of the Company's Secretary:

The consequences of this new and final plan are two in number. Firstly, if Lobengula looks on in silence and does nothing the Charter will occupy Mashonaland . . . If on the other hand, Lobengula attacks us, then the original plan [the armed invasion of Matabeleland] . . . will be carried out to the very letter . . . he must expect no mercy and none will be given him . . . If he attacks us, he is doomed, if he does not, his fangs will be drawn, the pressure of civilization on all his borders will press more and more heavily upon him, and the desired result, the disappearance forever of the Matabele as a power, if delayed is yet the more certain.[34]

The Shona chiefs had not been involved in any negotiations, and the arrival of the white settlers was for them unexpected. They assumed that these whites, like many before them, were transients looking for gold and trading opportunities before moving on. They treated them, on the whole, with their customary hospitality. Indeed, some of the Shona paramounts were concerned with the possibility of invasion not from the south but from the east, where the Portuguese were active, and where a Goanese, Gouveia, had established an expansionist independent kingdom modelled on African lines.[35]

However, the Shona were quickly given adequate evidence that the newcomers had rather more permanent intentions. It is important to note the characteristics of this early white–black contact, for it contains many of the ingredients which were to produce the modern racist state. The settlers immediately equipped themselves with self-justifying myths concerning the character and history of the Shona people, and proceeded to institutionalize the type of social relationships which appeared to provide these myths with validity. In 1890, as in 1973, the primary conflict was economic. From the start, the whites sought cheap African labour to assist them in amassing capital and seized the best land for white farming, irrespective of local rights or tribal customs. In 1890, as in 1973, the maintenance of the society depended not upon consent but upon the superiority of white force, subsequently regularized in a series of laws. The ensuing destruction of Ndebele and Shona military power gave whites a virtual monopoly over the necessary means of coercion.

In their administration of justice, the whites emulated the Ndebele even to the point of raiding the kraals of those who had offended them. But where Lobengula's impis had raided with assegais, the BSAC police raided with guns. One example will suffice. In 1892 a farmer named Bennet claimed that he had suffered a minor theft. Captain Lendy of the BSAC police took an armed party with a seven-pound maxim Nordenfelt gun to the kraal of the accused chief and killed the chief together with twenty-one other Africans, an action which caused even the Colonial Secretary to protest that the Shona were not British subjects and that, in any case, the discrepancy between the alleged crime and the punishment was disproportionate. No action was taken against Lendy, who soon became Magistrate of Fort Victoria. The whites followed similar arbitrary policies in seizing African land, conscripting labour and terminating the Shona's existing trading patterns with the Portuguese.

Ever anxious to reduce its administrative costs, particularly since Mashonaland had not yielded the expected golden bonanza, the Company cut its paid officials to the limit and frequently relied on white settlers to exercise its responsibilities. This created a situation where white conflicts with the African population were not so much controlled as resolved in favour of the whites, who became plaintiff, police and judge in their constant efforts to make money out of Mashonaland. Alleged disputes with the local chiefs were used as the occasion for a white raiding-party to seize African goods. With the whites increasingly exercising a monopoly of power, they inevitably became drawn into local African conflicts, and in return for a share in the proceeds, would frequently enforce one African's claim against another (as in disputes over *Lobola*, the bridal dowry which on the break-up of a marriage could be reclaimed by the bride's family).

In 1894 the Company imposed a tax of 10 shillings on each hut. This tax, on an independent and unconquered African population, naturally created considerable hostility. It also gave the Shona a clear indication that the whites were not only intending to settle permanently but, further, regarded themselves as the rulers.

The conquest of Matabeleland

The B S A C's major difficulties were initially not with the Shona but with the Ndebele, perhaps because the scattered and divided Shona paramounts, unfamiliar with the background to white settlement in Mashonaland, needed longer to make a response than did the centralized Ndebele state. The ostensible cause of the conflict was the continuation by the Ndebele of their raids on the Shona communities, raids often provoked by the fact that some Shona chiefs took advantage of Company rule to refuse to pay the traditional tribute. The effect of these raids for the Europeans was to disrupt labour supplies and create a general climate of uncertainty, though, anxious to avoid war, Lobengula carefully avoided clashes with the whites. Yet war with the Ndebele was always viewed by the Rhodes group as inevitable and desirable, a view reinforced by Lobengula's tenacity in opposing the Charter.

It was clear that the transformation of the warlike Ndebele into cheap labour for white farms and mines could not be accomplished peacefully, and the disappointing mineral discoveries in Mashonaland encouraged the belief that the real mineral wealth must lie in Matabeleland. The only question was when the war should take place. The Company naturally wished to avoid it until the settlement of Mashonaland was complete and white fire-power would be adequate to ensure a quick victory.

The actual occasion for war was provided in June 1893, when Lobengula sent an impi against a chief in the Fort Victoria area who had stolen some of the King's cattle and, according to Lobengula, stolen telegraph wire from the B S A C and fomented trouble between him and the Company. Jameson, the chief administrator for the Company, stated the problem very bluntly: 'The serious part is that every native has deserted from the mines and farms ... there is no danger to whites but unless some shooting is done, I think it will be difficult to get labour even after they have all gone ... The natives will not have confidence in the protection of the whites, unless we actually drive the Matabele out.'[36] That is exactly what Jameson did. He ordered the Ndebele impi out of Mashonaland and sent Lendy to see that his orders were obeyed. Lendy came upon the rearguard of the Ndebele party, apparently attacking a Shona kraal, and opened fire, killing a number of the party.

Jameson and Rhodes now made serious preparations for war and raised a column to attack Matabeleland. Recruits were each promised 6,000 acres of land, mining rights and a share in the loot, principally the Ndebele cattle. While the Company prepared for war, Lobengula tried to maintain peace and appealed to the British government against the Company, but without success. Two of his messengers, under safe conduct from the British Commissioner, were arrested and killed by the British Bechuanaland police while trying to escape.

The British government opposed any attack against the Ndebele unless the settlers were attacked first. Sir Henry Loch, the Cape Governor, was more concerned to ensure that imperial troops secured Matabeleland and therefore authority in the area. In the event, Jameson was able to conjure up an imminent, if fictitious, Matabele attack; and in October, he marched on Bulawayo, outmanoeuvring Loch and the imperial forces. With little fire-power and tactics unsuited for fighting the mobile white column, Lobengula was easily defeated and died in retreat on the Zambezi river. His last peace offering, of gold, was stolen by white soldiers. The invaders killed Ndebele prisoners. When the 'savage' Lobengula had burned his capital, before retreating, he had ensured that none of the whites was harmed.

The consequences of the white occupation

The fact that the victory over the Ndebele had been achieved largely by a volunteer army rather than by imperial forces was to have profound consequences for the future of Rhodesia. The nature of the victory was in itself indicative of the fact that in Rhodesia, unlike the majority of Britain's African colonies, settlers always provided the major political impetus. The whites who had first settled in Mashonaland, and now conquered Matabeleland, were not eager to listen to advice from London. Indeed, their very presence created a whole series of conflicts with the African population which, in principle, should have made the British government put a premium on a disinterested and impartial administration.

Loch's efforts to achieve Crown control over Matabeleland were easily thwarted, and the High Commissioner had to settle for the limited protection afforded to the indigenous population in the Matabeleland Order in Council of July 1894. Terence Ranger, who has given a superb account of the background to and conduct of the revolts of 1896–7, writes: 'The history of Company administration in Matabeleland in 1894–1895 is largely the story of how these protective provisions of the Matabeleland Order in Council were flouted and evaded with regard to both land and cattle.'[37] In short, the Ndebele were robbed of most of their cattle, which were divided as loot, and of the best land. Two totally inadequate reservations were set aside for them. The land on which the Ndebele kraals were situated was given to the volunteers or sold off to farmers and speculators; the indigenous occupants were told to work for the new owner or move on. Presented with a *fait accompli*, the British government acquiesced – a pattern which was to become characteristic of relations between the imperial government and the settlers when African interests were at stake.

The growth in farming and mining naturally increased the demand for labour. It was a demand which the African population was not eager to meet, least of all at the rates paid, which were significantly less than an African would have gained by working on his own land. In part, the problem was tackled by *ad hoc* arrangements. Europeans needing labour would, sometimes with the assistance of the local administration and the hated African police, simply seize available able-bodied males from the local kraals and force them to work. Non-payment of wages was almost as regular a part of the system as the flogging of reluctant workers. In its essentials, the system of labour recruitment and control was akin to slavery. Since the Africans could not be enticed into the European market, they were to be compelled. The 1894 hut tax was popular with the Company as a means of raising revenue to cover its administration, and popular with the Europeans since it forced some of the Africans onto the labour market to earn enough for the tax. The tax proved, however, an insufficient spur. Many Africans sought to reduce the tax demand by crowding into fewer huts and then paying out of produce sales. More direct forms of forced labour came to predominate.

Naturally these practices had important effects on race relations. John Rex suggests that there is a close correlation between the level of violence and coercion used in obtaining labour, the destruction of traditional socio-economic systems and in consequence the loss of economic and social independence which the indigenous population experience, and subsequent levels of racism. 'Having lost the means of fending for himself in the world, he [the slave] was forced into a Sambo stance doing what his master bade him, being pathetically grateful for any kindness, and not even aspiring to any kind of independent life.' On domestic servants, an occupational category which was increasing even faster than the settler population, Rex writes:

There are a number of aspects of the domestic servant's situation in the colonial context, moreover, which are suggestive of slavery. There is a tendency to tie him to his job through the introduction of penal sanctions against the servant who decamps. There is considerable limitation on his own family life, since very often he is required to live in single quarters, and there is considerable similarity, very often, between the way in which a master talks of his servant or is permitted to punish his servant, and what occurred under the slave system.[38]

The difficulties which white settlers experienced in persuading Africans of the virtues of hard work – on somebody else's account, of course – were not unique. Max Weber noted:

A man does not 'by nature' wish to earn more and more money, but simply to live as he is accustomed to live and to earn as much as is necessary for that purpose. Whenever modern capitalism has done its work of increasing the productivity of human labour by increasing its intensity, it has encountered immensely stubborn resistance of this leading trait of pre-capitalistic labour. And today it encounters it the more, the more backward (from a capitalistic point of view) the labouring forces are with which it has to deal.[39]

Yet the response of the African population to the labour market was in many ways a model of capitalist reasoning. They avoided wage labour because it was more profitable to do so.

Having conquered and settled the country, the whites proceeded to create a social system in which the African population would live up to the white man's image. Since the African would not work for the white man, he was lazy; since he could not understand orders in English, he was either insolent or stupid; since he was only employed in menial tasks, he was only capable of these. Sir Robert Tredgold, a one-time Chief Justice of the Federation of Rhodesia and Nyasaland, waxed sentimental about his father's African stable-hand: 'Dear old Chiliboy, I wonder how much of my feelings for the Africans stems from the memory of you.'[40] For some whites, as for Tredgold, this relationship gave rise to paternalism; for others, to more vicious brands of white supremacy.

The defeat of Lobengula had left the Company with the task of pacifying Matabeleland, many areas of which were still in a state of armed rebellion. Any Matabele seen with a gun could be shot on sight. Ranger writes: 'For most of 1894 the administration of Matabeleland had amounted to frank military despotism by Jameson's white police.'[41]

The Matabele had not only lost their land and cattle and been conscripted into labour for the whites, they were also vulnerable to the caprice of practically any white man. Rhodes himself referred to one aspect of this: 'It was very widely said in South Africa that the native rebellion had, as one of its causes, the treatment of the native women by white men and also by native police.'[42] Strict Victorian morality would not even countenance discussion of sex; but the repressiveness of the culture combined with racism to produce numerous sexual assaults. Africans were, after all, not full human beings. One official of the Company who compelled a chief to hand over his daughter, was dismissed; but within nine months he held a position in the force organized to crush the African uprising.[43] Philip Mason argues that this indicated the willingness of the Company to discipline its own employees, but the mildness of the punishment was in marked contrast to that meted out to African offenders. In 1910 an African convicted of assault on a white woman was sentenced to hang, and his reprieve by the British High Commissioner produced a storm of settler protest.[44]

In contrast to Matabeleland, the Shona in Mashonaland had never been conquered. Formally at least, the Company was still obliged to respect local customs and tribal practices, and the Shona were still allowed to carry arms. Conflicts between the settlers and the Shona continued to grow, as the question of who should rule remained unresolved.

The war of 1896

The opportunity for revolt was provided in January 1896, when Jameson led an abortive invasionary force to stimulate a rebellion against the Boer President, Kruger, in the Transvaal Republic. His force surrendered, leaving most of Rhodesia's white police imprisoned in the Transvaal. The organization of the revolt and its subsequent conduct were largely directed by the Ndebele and Shona religious hierarchy. The religious leaders were able to provide the unity which the Ndebele had lacked since Lobengula's death, and the Shona since the fall of the Rowzi empire.

The revolt came as a complete surprise to the whites, who preferred to believe that the destruction of Lobengula's power had been welcomed by most of the rank-and-file Ndebele, while the Shona were presumed to be grateful for white protection and in any case were regarded by the settlers as a wretched and cowardly people. In the circumstances, it is appropriate that the first shots fired in the war came from the Shona of East Belingwe Matabeleland, who were former Ndebele tributaries. These were the very people who, according to white ideology, should have been most satisfied with settler rule.

This incident took place in early March 1896. Three weeks later, on 24 March, the uprising in Matabeleland began. The key role in organizing it had been played by the main Ndebele religious officer, who was able to call on the old Ndebele regimental system that had never been successfully broken up after 1893. The Ndebele could not agree on a successor to Lobengula; and, from the start, the revolt lacked adequate central direction. On the other hand, the Ndebele had improved their tactics since 1893, and Ndebele fire-power was helped by an influx of deserters from the native police.

In 1893, the Ndebele had received no support from their Shona tributaries, but in 1896, through the support of the Mwari and Mlimo cult officers, an alliance was achieved. The influence of the religious officers was strengthened by the power-vacuum at the heart of the Ndebele nation and by natural calamity. 1894, 1895, and 1896 had been years of drought, and Rinderpest had wiped out many of the cattle. Indeed, to many it must have seemed that the presence of the white man had deeply offended the spirits.

The scale and organization of the risings led one historian to describe them as 'genuinely national revolutions in which for a time the traditional political leaders were set aside'.[45] Terence Ranger writes: 'Not only did these risings involve both Shona and Ndebele, they also involved almost everybody in the rebel areas ... children and women and old men; the lower castes and the subject peoples as well as the Ndebele aristocracy.'[46]

The Ndebele rising caught the whites unprepared. Many isolated farmers were killed and Bulawayo was besieged. The position of the whites, precarious enough since the Jameson Raid had depleted the white police-force, was further complicated by the Company's desire to maintain confidence among its shareholders and to restrain the British government from becoming involved, which led it to minimize the danger. The Company also wished to suppress the revolt at the lowest possible cost. Its failure to afford adequate protection in the early days of the revolt was to have a lasting effect on the settlers' relations with the Company.

In the end, the Ndebele proved no match for white fire-power, and in two decisive engagements outside Bulawayo, on 25 April and 5 June, they were beaten. But the whites were not yet strong enough to press home their advantage. There were sufficient troops to secure Bulawayo, but not to pursue the Matabele into their strongholds or to defend outlying areas. This was the situation when, in the third week of June, the rebellion spread into Mashonaland, an area presumed so safe that many of the whites were away fighting in Matabeleland. As Native Commissioner Edwards declared: 'I hadn't the faintest idea that within a week, the country would be in a blaze of rebellion.'[47] The first white explanations had a tone which was to become common in Rhodesia: the Mashona had been intimidated into rising by the Ndebele. Then, as now, so sure were the whites of the justice of their rule that any other explanation was inconceivable.

In Mashonaland, again, the role of the religious hierarchy was of key importance. The Mwari cult and the spirit mediums both played a major role in organizing and sustaining the revolt. The Shona remained much more divided than the Ndebele. Their forces were generally grouped under the local paramount and were engaged largely in a defensive strategy. In the early period they successfully blocked the roads but the structure of their organization prevented them from raising any large offensive standing armies. It can be argued that this robbed the Shona of any chance of victory; but it also made the job of the settlers more difficult, for each kraal had to be taken and each paramount defeated individually.

The remaining possibility of an African victory receded when, after a further success against the Ndebele in July and a series of indecisive skirmishes in the hilly Matopos, Rhodes sued for a separate peace with the Ndebele. The entry of Mashonaland into the war, the danger of further imperial involvement which might result in the loss of the Company's charter, and the heavy expenses incurred, all prompted Rhodes to seek a settlement. On 21 August Rhodes held what was to become a famous 'indaba' with the senior Ndebele indunas. Peace was made after Rhodes agreed to disband the Ndebele police and reform the administrative system. Rhodes also agreed that no charges would be brought against the senior indunas.

This settlement angered many of the settlers who were still eager for revenge, and it was not to be the last time that settler prejudices would run contrary to the needs of *Realpolitik*. The British government who had wished to conduct their own peace negotiations and impose their own terms, were confronted with a *fait accompli*. Rhodes, again much to the disgust of many white settlers, proceeded to consolidate the peace. Food and cattle were sent to the Ndebele; the leaders who had remained loyal were made salaried indunas; and some of the rebels were offered a similar prospect for the future.

The surrender of the Ndebele had taken place against the wishes of those leading the Mlimo cult, who waged a rearguard action against surrender. Mkwati, the most important of these, escaped into Mashonaland to continue the rebellion from there.

The relatively generous peace which Rhodes had made with the Ndebele – prompted by his concern for the future of the Charter – was matched by the bloody repression of the rising in Mashonaland. There, in spite of imperial reinforcements, the revolt continued until the end of 1899 because the British government representatives, who wanted total pacification as a prelude to a reformed administrative structure, were able to prevent acceptable peace terms from being agreed. The Shona retreated into caves in the mountains, which were dynamited by the white troops. Makoni, a Shona paramount, who had asked for peace terms and been refused any which did not amount to an abject surrender, was captured and shot after a summary and irregular court martial.

The Shona generally showed themselves much less ready to compromise than the Ndebele and, in late 1896, an attempt was made to regroup the paramounts under a new Mambo. Not until November was the resistance broken with the capture of the Kagubi and the Nehanda mediums. For leading the African people against the summary occupation of their country, the mediums were tried and executed.

The white conquest was now complete. What remained was to realize the promise of gold and rich profits which had spurred on both local settlers and B S A C investors in London.

2 The basis of white society

Constitutional development: a summary

In 1898, the Southern Rhodesia Order in Council established a legislative council to govern the colony. This consisted of four elected members and five B S A C appointees, with the Company administrator as President. The abortive Jameson Raid and the revolts of 1896 and 1897 had prompted the British to take a more active interest in the colony. Close control was exercised over the police and the armed forces, and the Resident Commissioner was empowered to keep a watch on legislative and administrative activities.

The failure of the anticipated gold boom encouraged the Company to make concessions to the settlers. In 1907, following a visit by its directors, the Company began to encourage European land settlement, hoping to recover its investment from the sale of land. In the same year, the settlers were given a majority in the legislative council.

The recognition that farming would form a major sector of the economy meant that the realization of profit would be a much slower process than originally anticipated. The charter expired in 1914, and settler support was essential for its renewal. A supplementary charter was granted, which provided for self-government if it was demanded by the settlers and if the Crown was satisfied with the financial and administrative condition of the country. The demand for self-government grew, and the decision by the Judicial Committee of the Privy Council, that title to the land belonged not to the Company but to the Crown, terminated the Company's interest in continuing the administration.

Both the Company and the British government favoured union with South Africa, which appeared to offer the best economic prospects and immediate settlement of the Company's claim of

£3¾ m. for administrative expenses. Union was, however, opposed by the white working class and farming interests. The white working class feared competition for jobs from poor whites in the south and opposed Smuts, the Union Premier, who had ruthlessly broken an armed rising by white mine-workers on the South African Rand. Farmers feared that union with South Africa would raise the level of African wages by forcing employers to compete with the higher African wages paid in the Union. In addition many Rhodesians wished to protect themselves against the danger of Afrikaner dominance and the possibility that Rhodesia's development needs would be neglected by a larger Union government. The growth of a relatively stable and stratified white society and the expansion of its economic base provided the preconditions for self-government. There were few whites who wished to see a strengthening of imperial control. The argument was rather between the larger entrepreneurs who saw economic advantages in union with the south and those who saw their interests best protected by a national government over which they could exercise more direct command.

In November 1922 a referendum gave a large victory to the group in favour of responsible government. In 1923 Company rule was terminated, and Rhodesia became a self-governing colony, a step which was to be of overwhelming importance in Rhodesia's future development.

The British government retained control over foreign policy and ostensibly over policy affecting Africans. The Assembly was barred from changing certain aspects of African administration; legislation containing clauses which discriminated against Africans had to be reserved for British government approval. Britain also retained the power to legislate directly for Rhodesia. These constitutional provisions provided the basis for the government of the colony until the Constitutional Review Conference of 1961.

The powers retained by Britain were intended to protect the African majority, and to restrict the exercise of self-government to European affairs – since, with few exceptions, Africans were not eligible for the vote. But Britain's reserve powers were

rapidly eroded both by convention and subsequent legal change.
At no time did the British government veto legislation emanating
from the Rhodesian Assembly or initiate legislation for the colony.
In practice, the Rhodesian government consulted Britain before
putting measures before the Rhodesian Parliament and secured
approval in advance. And in general, as a glance at the battery
of discriminatory practices demonstrates, British control was
slight, though on occasion it had some influence, as in dissuading
the Prime Minister, Huggins, from excluding Africans from the
common roll after the Second World War. D. J. Murray has
written of the legislative Assembly: 'Instead of being treated as
an instrument of self-regulation for the enfranchised minority,
it was regarded from the first both by the enfranchised minority
and the government in the United Kingdom as the rightful
legislature for the whole population of the colony.'[1] The
'Constitution Letters Patent' were amended when the need
arose, as in the integration in 1937 of the Native Affairs Department into the overall civil service structure, a move which gave
the Assembly full control over the activities of the civil servants
in the Department.

The franchise qualification involved both English-language
literacy and means tests. In 1914 the income qualification was
raised from £50 per annum to £100 and in 1951 to £240 per
annum. In 1957 the qualification for voters in the elections
for the parliament of the Federation of the Rhodesias and
Nyasaland was raised to £720 per annum, and in 1961 Southern
Rhodesia followed suit and established a similar income
qualification for 'A' roll voters in territorial elections. Initially
the property qualification was designed to exclude poor whites;
but with the establishment of a *modus vivendi* between white
capital and labour, it served essentially to exclude nearly all
Africans, with some Coloureds and Asians. In 1923, out of an
African population of close to a million (early census data on the
size of the African population are unreliable), there were only
30 registered voters, compared to 19,000 European voters out
of a population of 35,000 Europeans. Twenty-five years later
there were still less than 300 African registered voters out of a
total electorate of 47,000.

The development of the economy

When the white man came to our country, we had the land and they had the Bible: now we have the Bible and they have the land – African saying

The second Rand which Rhodes had hoped to discover did not materialize. The discovery of gold reef stimulated a temporary boom in the Company's shares, but by 1903 the country was in the midst of an economic crisis. Gold continued to play an important role in the Rhodesian economy, but it was clear that if the white settlers were to make their fortune in Rhodesia, it would be a much slower process than they had anticipated. There were, however, two other valuable assets at the settlers' disposal: the land and the people. The economic history of Rhodesia is largely the story of the exploitation of these two resources and the resulting conflict with the African population.

The seizure of the best agricultural land by the colonists deprived the African population of much of its traditional farming land. The subsequent development of white agriculture brought the white farmers into conflict with African producers. The monopoly of political power exercised by the whites ensured that the white farmers were victorious.

All whites in Rhodesia, farmers or gold-miners, housewives or builders, had an interest in ensuring adequate African labour at the cheapest price. Cheap African labour, like the seizure of traditional African farming lands and the imposition of the hut tax and later the poll tax, resulted in a shift of resources out of the African community. The surplus from African production, instead of financing African development, financed white development.

The development of white farming and the impoverishment of African farming

Initially land was allocated in an arbitrary fashion to the pioneers, would-be settlers, and land-speculators on request. The most fertile soil was largely centred in Matabeleland so that the Ndebele were the more immediately affected. Under the Charter granted by the British government, the Company was obliged to provide adequate 'reserves' for the African population. Africans resident in the designated reserves, which were generally situated on less fertile land away from the markets and the railway-lines, could continue to follow traditional farming patterns but were subject to growing population pressure, interference from religious and secular authorities and the payment of taxes. Taxes were increased in 1904 when the 10-shilling hut tax gave way to a £1 poll tax on each male African with a further 10-shilling tax on each wife after the first.

Latter-day whites are apt to quote the high proportion of the country's taxes that they pay and have even managed to relate this to the number of African voters allowed under the 1969 Constitution. In the fiscal year 1904–5 African taxes provided 41·4 per cent of the government revenue, an increase of nearly 15 per cent over the 1901–3 average, and a much higher proportion than that paid by the non-African residents whose contributions in 1904–5 amounted to only 27 per cent of the total public revenue.[2] In 1918 Africans were still contributing over one third of the total annual revenue of Rhodesia.[3] Europeans with incomes of less than £400 for a single man and £1,000 for a couple were exempt from tax. This was the crucial period of capital accumulation. The high African tax rates reduced the surplus available for African investment in agriculture and not only drove a significant proportion of the agricultural population onto the labour market – which was of course, the intention – but had the additional effect of reducing the European tax burden. The Company was thus able to use African tax revenue to subsidize the development of European mining and farming.

Africans living outside the reserves were initially allowed to remain in their traditional homeland – a decision which owed more to economic than humanitarian considerations. Selous, the famous white hunter and explorer, said in 1896: 'From the black man's point of view the white man is probably not essential in the prosperity of the country. He could get on very well without him. Unfortunately we cannot manage without the black man; he is absolutely necessary for the development of the country on the white man's lines.'[4] More explicitly, in 1911 the Native Affairs Committee of Enquiry commented: 'It would be very short-sighted policy to remove these natives to reserves as their services may be of great value to future European occupants.'[5] The presence of Africans outside the reserves was useful in providing a local labour reservoir for neighbouring farmers before the labour market had been fully developed. Moreover, the situation was made directly profitable to the Company and to the European landowners. After 1909 the B S A C received a rent of £1 per annum from Africans living on unalienated land.[6] Other landowners charged a variety of rents, in cash, in produce, in labour, or in some combination of the three, which enabled absentee landlords to make a profit without ever developing the land.

The development of the mining industry and other small enterprises in the white economy created a growth in the demand for foodstuffs. European agriculture was slow in developing; and in the early years, African farming, though it was not encouraged as was European agriculture, was nevertheless permitted to expand. The number of African-owned cattle increased rapidly at an annual rate of 12 per cent from 1905 to 1921; the output of maize, at an annual rate of roughly 25 per cent from 1904 to 1921.[7] Some whites observed that by buying African produce, the mining companies were in fact enabling Africans to pay taxes without joining the labour market. This added to the labour shortage, but for the moment mining companies were anxious to keep the price of food down and rely on other expedients to meet their labour requirements.

This period of relative prosperity in African agriculture was to be short-lived. As European farming developed, so did the pressure to make Africans move out of the European areas and to restrict African competition. It was at this point that the Company began charging rent to Africans living on 'unassigned' land. Furthermore, from 1909, the rate of eviction of Africans from European areas seriously accelerated. The proportion of the African population in the reserves rose from 54 per cent in 1909 to 64 per cent in 1922, and the rate of *per capita* African productivity began to decline. Traditionally Africans had relied on a form of shifting cultivation which avoided soil erosion, but with increased pressure on land resources, this was more difficult, and soil erosion increased. In addition a rise in the reserve population without any parallel rise in the size of the reserves forced Africans to bring poorer land into cultivation, again reducing the marketable surplus. The yield of grain per acre fell from 2·7 bags in 1920 to 2·2 in 1930, and the growth in cattle declined from an annual average of 12 per cent, to 6 per cent in the period 1921–31, and a mere 1 per cent in 1931–45. Even this increase was purely quantitative since the growing number of cattle led to severe over-stocking and a deterioration in quality. At the same time the urban economy became less dependent on African output. Between 1904 and 1921, European maize production rose from 46,000 bags a year to 1,200,000; the number of European-owned cattle rose from 30,000 to 905,000.[8]

Ostensibly Africans had equal rights to purchase land anywhere in the colony, rights guaranteed to them by the original terms under which the Company was granted administrative rule by Britain. In practice, the Company placed great obstacles in the way of those few who had the resources to buy, and by 1925, only 40,000 acres had been sold to Africans, compared to the 31,000,000 acres which had been sold to whites. The Company refused to sell land to leading Ndebele who saw this as one way of overcoming the land shortage problem. The Company also refused to sell land to the Fingo community, migrants from South Africa, many of whom had been promised land in Rhodesia by Cecil Rhodes in the hope that they might be used as a bulwark against the local black population. This refusal forged an alliance between the Fingos and the Ndebele which played an important part in the development of the African nationalist opposition.

Measures to support European farming

In 1925 the Morris–Carter Commission provided the basis for a permanent division of Rhodesia into African and European areas. When the Commission met, of the 96 million acres of land, 31 million acres were in the hands of Europeans; 21.5 million acres were reserved for Africans; and 43·5 million acres were still undistributed. In spite of African opposition, the Commission concluded that a division between European and African land was necessary; and with a characteristic Rhodesian sense of justice, the subsequent 1931 Land Apportionment Act allocated some 7·5 million acres to what became known as 'Native Purchase Areas' and some 17·5 million to the European area, with the remainder to continue as unassigned land. In time, much of the unassigned land, which was generally of very poor quality, was transferred to the African areas. A further guarantee against African competition was that African buyers in the Native Purchase Area would normally be limited to a maximum of 1,000 acres, thus ensuring that no African would ever be able to compete with large-scale white agricultural enterprises. In keeping with past tradition, the best land and the land closest to the market was again to be found in the European sector. The official geological map shows that by 1970, some 98 per cent of the land suitable for afforestation, fruit growing and intensive beef production lay in the European areas, as did 82 per cent of the land suitable for intensive farming; 100 per cent of the land unsuitable for any agricultural purpose lay in the African sector.[9]

Africans farming on what became European Crown land were given six years to quit. (In practice many of the Africans stayed where they were unless evicted by new European tenants, since with the pressure on land in the reserves few Africans would move there willingly.) The creation of Native Purchase Areas did little to relieve the pressure on African land, since Africans were already farming in them, and allocations of farms to African purchasers could only take place at the expense of existing tenants. In any case, allocation was slow – few Africans had the money to buy land. The depressed conditions of the thirties increased the European farmers' efforts to restrict African competition. European farmers were not eager to see the growth of a class of African farmers who would have a significant marketable surplus. By 1944, little over 1,500 farms had been purchased.[10]

The division of land between African and European farmers could hardly be justified by any general land shortage and even less by the real need of European farmers for land. Twenty-six years after the Land Apportionment Act, a parliamentary select committee found that of the 30 per cent of the land in the

European areas which was arable, only 3 to 4 per cent was actually being cultivated. The Land Apportionment Act did, however, provide a basis for the institutionalization of white rule. Segregation was seen as an essential method of preventing black competition. The Law gave Africans no rights whatsoever in the European towns or on land placed in the European area. Increased pressure on African land reduced the marketable surplus from African agriculture and therefore reduced African competition with white farmers. It also propelled a large number of African males into the labour market to provide cheap labour for European employers. These employers included European farmers who were able to consolidate their market position by employing cheap labour.

The Land Apportionment Act was not the only weapon in the European farmers' arsenal. In 1903 a Department of Agriculture had been established to help the farming industry, and it worked closely with the white farmers. As one student of the Rhodesian political system wrote in 1970: 'Up to the recent past, the administration of agriculture has depended upon a partnership between the Government, the Department of Agriculture and the Rhodesian National Farmers' Union.'[11]

In the early years, the B SAC provided a considerable amount of assistance. Specialists were engaged from the United States to advise on tobacco growing; warehouses were leased for the handling, grading and sale of tobacco; central farms were established to teach new settlers how to produce flue-cured tobacco. A suggestion by a native commissioner that the government should train Africans in the preparation of African tobacco for sale was rejected.[12]

The Company also set up a bacon factory at Salisbury to expand pig production. The Company assisted in the formation and financing of the Rhodesian Farmers' Union. In 1924 the government reached an agreement with the Imperial and Cold Storage Supply Company to facilitate the export of frozen meat and paid a bounty on the export of cattle. In 1928, when 10m. lb. of the 28m. lb. tobacco harvest could not be sold, the colony's government provided a £½m. subsidy.

Faced during the thirties with declining exports, European

farmers found these privileges insufficient. In spite of their existing advantages over African producers, they demanded more positive protection. They secured this in 1934 with an amendment to the Maize Control Act, the effect of which was to give a disproportionate share of the higher-priced domestic market to the small European farmers at the expense of large European producers and, above all, the Africans. Justifying this, the chairman of the 1934 Committee of Enquiry into Agriculture, stated: 'The native, owing to free farm land and labour, low standard of living and methods of farming, can produce at a cost under recent overseas parity ... It therefore seems equitable to treat native grown maize as export maize.'[13]

Africans were unable to sell cattle to the Cold Storage Commission for export, but they could sell to European farmers, who could then sell to the Cold Storage Commission. While cattle for export were subsidized between 1935 and 1937, a levy was placed on domestic sales which consisted largely of African cattle. A destocking scheme was introduced in the African reserves, allegedly to improve the quality of the African herds by reducing the pressure on grazing lands. The scheme served to limit competition with European farmers by reducing the overall supply of African cattle and allowed European farmers to profit by fattening up the cullings from African herds.

In the harsh days of the 1930s, these pioneering champions of free enterprise and rugged individualism did not stop at simply shifting the burden of the slump onto the Africans; they sought further support from the government. In 1933, a three-year moratorium was declared on payments for the purchase of Crown lands; subsidies for road building, soil and water conservation were obtained; and loans were secured under the Farmers' Debt Adjustment Act.

Despite the systematic expropriation of the surplus produced in African farming, the *de facto* and later *de jure* restrictions on African land holdings and produce sales, and the active assistance given to white farmers, Lewis Gann, a prolific pro-settler historian, wrote of the early period: 'The discrepancy between the extent of land holdings in white and black possessions owed much to the operations of a free and unfettered land market.'[14]

The outbreak of the Second World War created a boom in demand for agricultural products, and overt attempts to restrict African competition were of decreasing importance. Growing population pressure in the reserves restricted any significant growth in the African marketable surplus, while the aid which the government offered the white farming community continued.

The white farmers, always in possession of the best land and in closer proximity to the railroads and markets, had their access to the market steadily improved by road-building schemes. In 1952–3 expenditure on roads in the African areas amounted to less than 1 per cent of capital expenditure on roads in the European areas.[15] Africans farming at a distance from the market frequently had to sell their products to traders who maintained large profit-margins. A tax which was imposed on African produce, to support the Native Development Fund, meant that the purchase price paid to Africans remained lower than that paid to European farmers.

The failure of the attempt to rationalize African agriculture

In 1951 the Native Land Husbandry Act was introduced. It was directed at transforming the pattern of African farming by ending the distribution of land, currently at the discretion of the chief, among all those living on the reserves. The advertised intention was to create a class of independent small farmers with fixed farming plots which could not be subdivided among their heirs but which could be sold. Tenure was dependent on good farming methods. But this was far from the whole story. The division of land under the Act would terminate the land rights of urban Africans, and the prevention of subdivisions would ensure that the increasing African population would be compelled to leave the reserves for work in urban areas.

This Act should be seen in the context of the attempt by the more far-sighted elements in the white community to create an alliance with the emergent African middle class, which would be encouraged to act as a bulwark against the African masses. In his report for 1954, the Chief Native Commissioner argued that:

Rapid implementation of government policy, by application of the Native Land Husbandry Act, right throughout all the Native reserves and rural areas, is vital to establish and ensure a contented and progressive Native peasant . . . inevitably he will disregard the political sirens of the urban areas, who themselves are making no headway with their self-aggrandisement schemes.[16]

Nationalist comment was rather more blunt. In the words of Joshua Nkomo:

The Native Land Husbandry Act was ostensibly intended to produce a middle class of African small farmers, holding land in freehold instead of communally. But so far its main result has been to force thousands of Africans off the land – providing a useful float of labour for European enterprise.[17]

The newly landless young Africans responded to this situation by forming the militant City Youth League (see below, Chapter 4, p. 101).

The failure of the labour market to expand at a rate anything like sufficient to absorb the surplus African population, and the existing overcrowding in the reserves, led to serious difficulties in the implementation of the Act. The size of the plots allocated under the Act had in practice to be calculated not on the basis of the requisite amount of land required to create and support independent farmers and their families, but through a process of reverse reasoning. Farm sizes were determined by a rough division of those having a claim to land under the Act (i.e. those permanently resident in a particular reserve), into the available area. A *post facto* justification sought to demonstrate that this was adequate. Ken Brown, a former employee of the Southern Rhodesian Native Agriculture Department, has argued that the plots so created might realize £50 a year profit, while £88 constituted the minimum budget which a family of five would need to lead a 'healthy life'.[18]

The investment which would have been necessary to improve farming methods to the extent envisaged under the Act was not forthcoming. Between 1952 and 1960, £17m. were spent on the scheme, of which a third came from the Native Development Fund, financed out of African taxes. Half of the £17m. was spent in resettling Africans who had been farming in European areas.[19] The boom in European immigration in the postwar years and the rapidly growing export market for tobacco increased the pressures on Africans farming in the European areas. Between 1950 and 1960, some 110,000 were expelled from the European areas.

These expulsions exacerbated the situation in the African reserves, where the normal growth in population was already placing a heavy strain on land resources. The urban labour market failed to expand at a rate fast enough to absorb the surplus rural population, and in the late 1950s the government came at last to realize that it was impossible to continue implementing the Act.

It was calculated in 1959 that no land would be available for some 30 per cent of those Africans who were entitled to it.[20] The failure of the industrial sector to absorb the increasing African population was reflected in the rise in the proportion of Africans resident in the rural areas, where the African population doubled between 1953 and 1968.[21]

The growth in the population dependent on agriculture has inevitably been reflected in a declining standard of living in the rural areas. Malnutrition is widespread, and it is reported that traders who used to barter consumer goods for locally produced foodstuffs are now on occasion selling maize for cash sent in from relatives working in the towns – a fitting testimony to the benefits which the bulk of the African population enjoy after nearly eighty years of white rule.

From the vantage point of White Rhodesia, the African farmers are of little economic importance; in 1970 African rural sales amounted to only £6m.[22] The importance of the reserves is rather that they provide an area in which the growing African population which is surplus to the needs of a stagnant economy can be confined. Unemployment in the towns becomes underemployment in the reserves, which avoids the security problems posed by large-scale urban discontent or the need for welfare measures. The consequence will inevitably be a continued decline in African rural income, estimated to have fallen already from £15 *per capita* in 1956 to £11 in 1968.[23] The Rhodesian Front Government has made no effort to ameliorate this situation. The Land Tenure Act of 1969, which replaced the Land Apportionment Act, shifted 8 million acres of land from the 'unassigned' category into the category of 'European area'. Section 5 of the Act provides that 'the total extent of all land in the European area shall not differ by more than 2 per cent from one half of the combined extent of both the European and African areas'.

White Rhodesia, having taken from the Africans the best land and expropriated the surplus from the earlier periods of African agricultural prosperity, now proposes to give the impoverished reserves, renamed Tribal Trust Lands, a measure of clocal self government. The white élite's sudden conversion to the idea of a limited democracy for the Africans has, of course, a hard economic base. The Tribal Trust Lands are not only to be given a greater degree of local control; they are also to be made responsible for raising locally the revenue to administer services, a decision which has already resulted in the closing of many African schools. No doubt any decline in services will be proclaimed by Europeans as further evidence of the African's incompetence at self-government and self-reliance. An alternative way of viewing it might be to suggest that having reduced the Africans to poverty, White Rhodesia is now prepared to let them pay for and organize their own funeral.

Legislating for cheap labour

The early settlers experienced considerable difficulty in securing a steady supply of African labour at the wages which they were willing to pay. Several solutions existed. Wages could be increased and working conditions improved to make the labour market more attractive in comparison with agriculture. Tax demands on the Africans could be raised so as to compel more Africans to seek cash employment. Constraints could be imposed on African agriculture to reduce its profitability and in consequence raise the relative economic advantage of entering the labour market. Workers could be sought outside the colony. And, finally, Africans could be compelled to work by the exercise of overt or discreet compulsion.

At one point or another, all of these stratagems were used.

Initially, direct labour recruitment was paramount. Those who needed African labour would, generally with the help of the police or the Native Commissioner, approach a village chief or head-man and indicate their requirements. African messengers were employed to assist the Native Commissioners. The resident British Commissioner, Sir Richard Martin, described the system as 'compulsory labour . . . a system synonymous with slavery'.[24]

In the face of criticism, and prompted by the need to regularize labour supplies, the B S A C set up, in 1903, a Native Labour Supply Bureau, which sought to recruit labour both inside the colonies and in neighbouring countries, particularly Northern Rhodesia and Nyasaland. The element of compulsion, however, remained. The 1901 Master Servant Act, which excluded white workers, created a whole range of legal penalties for workers who failed to perform to the satisfaction of their white masters. Under the Act, an African who left his employment was subject to a fine or imprisonment of up to six months, after which he was obliged to return to serve out the rest of his contract plus the time equal to the length of his imprisonment. An employee found guilty of 'performing his duty carelessly or improperly' or of being 'abusive or insulting . . . to any person in lawful authority over him' was liable to a fine of £4 or one month's imprisonment.

Many Africans who signed contracts, particularly migrant workers, were unaware of the conditions. They could be placed in the charge of a brutal employer, where they suffered inadequate food and housing and free use of the *sjambok*. The Master Servant Act ensured that once the contract was signed the employee was, in the words of one moderate commentator, 'some employer's short term slave'.[25] The Act was relentlessly enforced and provided a crucial element in the control of African labour. In the first six months of 1943, for example, one in nine of the African employees in Bulawayo went before Native Commissioners' Courts in 'Master and Servants' cases.[26]

The generally low wages paid and the possibility of meeting tax demands and making purchases through agricultural sales created a continuous labour shortage in the first two decades and became one of the major concerns of white farmers and

mining companies. It was calculated in 1903 that 'a woman cultivating one or two acres, could make as much money in a month as
her husband (working in the labour market) in three'.[27] A number of attempts were made to bring indentured foreign workers
from India, China, Abyssinia and Aden, but working conditions
in Rhodesia made the imperial government and other colonial
governments reluctant to cooperate.

In 1903 there were already some 3,000 or 4,000 migrant workers in Southern Rhodesia, largely from Northern Rhodesia and
Nyasaland. In 1926, when the total number in wage employment had risen to 172,000, some 96,000 were from outside the
colony; and by 1946, when the number in wage employment had
risen to 363,000, there were 203,000 migrant workers.[28]

The supply of labour from Nyasaland and Northern Rhodesia
was in large part ensured by the need of the Africans from those
countries to earn sufficient income to pay taxes imposed by their
own governments; and since Northern Rhodesia was under the
control of the British South Africa Company until 1924, this
was naturally a factor which entered into tax calculations. These
migrants ensured that the labour market was able to meet employers' demands without any large wage increases. Eduardo
Mondlane described the significance of cheap labour in the
development of Mozambique in terms readily applicable to
Southern Rhodesia:

During the early development of the colony, agriculture and the
search for minerals yielded relatively small profit. But there was one
resource which could be profitably exploited: Labour. It was on labour
that all other enterprises were founded; the exploitation of labour was
essential to the whole development of the colony.[29]

Low wages served to increase the profits of white employers
and, therefore, the surplus available for investment, as well as
keeping in operation many farms and businesses which, with
higher wages, would have gone bankrupt. In 1943, when 50 per
cent of the national income was derived from gold-mining, a
government committee was informed that 80 per cent of the
country's gold mines would be unable to operate profitably without black labour.[30]

Cheap African labour was the prerequisite of white Rhodesian prosperity. Ethel Tawse Jollie, a member of the Southern Rhodesian Legislative Assembly after self-government, included in her praise for the country: 'Living is cheap when one reflects that the poorest white man employs servants, and the middle class woman expects to live in a style only possible to the rich at home.'[31] Cheap African labour was not merely important for European comfort, it was crucial to the whole economy. Huggins told the Legislative Assembly on 30 November 1944: 'We cannot exist for five minutes without the native today. He is absolutely essential to our wage structure, if nothing else ... if we went on a purely European basis with the present conditions of living and pay ... the country would be sub-economic and down and out in five minutes.'[32] On another occasion the Prime Minister told the Assembly: 'The Europeans could not have the standard of living they have today if it were not for the fact that we have a big native population who are doing a great proportion of the work of this country.'[33]

In addition to the introduction of the hut tax and subsequently the poll tax, which forced Africans into the cash economy, the white employers also benefited from the down-turn in African agriculture. At the same time, the penetration of African markets by European products not only created a demand for these products, but also led to a decline in home production in favour of European manufactures, for example in clothing. Where these demands could not be met by crop sales, again Africans were stimulated to seek wage employment. As a more direct method of securing the desired result, in 1926 the Native Juveniles Employment Act was passed, which provided for the compulsory indenturing of Africans found 'loafing' in urban areas.

To facilitate control over the African population, every African over 14 was required to carry a registration certificate, which both served as a tax receipt and could be endorsed with a labour contract. The 1936 Native Registration Act tightened control over the urban African even further. The Act obliged every adult male African in an urban area to have proof that he was working in the town, a pass to seek work, or a visiting pass.

The low wages in the urban areas before 1950 were based on

the assumption that an African was only a temporary resident in the towns. An African's urban wages were regarded as a supplement to the income, principally in kind rather than cash, which his wife obtained on the family plot in the reserve. The overwhelming majority of the Africans in the towns were males, and there were few provisions for Africans to live with their families. Accommodation for single males was generally provided in barracks by employers, or, in the case of domestic servants, in small 'out-houses'. In 1941 Robert Tredgold, Minister of Justice and Defence, reflected the popular view when he told the Legislative Assembly not to think 'that a native's wages and a white man's wages are on the same footing because they are not. The native's wages are pocket money.'[34]

Africans were restricted to unskilled work, and European artisans ensured that Africans, far from acting as a competitive element, in fact bolstered white wages. The strict colour-bar placed European workers in a strong bargaining position, since there was a constant shortage of skilled labour. Employers were able to meet European wage demands only because African labour was so cheap.

The depression in the 1930s brought demands for the stricter institutionalization of this system to ensure that employers did not seek to economize by using black labour. The 1934 Industrial Conciliation Act established industrial boards, composed of unions and employers in the industry in question, which were empowered to agree on wages and conditions. Africans were not recognized as employees under the Act and could not take part in the bargaining process. Nor were African unions legally recognized. The European unions gained control of apprenticeships in the industry and were able to exclude Africans. The effect of the Act was to lay down a rate for the job which meant in theory that African and white wages for the same job would be equal. In practice no employer would employ an African at the same rate as a European, since there would be no economic advantage, and in any event no union would have allowed it. In 1944 the government committee on African labour found that one effect of the Act had been to keep African wages below the poverty line.

Training the African labour-force

*In the colonial society, education is such that it serves the colonialist ...
In a régime of slaves, education was but one institution forming slaves*
– FRELIMO, Department of Education and Culture[35]

Neither individuals nor races are born with equal facilities or opportunities – Resolution of the Rhodesian Anglican Synod, 1903

The African educational system was designed to meet white requirements in the economic sphere; and in this, wittingly or unwittingly, the churches were helpers. In the early years many of the denominations had been provided with land by the British South Africa Company to establish mission stations; and, no doubt, the Company saw religion as a valuable means of controlling the African population. The churches were quick to take advantage of the pacification of the Shona and Ndebele, and the disruption of their traditional culture, to spread the Gospel. Since the mission had considerable powers over those who lived on its land, the task was greatly simplified.

The established churches protected their position. In 1903 the African Methodist Episcopal Church, which had its origins in the United States, requested permission to set up a branch in Southern Rhodesia. In opposing the application, the Bishop of Mashonaland commented that the church 'would appear to have aroused in the minds of a considerable section of the natives of South Africa political and social aspirations ... It advocates "higher" education, makes comparison between the political and social position of the American Negro and the African native.' In short, its view of evangelical work was hardly consistent with the role played by the existing missionary organizations. The church's leaders were refused entry; though in time the church penetrated into Southern Rhodesia by way of African migrant workers.[36]

The first Educational Ordinance of 1899 gave mission schools 10 shillings per African student providing certain conditions were fulfilled, one of which was that 'school is kept for not less than four hours daily of which not less than two hours should be devoted to industrial training'.

The 1903 Educational Ordinance established as the object of African education that 'pupils are taught industrial work, receive a sufficient knowledge of English and are trained in habits of discipline and cleanliness'.[37] Ethel Tawse Jollie wrote: 'There is only one way to force him [the African] to play his part in the economic life of the country; that is by civilizing him.'[38] It was a very Rhodesian civilization that Tawse Jollie had in mind. In 1927 she told the Legislative Assembly: 'We do not intend to hand over this country to the native population or to admit them to the same society or political position as we occupy ourselves ... We should make no pretence of educating them in exactly the same way as we do the European.'[39]

Africans who received more than the rudimentary education designed to equip them for the needs of the European economy were a threat to the government. They were unable to utilize their skills in the labour market and were often driven into opposition, providing the leadership for various African protest movements.

This strictly functional approach to African education continued even as Rhodesia entered upon 'partnership' in the Federation. The governing United Rhodesia Party's policy was that 'the emphasis in African education should be on character, and the inculcation of a sense of responsibility and pride in work efficiently performed'.[40]

Changes in the colony's economic base

The promised golden bonanza did not materialize, but gold mining did play an important part in the economy of the colony.* Gold production rose from 55,000 ounces in 1900 to 854,000 ounces in 1914. In addition to gold, a large coal deposit was found at Wankie, and deposits of lead, chrome, tungsten and asbestos were discovered. Mining provided the major stimulus to the economy, generating hard currency for necessary imports and providing a market for agricultural produce. In 1926

*In the meantime, Rhodes and other B S A C directors had made a considerable fortune in share dealings on the strength of the earlier prospect of a second Rand. After the defeat of the Matabele in 1893, the Rhodes–Beit group made an estimated £3m. capital gain by selling at the peak price before they again plummetted.[41]

minerals accounted for £4m. of the country's £5.4m. exports, with the remainder made up by agricultural produce; and even in 1943 it was estimated that 50 per cent of the national income was provided directly or indirectly from gold.[42]

Initially the secondary sector was largely composed of plants processing the agricultural produce; the construction industry; and the railroads, which provided valuable income from shipments through Southern Rhodesia of Northern Rhodesian copper and supplies.

The subsequent development of the manufacturing sector in Rhodesia was stimulated by five main factors. The depression in the early 1930s encouraged economic diversification. The Second World War made import substitution imperative as tradtional sources of supply became less accessible. At the same time, the demand for minerals and the economic impact of the large British air force base in Southern Rhodesia created a boom in the colony's economy. Postwar immigration and the natural growth in the white population extended the size of the internal market, particularly in the construction industry, and made the manufacture of import substitutes more profitable. Between 1946 and 1951 the net immigration amounted to 47,187; the highest figure in any previous five-year period had been recorded between 1926 and 1931, when a net immigration of 7,421 took place. The increase in the size of the African labour-force and the improvement in real wages, particularly in the urban sector, expanded the African market, which was the main target for many manufacturers, particularly in the textile industry. Manufacturers could not hope to compete with high-quality European imports nor to overcome European consumer preferences for imported goods.

The entry of Southern Rhodesia into the Central African Federation not only extended the size of the market for manufactured products but gave Southern Rhodesia access to a share of the growing revenue from the Northern Rhodesia copper belt which was used to improve the economic infrastructure of the country. As the table below indicates, by 1945 manufacturing had already overtaken mining and agriculture in the value of its gross output.

The rapid growth in postwar agriculture was largely due to the growth in tobacco production, which overtook gold as the country's most important export item.

Gross value of output in European agriculture, mining and manufacturing at market prices in £m.

	European Agriculture	Mining	Manufacturing
1938	3·8	7·7	5·1
1945	9·8	8·1	14·1
1951	21·2	15·1	51·0
1957	41·8	25·8	105·1

(Source: L. Tow, *The Manufacturing Economy of Southern Rhodesia*, p. 4.)

Rationalizing the labour market

The expansion in the manufacturing sector resulted in the rapid growth of the African urban labour-force. The African population in the urban areas rose from 1 million in 1946 to 1·5 million in 1953.[43]

In 1944 Prime Minister Huggins told the Assembly that secondary industry needed 'an efficient, stable labour force . . . In practice the provision of decent accommodation for married natives is essential if the native is to become more efficient and good at his job.'[44] In 1946 the Native (Urban Areas) Accommodation Act empowered municipalities to set aside Native Urban Areas in which to provide adequate housing for all Africans not housed on the private premises of employers. Rents were to be paid by the employer and were to be the same for married and single Africans. This rule was intended to encourage provision of married accommodation, since it equalized costs between those who employed single and those who employed married workers. It was intended to stabilize the African labour-force by encouraging the residence of families in the urban areas – a decisive break with past policies. The Act also provided for the election of African advisory boards who would work with municipal councils and, it was hoped, reduce friction in the urban areas; though effective power would remain in white hands.

Rhodesian Railways was one of the first industries to take advantage of the economic benefits to be gained from a stable labour-force. A large house-building scheme was started, and the management sought to obtain 75 per cent married strength 'in order to stabilize labour and obtain greater effectiveness'.[45]

In 1947 a Native Labour Board Act provided for the establishment of boards to lay down wage rates for Africans in different industries. In 1949 the Railway Act provided for the recognition of the Railway Workers' Union, a reflection of the strength of the black proletariat in that industry. Most African workers had to wait a further ten years before they could form legally recognized unions.

African wages, which had actually declined since the early 1930s despite the growth of the economy, finally began to rise – a rise which again had its origins in the changing nature of the African work-force. African wage increases were predominantly in those sectors where the benefits of a stable African labour force were most marked: in manufacturing, transport and communications. Wartime scarcities of white labour had forced employers and unions to allow a larger number of semi-skilled jobs to be filled by Africans. European job categories were subdivided, and Africans recruited to fill the new categories so created. The new jobs were generally at a higher level of pay than that otherwise enjoyed by Africans, though still well below European pay scales.

Industries which depended on a higher level of skill found that a high labour turnover was unprofitable. Low wages forced Africans to be partially dependent on agricultural production in the reserves to support their families. Higher wages and improved accommodation in the urban areas were clearly the essential prerequisites for a permanent skilled African labour-force. The same industries which would gain most from a stable labourforce were also those most susceptible to the growth of African trade unions. Labour militancy added to the upward pressure in wages and provided white employers and politicians with a further reason to improve the conditions of the urban labour-force.

The railway strike which started in Bulawayo in 1945 had alerted the white ruling class to the need for a mechanism for dealing with African wage demands. Hence resulted the 1947 Native Labour Boards.

Nevertheless, these changes did not create any overwhelming improvements in conditions for the African proletariat. In 1948 the National Native Labour Board set up a new minimum wage in the urban areas which, including rations, amounted to £3 per month. A 1943 survey by the Native Welfare Society had established a necessary minimum wage level of £5 for a single African and £7 10 shillings for a married man. Ten years later, according to a report from the Urban African Affairs Commission, a sample of Salisbury households showed that 57·1 per cent came in the category of 'extremely impoverished', with incomes at least 35 per cent below the Poverty Datum Line, while only 23·5 per cent had incomes above the line.[46]

From 1946 to 1956 there was a rapid growth in wage employment in the agricultural, mining and manufacturing sectors, reflecting the postwar boom and the rapid economic growth in the first years of the Federation of Rhodesia and Nyasaland. African wage employment rose from 363,000 in 1946 to 564,000 in 1956. Much of this increase was, of course, in migrant labour, but the number of Southern Rhodesian Africans in wage employment rose from 161,000 to 267,000.[47]

African earnings outside agriculture and domestic service continued to show a marked rise thereafter, but the growth in the urban labour-force slowed considerably. This was partly a result of the down-turn in the economy precipitated by the fall in world copper prices in 1956–7. Subsequently the political uncertainty over the future of the Federation and later of Southern Rhodesia itself discouraged investment. The slower growth-rate of the labour-force was also a logical consequence of the higher price of African labour. This encouraged the more efficient use of African manpower and made automation relatively more attractive, since the cost was now judged against potential savings on a higher wages bill.

Arrighi, while recognizing the role that trade union militancy had played, argues that the main explanation of the rapid growth in African urban wages was that '"stabilized labour" commanded a premium determined by the difference between the cost of the means of subsistence of single men during their working life in wage employment and the cost of the means of subsistence of a worker's family over his life cycle'. Large enterprises, especially those operating in secondary and tertiary industries which could introduce labour-saving methods in production, began to find it profitable to pay this 'premium' because higher wages were more than compensated for by the higher productivity of a permanent labour-force.[48]

The proportion of the African population in employment has fallen, and continues to do so, resulting in a growing population concentration in the Tribal Trust Lands. In 1958, 11·8 per cent of the total African population was in employment outside European agriculture; by 1971 the figure had fallen to 9·1 per cent.[49]

In 1956, some 56 per cent of the African population was estimated to live in the rural areas; by 1967, the figure had risen to 63 per cent.[50] The rise in wages in the manufacturing sector was paralleled by a decline in the subsistence level in the rural areas. Average urban incomes which were 1·6 times the average rural income in 1949, rose to 4·5 times the average rural income in 1968.[51]

It is worth exploring the political implications of this shift. The African proletariat, benefiting both from the desire of employers to stabilize the labour-force, and from its own bargaining position, has managed, relative to the rural peasantry, to secure a substantial increase in its standard of living. The rural peasantry had in many ways become expendable from an economic point of view, the rural areas serving more and more as merely a trap for the surplus population from the towns. In contrast, the black urban proletariat is still the key factor in white prosperity. And, relatedly, their concentrated presence in the urban areas makes them a volatile political force. Indeed it seems reasonable to suppose that one of the operative factors has been a desire to stabilize the black labour-force not only economically but politically.

In 1959 the Industrial Conciliation Act was amended to include African employees, with the significant exceptions of those in agriculture and domestic service. As from 1960 Africans could, in theory, join European unions; and where no union existed to cover them, they could form their own. Like much Rhodesian legislation which does not specifically distinguish between the races, however, the amendment in fact created African trade unions, since the European trade unions had no intention of opening up 'European jobs' to Africans. Still, African unions were for the first time able to take part in the collective bargaining process, and the amendment should be seen as an important move by the more far-sighted sections of the whites to institutionalize and legitimize economic conflict between white capital and the black proletariat. Significantly, too, unions which gave funds to political parties or allowed their facilities to be used by such, were ineligible for official recognition. The imprisonment of some 500 African National Congress members in 1959, which was allegedly prompted by the threat to security posed by nationalists in the three territories of the Federation, was also a precautionary move to prevent the nationalists from using the new Act to increase their influence over the black proletariat. An immediate consequence of the Act was a rapid increase in the unionization of black workers which added to the upward pressure on black urban wages.

The following figures give some idea of the continued movement of African wages in different sectors of the economy. In 1958 wages in Agriculture and Forestry stood at an annual average of R$104; in the private domestic sector at R$176; in manufacturing at R$215; and in transport and communications at R$273. In 1971 the respective figures were R$124; R$260; R$485; and R$717.[52] In agriculture, where there is little to be gained from a stable work-force and where many of the labourers are migrants from neighbouring countries, wages are low and rise slowly. By contrast, in the manufacturing and the transport and communications sectors, where the workers have a stronger bargaining position and where employers seek a more permanent work-force, wage rises have been rapid.

The role of the national bourgeoisie in development

In this discussion of Rhodesia's development, one key element should not be ignored. Unlike most colonies, Southern Rhodesia had a national ruling race. The colony was not administered primarily in the economic interests of foreign investors but rather in the interests of a multi-class white alliance. As we shall see, there were indeed conflicts within white society; but on the necessity for development and the creation of a diversified industrial base, there was usually a wide measure of agreement. Foreign capital had an important influence on the policies adopted, but not always a determining one. Ultimately the government was responsible neither to foreign investors nor to Britain but to politically conscious white electors who had every intention of building a stable, white-dominated society in Central Africa and who demanded that the government support them in that aim. Giovanni Arrighi and John Saul argue:

> The development of an organic industrial base in South Africa and Rhodesia which is a key dimension of the area's strength must be traced to the presence in these countries of a national bourgeoisie (the settlers) sufficiently strong to support a 'national' interest *vis-à-vis* the metropolitan countries. This class, by promoting important structural changes in the economies in question, has in fact restrained that 'development of under-development' which is a normal phenomenon in centre-periphery relations. [53]

In order to promote national development, the government intervened vigorously in the economy, both in support of various sectional interests and in pursuit of overall development. Already cited has been the assistance which the government gave to white farmers, a policy which was paralleled in the mining field. One economist writes:

> The government has employed a number of devices, with varying success, in an effort to keep the small worker in operation. It has attempted to lower his cost by making equipment available to him at a subsidized rental. It has attempted to increase the efficiency of his operations by providing a government-owned plant for processing low grade ores. It has even attempted to increase the income of the small worker by subsidizing the price of gold. [54]

In 1933, in response to pressure from the mining industry, the government paid £2m. to buy out the mineral rights of the BSAC.

In pursuing general development, the government sought to create a comprehensive economic infrastructure, and, where private capital was reluctant to invest the government stepped in. Faced with a steel shortage during the Second World War, the government nationalized the Bulawayo Iron and Steel Works. Huggins wished to increase wartime production and to ensure that ISCOR, the South African Steel Trust which held shares in the Bulawayo Works, would not, in the event of a postwar slump, cut back production in Southern Rhodesia for the sake of the South African enterprise.[55] In 1942, faced with difficulties in selling the local cotton crop and securing cotton imports, the government set up a Cotton Research and Industry Board. Within a year the Board was able to undertake the ginning and spinning of cotton for private enterprise, which completed the manufacturing process. In 1944 the government took over the Triangle Sugar Estates and established a Sugar Industry Board.

In pursuing these policies Huggins was going beyond the wishes of private enterprise. Murray comments: 'The reaction to these measures among those engaged in commerce and industry was out-right opposition. To nationalization they were adamantly opposed; government assistance was desired but not public ownership.'[56]

However, Huggins, reflecting his multi-class settler political support, did much to develop a national industry and lay the basis for industrial diversification

The encouragement of immigration was also seen as a means of stimulating economic development and of increasing the strength of white society and, therefore, the permanence of white rule. In fact, immigration had a dual impact. It increased the size of the money economy – as distinct from the large African subsistence economy – but it also absorbed scarce capital resources in the provision of new housing and services. This meant that a high rate of immigration in the short term served to reduce the surplus available for industrial investment. This argument, however, is only valid in contrast to an alternative approach: the training of the indigenous labour-force and the expansion of the internal market by removing the barriers against African economic advance. Before 1953 this was never considered as a serious possibility; and after 1953 the opposition of those whites who felt most threatened by African advance hindered efforts in this direction.

It is worth noting the economic consequences of racism for overall capital growth, consequences which resulted in the continued dependence of the economy on the export trade and, in the absence of expansion, on the export sector. The scarcity of imports after the imposition of sanctions resulted in some successful attempts at economic diversification; but the economy still faces serious difficulties, not the least of which is the continued limitation on the growth of a prosperous African market.

Ultimately, self-sustaining economic growth had to be based on a growth of the domestic market for consumer products. The artificially inflated wages paid to white workers resulted in the higher cost of goods and services. In 1926 one railway administrator estimated that the wages bill of the Engineering and Locomotive Department could be halved if more work were given to Africans, and reduced even further if Africans were trained for fully skilled jobs.[57] Such savings would have increased both the investable surplus and the international competitiveness of Southern Rhodesia.

Other consequences of the discriminatory policies were equally destructive to overall growth prospects. In spite of its agricultural resources, Southern Rhodesia was a large food importer, a situation which could have been transformed if Africans had been able to farm the unused acreage in the European areas. Provision of segregated facilities led to duplication and waste. Surplus capacity in European schools went hand in hand with overcrowding in African ones.*

*For a fuller consideration of the issues raised in this section, see G. Arrighi, *The Political Economy of Rhodesia*, (The Hague: Mouton, 1967), and 'Labour Supplies in Historical Perspective: A Study of the Proletarianisation of the African Peasantry in Rhodesia', *Journal of Developmental Studies*, Vol. 6 (1969–70); and R. B. Sutcliffe, 'Stagnation and Inequality in Rhodesia, 1946–1968', *Bulletin of the Oxford University Institute of Economics and Statistics*, Vol. 33 (1971).

3 The development of white politics

Discussing the historical significance of the settler element in colonialism, Arghiri Emmanuel has written:

Beyond the causes that are so to speak 'inherent' in capitalism, there exists another independent motive force that generates the colonial phenomenon ... this motive force proper to colonialism is none other than the settlers themselves ... For these people, the colonial adventure was ... the main spring of their existence and their supreme justification.

The presence of a strong settler element substantially altered the course of those societies which were affected:

Big capitalist enterprises were able to come to terms with the essential aspirations of the local élite ... the settler community could not come to terms with anything; neither with the trusts, nor with the metropolitan country – far less with Africanization or independence. It could be saved only by secession from the metropolis by setting up an independent 'white' state.[1]

In many ways this argument sums up the Southern Rhodesian experience.

An understanding of white politics in Southern Rhodesia has to be based on an appreciation of the conflicting interests of the different groups in white society and their relative historical strength. The crucial issue has been the attitude of the different white social classes towards the African population. White wage workers and farmers have always opposed the possibility of African competition either in the labour or in the produce market. They vigorously fought any move which would raise the general level of African wages or reduce the supply of African labour. In contrast, the interests of the manufacturing sector, which grew rapidly in importance after 1939, were, in many ways, convergent with African ones. Manufacturing interests sought to increase the size of the African market and therefore supported moves to increase African productivity and wages. Many industries also favoured increased competition in the labour market to reduce the upward pressure on wages caused by the white artisans' monopoly of skilled work. For the large mining companies dependent on an export market, the issue of African advance was not crucial, except (and this was even more true of Northern Rhodesia) in the political sense. A rise in African wages could be met either by increased automation and a reduction in the workforce, or by fragmenting 'white' jobs and filling them with Africans at lower rates of pay.

White class contradictions and their resolution

The conflict between the white working class and the bourgeoisie was particularly strong before 1933. In that year the election of a Reform Party government resulted in an inter-class governing alliance which lasted until 1962.

The first years of white settlement were years of considerable economic hardship, a hardship which was often reflected in opposition to BSAC policies on land sales, mineral rights, and railway charges, and the Company's failure to secure an adequate supply of cheap African labour. Gann and Gelfand conclude that, in this period, 'the challenge to the established order came from the poorer European settlers who now questioned both the Chartered Companies' political position and the traditional economic rights of capital'.[2] Working-class opposition found expression in the formation of trade unions and later in the founding of the Labour Party.

In 1916, taking advantage of the tight labour market created by the First World War, railway workers took successful strike action, and in the same year formed the Rhodesian Railway Workers' Union. The railway industry, which employed the largest group of white workers, provided a natural vanguard for the white working class, as thirty years later it was to do for the black working class. In 1919, the Rhodesian Mine and General Workers' Union organized a strike, and the railwaymen blacked Wankie coal. In 1920, a second rail strike secured an eight-hour day and improved wages. Unions developed in other sectors, and organized labour was active in the campaign to prevent union with South Africa. But, although this succeeded, the early years of self-government saw labour on the defensive.

The bourgeoisie, which had favoured union with South Africa, was quick to cut its losses: 'By 1925 the General Manager of the British South Africa Company, the Manager of Wankie Collieries, the Manager of Rhodesian Railways and others from the Chamber of Mines were all Rhodesia Party members of the Assembly.'[3] In contrast, organized labour had no representation in the early years. After the success of the campaign for responsible government, a Labour Party had been formed; but all the candidates were defeated in 1924, as a result of the decision to have two-member constituencies, which negated the concentrated working-class vote.

The Rhodesia Party governments of 1924–33 reflected the interests of the major businesses in the colony, particularly the mining industry. After the death of Coghlan, who had led the campaign for responsible government, the Rhodesia Party was led first by Howard Moffat, former General Manager of the Bechuanaland Exploration Company, and subsequently by George Mitchell, a former President of the Chamber of Mines, which represented the large mining companies. Confidence in the government was not increased when Moffat, after negotiations with Sir Edmond Davis, Chairman of the Bechuanaland Exploration Company, announced the payment of £2m. for the B S A C's mineral rights. Many Rhodesians had demanded that the government take over the rights without payment of compensation.

The employers mounted a counter-offensive against the unions. They played off the Amalgamated Engineering Union, a craft union, against the industrial unions, mainly the Rhodesia Railway Workers' Union and the Rhodesian Mine and General Workers' Union. By 1923 the Rhodesia Mine Owners' Association had broken the Rhodesian Mine and General Workers' Union. Then the employers, having no further use for the Amalgamated Engineering Union, refused further cooperation; and it, too, had closed down all its mine branches by 1926.

The Railway Workers' Union managed to survive through the twenties, but only in a much weakened form. The Union was forced to accept wage cuts in the industry and was compelled by its own rank and file to sever its formal links with the Labour Party. The Depression increased working-class insecurity and encouraged demands for more vigorous protection from African competition. The main fear was that, faced with falling profit-margins, the employers would seek to economize by using African labour in the place of white. The demand for the legal entrenchment of the privileged position of white workers found support in other sections of the white community. Many were anxious to preserve white standards to ensure that there was no loss of face before the African population. Ranger notes the concern voiced during the railway workers' strike in Bulawayo in 1929, and quotes a contemporary writer: 'What about the natives if the white population starts rioting? What about the Matabele? ... It is not such a long time since 1896 ... when all is said and done we are only a handful among an immense native population.'[4] The armed rising by white miners on the South African Rand in 1922, in protest against attempts to under-cut white wages by recruiting African workers to skilled positions, had served as a warning to employers who might have similar plans for Rhodesia.

If no compromise could be reached between white labour and capital, then the possibility of a working-class alliance across the colour line was always an option. But, such an alliance would have only been considered by white labour as a last resort. A far greater threat was seen from the African masses than from the white bourgeoisie. The strategy of the white unions and Labour Party leaders was to turn the white proletariat into a labour aristocracy, not a revolutionary vanguard. Nevertheless, if a black–white working-class alliance was not white labour's preference, it certainly offered a far greater threat to the white bourgeoisie and the other sectors of white society: a threat directed at the very basis of Rhodesian society. The growth of African militancy in the late 1920s naturally made the threat seem more immediate; and, indeed, there were fleeting instances of black–white co-operation in the union field.

Since the Rhodesia Party government reflected business thinking, its racial policies were less stringent than those demanded by many settlers. Indeed Moffat, according to Huggins's biographers, 'stood out as a sincere believer in African development'.[5] This issue became crucial in the 1933 elections, when the Rhodesia Party was defeated by the Reform Party under Godfrey Huggins. Huggins was elected on a promise to implement a 'Two Pyramid Policy', which was the 'gradual differential development of the European and Native races on a territorial basis'[6] – a policy similar to apartheid.

After his election, Huggins rapidly moved to satisfy the demands of the white electorate. The position of white workers was insured by the introduction of the 1934 Industrial Conciliation Act. Huggins's biographers comment: 'The machinery of law now swung into operation on their [the white workers',] behalf, the first prosecution ever under the new Statute actually being directed against an employer who underpaid a white South African immigrant.'[7] The Reform Party accepted the underlying Labour Party policy that 'in the white area, no European engaged in the agricultural, mining, or other industries shall be affected by the lower civilization and economic standards of the natives'.[8]

In 1934, the stabilization of white society was completed when Huggins, faced with dissent in the Reform Party, joined with Rhodesia Party members to form the United Party, which held power until 1962. The United Party was effectively a coalition of white class interests, a coalition reflected in the postwar election slogan: 'Neither Socialist nor Capitalist – The People's Party'. Many white workers continued until the late 1940s to vote for the Labour Party, and those dissatisfied with the government's commitment to racial supremacy voted for a series of opposition parties. Huggins's success was to ensure that these conflicts were brought within acceptable limits. The conflict between labour and capital would for the next thirty years be played out constitutionally and within a framework which did not jeopardize white rule.

The experience of the Rhodesia Party government from 1924 to 1933 had demonstrated that the white bourgeoisie could not govern the country in opposition to other important interests, particularly those of the farming community and the white working class. The government's defeat also demonstrated the operation of what Colin Leys has called 'The Inner Law' of European politics in Southern Rhodesia. Leys, who has written an unparalleled analysis of white political dynamics in Rhodesia, argues that the key issue in Rhodesian electoral politics was the 'racial fear' of the European electorate: 'Nothing is more striking in Rhodesian politics than the way in which, under different party labels, the opposition has consistently based its electoral appeal on the doctrine of European supremacy.'[9]

Federation: the consolidation and decline of white power

The establishment of a closer relationship with Northern Rhodesia had been considered intermittently for most of the first half of the twentieth century. Until 1923 Northern Rhodesia, like Southern Rhodesia, had been administered by the BSAC. But unlike Southern Rhodesia, her much smaller settler population had been unable to take over government after the Company's withdrawal, and this had passed into the hands of the Colonial Office. White settlers and later the indigenous population came to exercise a growing share in policy, but decisive political power remained with the Colonial Office.

Nyasaland, while not administered by the BSAC, had not entirely escaped Rhodes's interest. In 1889 he had promised Harry Johnston, formerly Vice-Consul in the Cameroons, £9,000 a year from the BSAC to set up an administration in Nyasaland, which Rhodes wanted to secure from Portuguese influence. Rhodes paid the bills, and the British government provided Johnston with the title of Consul for Portuguese East Africa. Johnston, however, proved to be an opponent of Company plans for the area, which became a British Protectorate. In any event, the absence of significant mineral wealth or attractive farming lands made Nyasaland marginal both to Company and, later, to settler considerations. When the Federation was established in 1953, Nyasaland offered neither wealth nor a significant white population and was only included at British insistence.

Initially the settlers were opposed to the amalgamation of Northern Rhodesia and Southern Rhodesia, as the B S A C discovered in 1917, when it tried to put through a proposal on those lines. Northern Rhodesia's mineral wealth was largely undiscovered, and whites in Southern Rhodesia saw no advantage in increasing the African proportion in the population. Settlers in Northern Rhodesia were worried that their interests would be ignored in a legislature dominated by Southern Rhodesia, while a few opposed any move which would extend Southern Rhodesia's pattern of race relations into the North. In the mid-twenties the new Southern Rhodesian government considered union with the North again, but the issue was not pursued to any conclusion.

The Hilton Young Commission, which visited the territories to consider some form of closer association, recommended against amalgamation. In 1931 the British government rejected immediate amalgamation, but left the possibility open for the future.

The Bledisloe Commission considered closer association between the Rhodesias and Nyasaland, and reporting in 1939, argued that the major barrier to amalgamation was the segregationist racial policy of the Southern Rhodesian government. On the other hand, the Commission recommended immediate amalgamation of Northern Rhodesia and Nyasaland. Africans in Northern Rhodesia and Nyasaland, many of whom, as former migrant workers, had first-hand knowledge of Southern Rhodesia's racial policies, were quick, then as later, to reject any closer association with Southern Rhodesia.

Northern Rhodesian settlers came to see amalgamation with Southern Rhodesia as the quickest route to freedom from Colonial Office control. The 1930 Passfield Memorandum, which in essence had done no more than restate British policy on colonial affairs, had proclaimed as paramount the interests of the indigenous population in any conflict with those of an immigrant population. 'With the publication of the Passfield

Memorandum, differences of opinion on the questions of amalgamation vanished. The urgent over-riding need was to escape from the clutches of the Colonial Office.'[10]

The increase in the European population of Northern Rhodesia, from some 10,500 in 1936 to 35,000 in 1951, strengthened the power of the settlers and their demand for more autonomy. The major stimulus to this rapid rise was the copper boom during the war and postwar years. The value of output grew from £7,990,000 in 1939 to £51,475,000 in 1953. This economic boom and the growth in Northern Rhodesia's white population increased the pressure for amalgamation not only in Northern Rhodesia but also in Southern Rhodesia. In 1953, Northern Rhodesia's export revenue was double that of Southern Rhodesia, and Southern Rhodesian whites saw in amalgamation or federation with Northern Rhodesia the opportunity to share in this growing revenue. In addition, as Huggins's biographers note: 'He and his supporters wanted Northern Rhodesia and Nyasaland as a protected market for their industries.'[11]

The desire to strengthen the position of the white population was also an important factor in Southern Rhodesia, where whites were anxious to avoid the possibility of a neighbouring black-ruled state or Colonial Office intervention in neighbouring affairs. Huggins said in 1948: 'We do not want our grandchildren to have as a neighbour a state such as Liberia which has no European guidance.'[12] J. M. Greenfield, Southern Rhodesian Minister of Internal Affairs, made explicit the argument for greater autonomy and a careful control of African advance: 'One of the principal reasons for having this Federation at all is to get as much power as possible out of the hands of people far away in London.' Dealing with the dangers of undue African influence in the proposed Federation, he continued: 'I cannot say that the common voters roll will persist ... if the common voters roll were retained and it became apparent that by means of the common voters roll Africans were being elected among those 36 people (the Southern Rhodesian Federal MPs) ... then a move would be made to change the constitution so as to reduce the number of representatives chosen to represent African interests.'[13]

The Second World War delayed any action on the Bledisloe recommendations, but it also brought strong pressures for inter-territorial coordination of the 'war effort'. In 1941, the Central African Council was established. The British Colonial Secretary, in announcing its establishment, said:

The Council will be consultative in character and its general function will be to promote the closest contact and cooperation between the three governments and their administrative and technical services ... His Majesty's Government realise that the Southern Rhodesia Government still adhere to their view that the three protectorates should be amalgamated. While, however, His Majesty's Government have, after careful consideration, come to the conclusion that the amalgamation of the territories, under existing circumstances, cannot be regarded as practicable, they are confident that the present scheme will, by ensuring a closer contact and cooperation, make an important contribution to the future prosperity of the Rhodesias and Nyasaland.[14]

Postwar approaches to the British Labour government and the Conservative opposition indicated that amalgamation was not an acceptable proposal, but that a form of federation would be considered. This, therefore, became the objective. The Labour government initiated discussions between itself and the other three governments involved which continued despite the outright rejection of the proposal by African representatives from Northern Rhodesia and Nyasaland. Whether the Labour government would have overridden this rejection is unclear.* Subsequently, in opposition, the party's leaders maintained that they would not have gone ahead without African consent. But the Labour Party in opposition, as we shall argue later, is no guide to the Labour Party in power. A sample of contemporary Labour thinking on colonial development was given by Sir Stafford Cripps:

The whole future of the Sterling group and its ability to survive depends in my view upon a quick and extensive development of our

*Welensky argues that Griffiths, the Colonial Secretary, was prepared to put through federation, and writes of Labour's subsequent opposition: 'I must confess I was a little shaken by the way in which Griffiths, in particular, seemed to have no qualms about attacking a measure which he himself, a year earlier, had been ready to put before the House of Commons.'[15]

African resources ... The further development of African resources is of the same crucial importance to the rehabilitation and strengthening of Western Europe as a restoration of European productive power is to the future progress and prosperity of Africa. Each needs and is needed by the other. In Africa indeed is to be found a great potential for new strength and vigour in the Western European economy and the stronger that economy becomes the better of course Africa itself will fare. We must be prepared to change our outlook and our habits of colonial development and force the pace so that within the next two to five years we can get a real marked increase of production in coal, minerals, timber, raw materials of all kinds, foodstuffs, and anything else that will save dollars or will sell in a dollar market.[16]

Cripps's view was remarkably similar to that of British capitalism expressed in regard to Central Africa in a speech by Sir Miles Thomas to the Engineering Industries Association in London in 1948.

In no single area is the upsurge of economic progress so apparent as it is in Central Africa today. Apart from its strategic position ... it possesses a great wealth of mineral potential that is of the utmost importance ... There is immense potential of hydro-electric power, and the possibility of oil made from coal. In fact the whole of that vast African territory – so much of it fortunately at a high altitude, enabling white men to live in reasonable comfort even in the tropical belt – is simply asking to be turned into both treasury and armoury, a source of dollar reserves in peace, a steadfast fortress in war ... I am a great believer in the value of the African as a contributor to the prosperity and security of the British Empire. He is a cheerful, loyal and good-tempered soul with a great sense of humour. When he is decently fed he will work hard. Provided that we can protect him from the virus of Communism – and the best way of doing that is to give him peace of mind and a full stomach – he has the manipulative dexterity and mental agility to enable him to become a useful operator in the agricultural and engineering field. In that way he will emerge as a wage-earning artisan who is a good customer for consumer goods.[17]

The Conservative government which came to power at the end of 1951 had in any case no scruples about the necessity for African consent; and, in September 1953, the federation of the three territories was completed. Those who had expressed fears of the racial consequences of federation could take little comfort from the fact that the new Federal Prime Minister was none other than Godfrey Huggins, now Lord Malvern, former Prime Minister of Southern Rhodesia. Two years earlier, Lord Malvern had told the Oxford Union:

... Even in such a vast country as Africa it seems unlikely that the Africans were not touched by some of the ancient civilizations, and this being so, it gives cause to wonder that they did not assimilate even the elements of culture and mechanical knowledge. Is there something in their chromosomes which makes them more backward and different from people living in the East and West, and if so, we have to ask ourselves, can this inherent disability be bred out? I do not know.[18]

This was the man who was to lead the Federation forward in 'partnership'.

One of the arguments popular in Britain among professedly liberal supporters of the Federation was that it would prevent Southern Rhodesia from falling under the influence of South Africa, where apartheid was being vigorously implemented. It is worthwhile recalling that Huggins had originally been elected to power on the 'Two Pyramid Policy' of separate development, a policy which in its principles was different from apartheid only in name, and a policy which Huggins continued to espouse until the late 1940s. In fact, the racial policies of Southern Rhodesia were not explicable in terms of such abstractions as South African influence, or the arbitrary opinions of individual politicians: they were explicable only in terms of the competition between whites and blacks for Rhodesia's resources. The situation reflected substantially the same developments as those at work in South Africa, although the smaller proportion of whites in Southern Rhodesia made a rigorous apartheid policy impractical. However, the British Labour Party had long since substituted pragmatism for any attempt at theoretical understanding of capitalism or colonialism; and it is therefore not surprising that Labour Colonial Secretary James Griffiths should, according to his own subsequent testimony, have been persuaded of the merits of federation in part by his civil servant's warnings on the dangers of the influence of South Africa.[19]*

*This contagion theory of Southern Rhodesia's racial patterns is widespread. A. K. H. Weinrich in a recent book, *Chiefs and Councils in Rhodesia*, writes of the

Attitudes to federation in Southern Rhodesia

In Southern Rhodesia, the major backers of federation had been the white élite, in particular the industrial and commercial corporations who looked to the larger markets which would be available and the valuable copper revenue. In 1949 with Huggins's encouragement, the United Central Africa Association had been formed to encourage public support for federation. Its first president was a past Chairman of the Associated Chambers of Commerce and Chairman of the Federation of Rhodesian Industries; other leading members came from the same milieu.[21] Two economists, writing in the early years of the Federation, considered 'the relief which a pooling of government funds may bring to the tax-payers of Southern Rhodesia and Nyasaland' to be the major advantage of federation.[22]

White opposition came from those who feared any increase in African influence as a result of adopting a policy of 'partnership'; they demanded, instead, adherence to the old policy of separate development. Indeed, this opposition secured 35 per cent of the vote in the Southern Rhodesia referendum on entry into the Federation. The white electors in Northern Rhodesia and Nyasaland were not called upon to vote; nor was the African population, with the exception of the few who were registered voters in Southern Rhodesia.

Africans in Southern Rhodesia were by no means as firmly opposed to federation as were their counterparts in Northern Rhodesia and Nyasaland. Largely on the initiative of the Northern Rhodesian African National Congress, an All-African Convention had been formed to unite different African groupings in Southern Rhodesia in opposition to federation, but the impetus was more one of loyalty to Africans in Northern Rhodesia and Nyasaland than indigenous opposition. In Southern Rhodesia, 'partnership' represented a step forward from the old segregationist approach. To the other territories it represented a

period after Company rule: 'The strong ties by which many Rhodesians felt bound to South Africa derived from pioneer days, when a significant number of Afrikaners took part in the occupation of the new country. Consequently, the racial policies of Rhodesia were modelled on those of the South.'[20]

step back from the Passfield Memorandum and the paramountcy of African interests.* Shamuyarira has described the mood:

> Particularly was it a time of optimism in Southern Rhodesia. A week or so before, the British House of Commons had approved the draft Order-in-Council setting up the Central African Federation ... For most of the hitherto oppressed Southern Rhodesian Africans a prospect of federation with the British protectorates of Northern Rhodesia and Nyasaland seemed full of promise: the new policy of partnership, which was to be inscribed in the federal constitution, would bring to a speedy end the segregation, humiliation and indignation which we had suffered for 40 years ... The Northern territories would help to break down the racial barriers and the Southern Rhodesian whites would even of their own accord, inspired by partnership, pass laws which would let us share political power and economic privileges and enjoy social justice.[14]

The economics of federation

Economically, federation served Southern Rhodesia well. On its establishment the Federation assumed £88·4m. of Southern Rhodesian debts, largely accrued as a result of the expensive postwar immigration drive. The tax revenues from Northern Rhodesian copper provided a high proportion of Federal revenue. Federal responsibilities were largely concerned with the European population. African affairs remained a territorial responsibility. This division of responsibilities favoured Southern Rhodesia, where the majority of whites lived. Leys and Pratt commented:

> The major expenditure items transferred to the Federal Government have been those which provide services primarily for Europeans. Not only did Southern Rhodesia have the heaviest concentration of European population in 1953, but it has also received the biggest share of post-1953 immigrants. In consequence, the relief given to its budget by Federation (which was from the first very substantial) has steadily increased.[15]

This point can be illustrated by comparing the pre- and post-Federation revenues of the Northern Rhodesian and Southern

---

*This doctrine, however, had already been subject to redefinition in terms of 'partnership' by the Labour Colonial Secretary, Creech Jones, in response to pressure from the unofficial members representing the Europeans in the Northern Rhodesian Legislative Assembly.[23]

Rhodesian territorial governments. In 1953 Northern Rhodesia collected 60 per cent of all central African revenue; in 1957–8 it collected only 20 per cent. Post-Federation revenue receipts in Southern Rhodesia fell from £22·3m. in 1953 to £19·7m in 1957–8. In Northern Rhodesia revenues fell from £39·9m. in 1953 to £19m. in 1957–8.[26] This fall in territorial revenue was, of course, more than matched by a rise in Federal revenue. For while Northern Rhodesia paid a disproportionate share in Federal revenue, Southern Rhodesia received a disproportionate share of the expenditure.

In addition to the tax benefits, Southern Rhodesian industry was able to turn Northern Rhodesia and Nyasaland into a protected market for its products, many of which were aimed at the African consumer. Indeed, Africans in the other territories were often forced to pay higher prices than those previously charged for cheaper imported products. In 1961, inter-territorial sales accounted for 41 per cent of the total output of toilet preparations in Southern Rhodesia, 29 per cent of the output of transport equipment, 35 per cent of clothing output, and 38 per cent of the output of rubber manufactures.[27]

The concentration of industry in Southern Rhodesia and the free access of Southern Rhodesian products to the Northern Rhodesian and Nyasaland markets militated against the development of any local secondary industry in these territories, which effectively became hinterlands providing mineral revenue, cheap labour and a captive market.

4 African opposition

For my part, the deeper I enter into the cultures and the political circles of Africa, the surer I become that the great danger which threatens Africa is the absence of ideology – Frantz Fanon[1]

The defeat of the Ndebele and the Shona in 1896 and 1897 did not mean the final pacification of Rhodesia. Local opposition was frequent; and if experience dictated that violence was likely to be unsuccessful, there were other forms of resistance – principally the evasion of government regulations and the refusal to pay taxes and meet requests for labour.

The administration had been caught unawares in 1896, and until after the First World War there were repeated rumours of impending African revolt. Between 1900 and 1901 Mapondera, a Shona chief who had not been involved in the earlier rising, attempted to regain control over his own territory by attacking both white officials and loyalist chiefs. With the exception of this unsuccessful episode, the rumours proved unfounded, however. Nevertheless, the mood amongst some of the Shona can be gauged from the fact that many of them crossed into Mozambique in 1917 to assist in the abortive revolt by neighbouring Shona tribes against Portuguese rule.

African protest movements took four main forms. There were the élite African associations, primarily concerned with improvements in the position of the emerging urbanized African intellectuals. Among the Ndebele, organizations were created to work for the restoration of the old Ndebele nation, at least in modified form, by obtaining permission to restore the kingship and secure land for an Ndebele home. The emergent working class provided a base for more modern kinds of organizing, most notably by the Rhodesian Industrial and Commercial Workers' Union. Finally and most significant, in terms of mass support, were the millenarian independent African Christian Churches, particularly the Watch Tower, the Zionists and the Vapostori Movement.

There were two related aspects which determined the response of the African population in the post-conquest period. The overwhelming issue for most Africans was the question of land, an issue especially important for the Ndebele whose traditional homeland, being more fertile, was more rapidly occupied by white settlers. The second was the contact of the African population with the European labour market. Traditional structures and beliefs were weakened, opening the way for new ideologies to emerge. The division of labour in the Ndebele tribal structure had left the higher-caste Ndebele free to follow martial pursuits. The imposition of white rule made these pursuits no longer practicable, and, as this went hand in hand with a reduction in available land and cattle, the Ndebele were propelled into the labour market at a faster rate than the Shona.

Since the Ndebele were more immediately affected by the land question and more rapidly exposed to wage employment, it was to be expected that their political response would be more sophisticated than that of the Shona. In formulating this response, they were aided by the homogeneity of the Ndebele and the continuity in leadership which had survived the 1896 rebellion.

The Ndebele combined traditional organization and leadership with modern tactics. Helped by the African National Congress in South Africa, the Matabele National Home Movement presented exhaustive defences of its positions, and organized petitioners and representations in Rhodesia at the British High Commission in South Africa, and even in London. Led in the most active period of its existence by Nyamanda, Lobengula's elder son, the Ndebele sought to restore kingship and obtain an Ndebele homeland. The issue of the kingship and the land united the Ndebele urban workers, the emerging intellectuals, the tribesmen and the royal family. In spite of this unity and the vigour with which the campaign was conducted, there were no concessions from the Company or the British government.

The Rhodesian Bantu Voters Association (R B V A), founded in 1923, was, as its name suggests, more concerned with the problems of the emerging African élite than with the African masses. It sought to use the tactic, which the African National Congress in the Cape had used with some effect, of bargaining black votes for commitment to legislation favoured by the organization. The major drawback of this policy was that African voting strength was insignificant and certainly not sufficient to force concessions from the settler government.

The ineffectiveness of the élite organizations like the RBVA, the Gwelo Native Welfare Association and the Rhodesian Native Association, as of the tribally based Ndebele Movement, was demonstrated in the result of the Morris Carter Land Commission and the subsequent adoption of the 1931 Land Apportionment Act. African demands, whether for a unified homeland instead of scattered reserves, a substantial increase in land, or equal rights to compete with Europeans, were systematically rejected.

The development of the trade union movement, like the Ndebele Homeland Movement and the élite associations, again owed much to South African influence. The Rhodesian Industrial and Commercial Workers' Union (RICU) was started in 1927 by Robert Sambo, who was sent to Rhodesia by the leader of the South African Industrial and Commercial Workers' Union, Clemens Kadalie. Though Sambo was deported by the settler government, the work which he had done took root, and the RICU brought to the African urban workers the first taste of class politics.

Characteristic of the élite and Ndebele movements had been their politeness, their eagerness to affirm loyalty, their anxious claims for respectability, and the regular assertions of their Christian principles. The RICU broke with this tradition by appealing to the black urban workers to set aside tribal differences and unite to fight for better conditions. In the largely Ndebele city of Bulawayo, the union had a Shona organizer; and in Mashonaland, a Ndebele one. While the RICU leaders would on occasion talk in terms of Christian morality, they were not slow to attack the missionaries and the established church for their cooperation with white supremacy.

The R I C U never achieved the importance of its South African counterpart. The South African I C U had used the strike weapon with great effect, but in Rhodesia, where the urban working class was more recent and where striking Africans could easily be replaced from the ranks of the unemployed, strikes were not favoured by the union. The collapse of the I C U in South Africa, the failure of the Rhodesian union to build an adequate financial base by recruiting dues-paying members, and the arrest and imprisonment of R I C U militants, led to the disappearance of the union in the mid-thirties.

The R I C U had never successfully resolved the problem of the relationship between the urban worker and the rural areas. For many urban workers, the issues of the rural areas and in particular the shortage of land were of much greater importance than their temporary condition as wage-earners. With more land, the urban worker might never have been forced to leave the rural area; and certainly, any urban worker could only view his stay in the town as transitory. The 1931 Land Apportionment Act merely formalized what had long been clear: blacks and whites would live separately. Africans in the cities were there at the white man's convenience. In these circumstances the development of a proletarian consciousness was inevitably delayed; and, indeed, it is arguable that in 1973 it is still difficult to talk of a fully proletarianized African labour-force. In appealing to the class instincts of the urban workers, the R I C U injected a new and important element into Rhodesian politics; but in ignoring the fact that these same workers had left much of themselves in the rural areas, the union missed an important dimension of their existence.

Though the union gained few if any tangible victories, it was in many ways a precursor of the later militant mass nationalist parties. The two major leaders of the R I C U, Mzingeli and Ndlovu, continued to play an active part in African politics, Mzingeli in the trade union movement, and Ndlovu in the A N C and later in Z A N U.

Political opposition also found its expression in independent religious movements. The close cooperation which the established churches maintained with the Company and later with the settler government, not surprisingly resulted in their being large-ly identified in African eyes with white domination. In general, this view was well justified, though there were some mission-aries, notably Arthur Shirley Cripps, who, to the general horror of their superiors, acted as strong advocates of African rights and critics of Company and settler practices.*

The white churches kept a careful control over their African converts. The activities of the Southern Rhodesian Missionary Conference of Christian Natives, which was established in 1928, were carefully circumscribed by the Rhodesian Missionary Conference. The churches did not limit themselves to narrow religious concerns. When the influence of the R I C U began to be felt, the Catholic Church threatened to excommunicate any of its members who joined the union.

The growth of the independent churches was strongly attacked by the traditional ones. The government accordingly considered itself encouraged to act against such subversive influences. In the early 1930s the Zionist church was proscribed, and in 1936 a Sedition Act was introduced to combat the Watch Tower move-ment. One astute native commissioner suggested in 1928 that 'the ideal corrective (to the spread of the Watch Tower move-ment) would be an immediate planned and intensive campaign by some strongly organized church, having as its objective the conversion to Christianity of all Natives in the area affected and the establishment of regular Native Churches under the authority of a governing body'.[2]

Concern was particularly intense in 1928, since this followed the first significant African strike in Southern Rhodesia at the Shamva mine. The Watch Tower movement had played a large role in organizing the strike, which, though it was quickly broken by the police, had caused some concern in the white community. However, in general the activities of the Watch Tower move-ment were more millenarian. It told its members: 'You must be strong, as the world will shortly be changed and the white people that have high positions will be our servants in heaven.'[3]

*One is tempted to say that the Anglican church at least has not changed much in seventy years. In 1973, the Anglican Bishop of Mashonaland could say: 'I believe this remains probably the freest country in an Africa where so much freedom dis-appears overnight.' (*The Link*, Salisbury, 1973.) The Bishop is white.

Two other independent African churches which developed later than the Watch Tower movement but proved more permanent were the Vapostori and Zionist movements. These churches were particularly strong in the rural areas of Mashonaland. Again they combined a religious and a political sentiment, condemning the white seizure of land and the exploitation of African labour.

The independent church movements were important as an expression of continuing hostility to white rule and to the conquered Africans they offered self-respect and hope for the future. They did not restrict their appeals either to the élite or to urban workers, but offered to save all who would follow their exacting discipline. In terms of their impact and the breadth of their membership, they were undoubtedly the most important among the African movements of this period.

The 1930s saw a surge in the growth of the independent African churches, but little development in the more explicitly political organizations. In 1934 the Southern Rhodesia African National Congress was founded; and while in the 1950s this was to be the chosen vehicle for a mass nationalist movement, in the 1930s it retained much of the élitist, self-deprecating approach of the RBVA.

The pattern of the thirties would soon be broken by the real changes taking place in Rhodesian society. The growth in African education was throwing up a new kind of leadership, while the expanding African work-force, driven into the towns by taxation and land shortages, would in a few years give birth to the first major industrial action by Africans.

Rhodesian nationalists had to deal of course, not with a distant colonial office and a politically and economically weak white settler population, but with a government whose existence was dependent on and devoted to building a prosperous and permanent white society at the African's expense. At a more day-to-day level, the strength and penetration of the white settlers was reflected in the extent of their real control over the territory. Southern Rhodesia does not contain the large unpoliced areas that Nyasaland had, or Angola and Mozambique still have, where colonial rule was always weak and intermittent. In 1935, a former member of the Southern Rhodesian police, while giving evidence before the Commission of Enquiry into the Copperbelt disturbances, compared the sophisticated control in Southern Rhodesia with the much less thorough policing in Northern Rhodesia:

> In Southern Rhodesia, you might say that every inch of the territory is policed, you have regular patrols. The European police are always in touch with the natives and go among them. I think it has a certain beneficial effect. They see they cannot get away with a crime, they are found out and brought to justice. Here it is only the line of rail really which is policed ... In Southern Rhodesia you are always among the natives, one might say you are in constant contact with their pulse, you can feel how they react to things, but here you never get amongst the natives.[4]

The dominating position of the white population was particularly critical in creating and maintaining a division between the rural and urban African masses, and the African élite. The members of this élite, faced with the apparent permanence of the white order, sought to obtain the best terms that they could for themselves, and were encouraged in the 1950s by the more far-sighted among their white rulers. This divorce between the potential leaders of the nationalist movement and the mass base was not overcome until the early 1960s. Faced with the prospect of federation, the élite equivocated; faced with the promise of partnership, they responded by joining the United Federal Party and later the Central African Party. Only with the defeat of Todd; with the framework of Federation crashing about their ears; with the rebirth of the mass nationalist movement; and with the growing strength of the white backlash reflected in the Dominion Party, did they finally come to terms with the reality that there could be no solution to the problems of the African élite without a solution to the problems of the African masses.

While the African middle class continued to pursue the mirage of cooperation with the white élite, the development of the black proletariat was delayed by similar illusions about the possibilities of black–white solidarity. The R I C U had attempted to build an inter-racial class alliance, and, indeed, in 1930 one of its meetings had been addressed by Bowden, a white labour leader. However, as Terence Ranger comments: 'Bowden's speech was very much a flash in the pan; the chance of a united working class movement, if it had ever existed, was passing away as the white establishment came to terms with white workers.'[5]

Ranger is undoubtedly correct in this assessment. Yet attempts at a black–white labour alliance were to be renewed in conjunction with some of the white Labour Party leaders during the Second World War, a war in which, as Doris Lessing has so eloquently argued, the conflict between the reality of Rhodesia and the ideology of an anti-fascist, anti-racist cause produced some very interesting political dynamics.

In 1941, at the request of Mzingeli, the Rhodesian Labour Party agreed to register an African headquarters. But opposition to African participation in the party grew rapidly, and significantly it was the trade union element which led this. It was not, of course, the middle-class members, socialist out of intellectual conviction, but the artisans, who saw themselves losing most from any improvement in the competitive position of black workers. From the electoral point of view, there was in any case little to gain from African support, since by 1948 fewer than 300 Africans were registered to vote out of an electorate of 47,000.

In 1944 the opposition to the inclusion of African members was sufficient to split the labour movement, which had recently become united in the Southern Rhodesia Labour Party. A breakaway all-white Rhodesian Labour Party was formed, with the support of the Trades and Labour Council. In 1948, with a growing white awareness of the threat posed by African competition. the Southern Rhodesia Labour Party collapsed.

Nevertheless, African labour leaders continued to believe, at least in principle, in a community of interests between black and white labour. In 1952 Joshua Nkomo, who was to become Rhodesia's most important nationalist leader, was General Secretary of the Rhodesian Railways African Employees' Association. He commented: 'It will be found in the long run that the interests of workers, be they black or white, are inseparable.'[6] Mzingeli demonstrated his continuing faith in the unity of the interests of the working class by leading May Day demonstrations until 1957, when his influence was largely displaced by the modern nationalist movements.

During the 1950s, in practice, the only inter-racial cooperation which took place was not between the white and black working class, but between the more far-sighted members of the white middle and upper classes and the African middle class. It was a cooperation which would prove fruitless for both sides, precisely because the white working class stood to gain nothing and to lose everything.

Post-war developments in African politics

In the early twentieth century, Southern Rhodesian African politics, boosted by South African influence, had developed at a much faster rate than African politics in Nyasaland or Northern Rhodesia. Arguably, South African influence had, in fact, caused the political superstructure to grow far beyond the base. After the Second World War, Southern Rhodesian African politicians were quickly outdistanced by their northern counterparts. Southern Rhodesian politics were not, of course, stagnant, but in comparison to African politics in the North, politics in Southern Rhodesia often seemed to lack unity, clarity and decisiveness.

The rapid growth in the African work-force, the urbanization and industrial development of the war and postwar years, and the continued decline in mass African living standards stimulated the rebirth of militant African political activity. Richard Gray writes: 'By the end of the Second World War ... the experiences of urban poverty and frustration were creating a new unity in which class became coterminous with colour, and at the same time the African initiative was passing to those leaders who made articulate the new demands and awareness of African labourers and their wives.'[7]

It was in the largest of the urban industries that the new mood of militancy first found its expression. In 1944, the Rhodesian Railways African Employees' Association was formed in Bulawayo. In October 1945, the railway workers in Bulawayo went on strike. Some 2,400 African workers were involved, and the strike soon spread to other railway centres in both the Rhodesias. It was two weeks before the strikes were ended, in return for a government's promise to set up a commission to investigate grievances.

In April 1948, what has been called 'the first general strike' broke out.[8] Again, Bulawayo was the centre of activity, but in this case it was the municipal employees who led the way, and a mass meeting of 13,000 Africans was held in the African location. Despite an apparent lack of centralized coordination, the strike rapidly affected most of the African employees in Bulawayo and spread to every urban and mining centre in Southern Rhodesia.

The militancy of the strike and the widespread support that it gained gave a considerable shock to the settlers. Richard Gray comments that 'to their surprise and indignation, many were suddenly confronted with the challenge and rivalry of their modern African neighbours'.[9] The response of many Europeans was to demand repression, but more intelligently the government planned reforms. Huggins told the Legislative Assembly: 'We are witnessing the emergence of a proletariat, and in this country it happens to be black.'[10]

The growing militancy of the African proletariat was reflected in the radicalization of the Southern Rhodesian African National Congress. The congress, though unable to control or direct the 1948 strike, did play a supportive role and participated in negotiations with the government on African grievances.

While the African élite sought to respond to rank-and-file militancy, a more important leadership was being thrown up from the base. In 1946, the old RICU was reborn under the name of the Reformed Industrial and Commercial Workers' Union. Mzingeli returned to the leadership of the union. In the first elections for the Salisbury Native Advisory Board in 1947 every RICU candidate was elected.

In Bulawayo, Benjamin Burumbo ran the British African Voice Association, which played a major role in the 1948 strike, organized rural opposition to cattle de-stocking, and later fought the implementation of the Native Land Husbandry Act. His organization succeeded in bridging the crucial gap between urban and rural discontent.

The revived RICU and later the City Youth League and African National Congress can be seen as the vanguard of the

African nationalist movement, but we should not exaggerate their influence. Many urban Africans continued to identify primarily with their local tribal grouping and joined welfare associations established on tribal lines which provided support and some cooperative social security in the urban areas.

The City Youth League was formed in Salisbury in 1955 by George Nyandoro, James Chikerema and Duduzo Chisiza from Nyasaland. With its formation, the African élite faced a significant and organized challenge. The élite were at that time epitomized by Mike Hove and Jasper Savanhu, who had been elected to the Federal parliament by an overwhelmingly white electorate. (Hove subsequently became Federal High Commissioner in Nigeria, and Savanhu a much-publicized Parliamentary Secretary to the Ministry of Home Affairs.) They adhered to the politics of partnership, and were, in fact, responding to the deliberate strategy of the white political leadership to foster the emergence of an African middle class, with whom they could then form an alliance

The Youth League also sought to break the power of Mzingeli, pressing confrontation politics where Mzingeli sought to convince white authority. Their early successes were spectacular: they swept the elections for the African Advisory Board in the Salisbury Harare township; and in August 1956, in protest against a rise in bus fares, they organized an effective three-day boycott. In Bulawayo the old ANC branch was revived; and on 12 September 1957, a day celebrated by white Rhodesians as the anniversary of the white conquest, the Youth League from Salisbury and the Bulawayo ANC met in Harare to launch a new national ANC with Joshua Nkomo as President.

The new ANC gained support rapidly, extending its influence in the rural areas by leading opposition to the implementation of the Native Land Husbandry Act. When in February 1958 Todd was removed from the premiership because of his relatively liberal racial politics – or, to be more exact, his liberal statements on racial issues – a number of Africans who had previously worked through the United Federal Party joined the ANC. Todd's removal and the subsequent overwhelming defeat of the United Rhodesia Party which Todd led in the June elections dealt a severe blow to those Africans who had held illusions about the promises of 'partnership'.

1958 saw a dramatic increase in nationalist activity not only in Southern Rhodesia but also in Nyasaland and Northern Rhodesia. Large-scale disturbances broke out in Nyasaland in the first months of 1959. In Northern Rhodesia the Zambian National Congress, a radical breakaway from the Northern Rhodesian National Congress, was banned. In Southern Rhodesia a state of emergency was proclaimed; the A N C was banned and 500 of its members arrested. In justifying the ban Whitehead, the Southern Rhodesian Prime Minister, paid an unintended compliment to the efficiency of the A N C. Commenting on its campaign against the Land Husbandry Act and against the powers of the native commissioners and government-controlled chiefs, he declared: 'Unless some effective measure were taken to stop the many deliberate lies that were being told ... the whole administration of the Native areas would break down.'[11]

Nkomo was abroad when the arrests were carried out, and this, combined with the repression in Southern Rhodesia, encouraged the development of a politics which has bedevilled the Southern Rhodesian nationalist movement ever since. Instead of concentrating, in spite of the repression, on building a strong national base, and developing an appropriate strategy, the nationalist leaders expended a great deal of effort in attempting to influence Britain and obtain support from other countries and the United Nations.

If Rhodesia had been a typical British colony, then this kind of approach might well have been effective. In the rest of Africa, Britain was in the process of discharging its administrative responsibilities into black hands; concerned only that the hands could be trusted to protect her economic interests. In Kenya and Northern Rhodesia, areas with significant settler minorities, the delivery would be more complicated; but the decisive political power over these countries was still exercised by Whitehall. In contrast, since 1923, Southern Rhodesia had had effective self-government, exercised by white settlers whose strength far exceeded that of their counterparts in other British colonies. This crucial element meant that the government of Rhodesia was not a

British possession, a present to give to whoever seemed best able to administer it in capitalism's long-term interest. However attractive a stable bourgeois black government may have seemed – and Nkomo had certainly gone out of his way to reassure the British government of his 'reasonableness' – it was not an option; since power in Rhodesia was in the hands of the predominantly working-class white voters, for whom anything other than white sovereignty spelt disaster. If, in fact, Britain was to be encouraged to intervene then this would be most likely to happen in the context of a severe internal crisis in Southern Rhodesia.

In short, the most effective pressure on Great Britain lay in local organizing to confront the white settlers who controlled the country. For, as long as there was no serious challenge to settler power, Britain was not faced with the question of intervention. And concentration on the strengthening of a local base was, of course, essential from a more important perspective: since effective power lay in settler hands, only a strategy aimed at their defeat held a sure prospect of success.

After the banning of the Southern Rhodesian ANC, Nkomo, who at least for the African masses was the unchallenged nationalist leader, stayed abroad until November 1960, when he returned to assume the presidency of the National Democratic Party (NDP), founded on 1 January 1960. Nkomo had made London his headquarters, though he had travelled in Africa and the US, and in October 1960 had visited the UN as an unofficial observer. Even after his return, he continued to travel extensively abroad until July 1963, when the split between the Zimbabwe African Peoples' Union (ZAPU), formed in 1962 to replace the NDP, which had also been banned, and the Zimbabwe African National Union (ZANU) formed by ZAPU dissidents, made his presence in Rhodesia imperative.

Nkomo's activities should not be seen merely as a reflection of his own proclivities, but rather as indicating the emphasis of the movement at that period. More significant than the foreign travels was the consideration which ZAPU gave to the establishment of a foreign headquarters. This issue came to a head in 1963 when Nkomo summoned the ZAPU executive to meet in

Dar-es-Salaam, apparently to prepare for the establishment of a government in exile. The move was opposed both by members of the ZAPU executive and by Nyerere and other African leaders.

It was this policy of concentrating the party's efforts outside the country which, according to Nathan Shamuyarira, precipitated the formation of ZANU in August 1963. Shamuyarira, who supported ZANU, writes: 'There was a fundamental difference of approach: Nkomo wanted to circumvent the situation at home and organize international support in hopes of bringing effective pressure to bear; Sithole and Mugabe saw as the great need more organization at home to crystallize the situation there.'[12] In any event, the subsequent split forced both movements to concentrate their efforts inside the country – efforts which unfortunately were increasingly directed neither at foreign opinion nor at the destruction of settler power, but rather at securing hegemony over the nationalist movement by one group through the destruction of the other.

It is easy, however, to be wise after the event. It is important to recognize the strong pressures which were operating to encourage this orientation. Organization in Southern Rhodesia was exceedingly difficult. Following the banning of the ANC, no meetings were allowed in rural areas, and the main leaders of the ANC, with the exception of Nkomo, were in gaol until 1963. The NDP was banned in December 1962; ZAPU was immediately formed to replace it and in turn was banned eight months later, though ZAPU continued to operate underground until the ZANU–ZAPU split forced Nkomo to create the People's Caretaker Council (PCC). Party leaders and activists were subject to harassment and the possibility of arrest. The Vice-President of ZAPU, Tichafa Parirenyatwa, an African doctor, died in mysterious circumstances. According to his chauffeur, his car had been stopped, and they had been attacked by whites. Doctor Parirenyatwa had continued driving and had died on the road.[13] John Day comments that, after the accession to power of the right-wing Rhodesian Front, 'Nkomo probably felt that the dangers of a right-wing government becoming independent and paralysing the nationalist movement made it more than ever necessary to put the national executive beyond the reach of the government outside Southern Rhodesia'. Day argues that in the face of repression in Southern Rhodesia, 'the web of foreign offices at least gave the nationalists the feeling that all their organization had not been paralysed by the government'.[14]

Even without the extensive oppressive apparatus, organization would have been difficult. Over half of the African labour-force continued to be drawn from outside the territory. On the one hand, this facilitated an interchange of ideas between the different nationalist movements in the Federation; but on the other, it fragmented the labour-force. Migrant workers from Nyasaland, Northern Rhodesia and the Portuguese territories did not always readily identify with the Southern Rhodesian nationalist movement. Those migrant workers who did become involved in Southern Rhodesian politics were liable to deportation, a fate which had rapidly befallen Chisiza in the early days of the Youth League. The difficulty of forging effective links between the different African reserves was exacerbated by the preponderance of migrant workers in the intervening farms. Widespread urban unemployment made strike action difficult, and there were few Africans with jobs which would not be jeopardized by an active involvement in nationalist politics. Finally the poverty of the African masses made fund-raising difficult, though financial support was provided by independent African countries.

The early sixties were a period of rapid decolonization in Africa. In 1960 the Monckton Commission recommended that the territories be given the right to secede from Federation. Nyasaland and Northern Rhodesia were given African majority governments. Nigeria and Somalia became independent, and the new Kenyan constitution paved the way for majority rule. At first glance Southern Rhodesian nationalists had every reason to be optimistic and assume that, with sufficient constitutional pressure, they, too, would obtain majority rule. As Shamuyarira wrote: 'Constitutional reforms, even independence, seemed imminent everywhere. The sky was suddenly bright.'[15]

The final factor which encouraged the nationalist movement's foreign activities was the very ambivalence of Britain's relationship with Rhodesia, for legally the final status of Rhodesia still lay with the British government. If this *de jure* power had also been a *de facto* one, then the policy of mobilizing British public opinion and world pressure may well have made sense, for clearly the British were more susceptible than were the local settlers. However, as we will argue, any exercise of British power would have meant a military confrontation with the settlers. It was simply not realistic to argue, as Shamuyarira does, that at the 1961 Constitutional Conference 'the great opportunity to settle Southern Rhodesia's problems peacefully, as Kenya's problems had been settled in their 1960 conference, was let slip away'.[16] Such a solution was never an option. To condemn Britain on moral grounds is justifiable; but it should be clear that for Britain these were not moral, but strategic, questions. What could be imposed on Kenyan settlers could not be imposed on Rhodesian settlers without risking a white revolt in Rhodesia. We will argue later that Britain could and should have used military force in Rhodesia. But if we are to learn from history, we should also understand both why it was never a serious possibility and why, without the use of military force, there was never any question of Britain imposing majority rule.

The strategy of internationalizing the Rhodesian conflict went hand in hand with concentration by the nationalists on constitutional rather than social issues. Shamuyarira writes: 'The NDP decided to lay greater emphasis than the ANC had ever done on constitutional and political development, and put a lower priority on attacking the Land Apportionment Act, the Land Husbandry Act, and other discriminatory laws.'[17] Initially this approach seemed to pay dividends; and following an NDP lobby in London, the British government said in May 1960 that African opinion would be consulted over any changes in the constitutional position of Rhodesia. In December 1960 the NDP attended the Federal Constitutional Review Conference in London, and, in January 1961, the Territorial Constitutional Conference in Salisbury. Nkomo said that though he would not endorse the proposed changes in the constitution, which would have in effect given Africans control of 15 out of 65 seats in the legislature, he would not oppose the plan. There was a swift reaction from the other NDP leaders. Nkomo was forced to reject the proposals, and the N D P subsequently boycotted the elections held under the new constitutional provisions.

This concentration on constitutional issues and foreign activities did not mean that the nationalists ignored local mobilization. By June 1959 seventy-one people had been arrested and charged with attempts to revive the banned A N C. After the arrest of three N D P leaders in July 1960, the N D P were able to mobilize over 25,000 people to march on Whitehead's office in protest, and after a widespread strike and serious rioting in Bulawayo, in which a number of Africans were shot and killed, the leaders were released.

The constitutional thrust of the N D P and the *de facto* recognition of its influence by the British government brought a number of African intellectuals into the movement who subsequently played an important role. But inevitably the constitutional emphasis had its negative consequences. Theodore Bull, a former editor of the liberal *Central African Examiner*, comments: 'The "intellectuals" who predominated in the N D P executive failed to recognize that this "egg-head" approach was creating a gulf between themselves and the semi-literate or illiterate masses of simple people, particularly those in the rural areas who the leadership tended to neglect.'[18] Nevertheless the N D P's unofficial referendum on the 1961 constitution demonstrated a sizeable support: 373,017 people voted, of whom only 471 were in favour of the proposed amendment. The subsequent election boycott reflected the N D P success in incorporating the African middle class – who were the potential voters – into the nationalist movement.

The split between Z A N U and Z A P U in 1963, and the resulting violence between the movements, gave the new Rhodesian Front government a ready excuse to ban them; and this it did in August 1964. The unilateral declaration of independence in 1965 found the nationalist movement divided, its formal organizations banned, and its leaders jailed or restricted. In consequence, African resistance was weakened and largely spontaneous, though in Bulawayo strikers held out for three days before the police regained control.

In many ways, the ease with which order was maintained

after U D I is the clearest indictment of the strategy that had been pursued by the nationalists. It is possible that their foreign publicity encouraged Britain's rather feeble response in imposing sanctions; however, the response of the independent African countries would itself have forced Britain into such a face-saving activity. If Z A P U and Z A N U, both of whom had anticipated a U D I at least since the election of the Rhodesian Front government in 1962, had concentrated on building up an effective political and military movement in the country, subsequent events would have been radically different. Wilson's dilemma would have been much more real, while Smith would have had great difficulty in stabilizing the situation in the crucial days after U D I, when the question of whether he could get away with it was relevant, not only to British policy makers, but also to many white Rhodesians and to South Africa.

Yet, in evaluating the history of the African nationalist movements, it is important to retain the perspective offered by the South African A N C:

Future historians may well be able to pause at some moments during the evaluation of our struggle and examine critically both its pace and emphasis. But, in general, without the so-called reformist activities of the previous half century, the prospect of advancing into the new phase would have been extremely small. This is so, because ... armed struggle becomes feasible only if there is disillusionment with the prospects of attaining liberation by traditional peaceful processes, because the objective conditions blatantly bar the way to change. There is readiness to respond to the strategy of armed struggle with all the enormous sacrifices which this involves.[19]

In the final chapter we will discuss to what extent the nationalists have since transcended the limitations of the earlier struggle.

5 In search of a solution

Changes in Conservative colonial policy

The colonial policy of the British government underwent an important change during the fifties. The Conservative Party had entered the 1951 General Election proudly proclaiming: 'The Conservative Party by long tradition and settled belief is the party of the Empire. We are proud of its past. We see it as the surest hope in our own day. We proclaim our abiding faith in its destiny. We shall strive to promote its unity, its strength, and its progress.'[1] The party gave unreserved support to the creation of the Federation, seeing in it a way of maintaining the Empire on a new basis of 'partnership' between the colonizers and the colonized.

In retrospect, the Federation can be seen both as the highest achievement of this up-dated colonialism and as its death-rattle. In 1954 Britain, in the face of back-bench Tory opposition, evacuated the Suez Canal Zone base, a move which enabled Nasser in 1956 to nationalize the Canal and resulted in Britain's abortive invasion. After the Suez débâcle, it became clear that the Imperial Lion could no longer strike at will. The Mau Mau movement in Kenya, which cost Britain a total of £70m. and was only suppressed after some 1,000 Kikuyu had been hanged and another 80,000 placed in concentration camps, dramatized the need for a swift reconsideration of British policy. It was clear that to hold on to the Empire would be an expensive and bloody business – a lesson which the French and the Dutch learnt in Indo-China, Algeria and Indonesia. In addition, the growth of European industry and trade made the old Empire seem less important.

Andrew Gamble has perceptively described the development: 'Britain's belated attempt (under Macmillan) to seek admission to the Common Market was the other side of the decision to with-draw from the Empire. It was the beginning of a search for a new national identity and a new world role.'[2] The new Tory strategy was to hand over power to stable indigenous govern-ments which would safeguard Britain's trading and investment interests. It was the strategy which the Labour government had been forced to adopt in Asia at the end of the Second World War. What had been important in the first wave of decolonization – the continued safety of British trade and investment – remained important. The British fought a costly eight-year war to ensure that Malaya could be handed over to a suitable bourgeois govern-ment. In British Guyana the victory of Cheddi Jagan's left-wing party delayed constitutional reforms until a more pliable heir apparent could be placed in office.

In Rhodesia it was not the threat of a socialist take-over that posed a problem to the would-be decolonizers, but rather the presence of a substantial minority of settlers, who would do all in their power to ensure that decolonization was far from orderly, and whose intransigence could only lead to a radicalization of the nationalist movement. It was a problem faced by the British in Rhodesia, the French in Algeria, and the Belgians in the Congo.

In West Africa there were few settlers, and independence was granted rapidly: to Ghana in 1957, and to Nigeria in 1960. In Kenya, Northern Rhodesia and Nyasaland, independence came only after a prolonged and bitter struggle with the white settlers. In Algeria independence was conceded only after a full-scale war of independence which threatened to destroy the political institutions of France. The nature of the Algerian struggle for independence resulted in the emergence of a government sub-stantially to the left of those in other former French colonies. In the Belgian Congo the rapid imposition of independence in opposition to the white settlers resulted in a prolonged and bloody conflict which for a time threatened to bring about the very kind of government most feared by the Belgian and interna-tional bourgeoisie.

The shift in Britain's colonial policy was not accomplished without substantial opposition. In 1961 the Monday Club was founded to commemorate the 'Black Monday' on which Harold

Macmillan had made his 'winds of change' speech to the South African Houses of Parliament in February 1960. Macleod's colonial policies and particularly his proposals for new Northern Rhodesian Constitution, were attacked in an Early Day Motion signed by over 100 back-bench M Ps. However, the opposition from the Tory backwoodsmen, though influential in delaying decolonization and, more importantly, in limiting the flexibility of the government, was not as troublesome as the resistance of local settlers. Arghiri Emmanuel has argued: 'The extraordinary haste with which independence was granted in many cases ... can only be explained by a positive motive, i.e. the home country's need at a certain moment to steal a march on their own settlers who were threatening nearly everywhere to secede and form white states.'³ It is an argument which seems certainly justified in the case of the Belgian Congo, which Emmanuel cites as an instance, and one helping to explain the vigour with which Britain pursued the break-up of the Federation and the granting of majority rule constitutions to Nyasaland and Northern Rhodesia. Not that the course to independence in Northern Rhodesia and Nyasaland was easy. In 1961, in the face of settler opposition to constitutional proposals which would have given Africans a majority in the Northern Rhodesian legislature, British troop-carriers were assembled at Nairobi. This move was rejected when consideration of it reached the British Cabinet; but it had been taken sufficiently seriously for Welensky to order counter-moves: 'I took immediate steps to ensure that, if the British launched an operation in Northern Rhodesia, Federal forces would be able to counter it promptly and effectively.'⁴

The conflict between the views of the white settlers and those of international capital was reflected in the contrary positions which were taken during the crises in the Congo. Welensky gave full support to Tshombe's settler-backed rebellion in Katanga while the Western powers supported a central government made malleable by their pressure. The divergence between Western policies and settler interests led Welensky to argue that

American policy in Africa and British policy (perhaps to a lesser extent under American influence) have unintentionally but actively assisted the fulfilment of Communist aims. ⁵

In fact, of course, what both Britain and America feared was that the intransigence of the white settlers would give birth to revolutionary, as distinct from reformist, nationalist movements.

Ultimately Britain was able to override settler opposition and grant the right to secession from the Federation to Northern Rhodesia and Nyasaland. In Southern Rhodesia, with a much stronger settler population, British policy was to work through the UFP government for a gradual transition to African rule. It was a policy that failed.

Horrowitz, reviewing Conservative policy on African decolonization, writes:

> The only territory to which the policy of disengagement and cooperation with African nationalists was not applied was Southern Rhodesia, where there was established, European-dominated self-government. Southern Rhodesia remained the exception because it was the only territory in which the two main themes of the policy of decolonization in Africa – disengagement without complications and coming to terms with African Nationalism – conflicted with one another.[6]

If Britain had been called on to intervene militarily to protect settler rule against a local guerilla struggle, then the question of independence under an African government would have presented itself more forcefully. In these circumstances, it is probable that British policy would have aimed at a deal with the African nationalists which would have resulted in majority rule. The Southern Rhodesian government were, however, able to maintain control with their own resources.

After the break-up of Federation, Welensky expressed the determination of white settlers not to capitulate to further British pressure: 'I can only proclaim my hope and my belief that we can and will if necessary *make a go of it alone*, however rough the road we may have to travel.'[7] This was a sentiment which came not from the Rhodesian Front, which led the fight for independence and ultimately proclaimed UDI, but from within the leading ranks of the 'moderate' Rhodesian National Party, the Southern Rhodesian successor to the UFP. The 'moderates' were soon to be overtaken by those for whom white supremacy was the *sine qua non* of existence. To the resulting declaration of UDI, a declaration as imminent as it was obvious, the British government, Labour or Conservative, could make little response.

Though the political dynamics seemed alarmingly clear, there were many who failed to recognize them. In 1960 Philip Mason, Director of the British Institute of Race Relations, advocated a transition to electoral parity in Southern Rhodesia and subsequently to majority rule. It was a move that he thought would enable the white professional and business classes to continue playing a major role in the economy; though

it is not so easy to see a future for the brick-layer or the lorry-driver... Those with lower skills will lose their present high rates ... Some would no doubt have to lower their standards of living or leave the country. This is sad ... What is sensible is to consider the alternative; if this choice is refused, all that remains is the South African way, which must surely mean, sooner or later, change even more violent and catastrophic.[8]

The fallibility of this prescription is obvious: for, from the perspective of most white voters, if the choice lay between leaving the country or consolidating white supremacy there, the decision would be for the latter.

Patrick Keatley concluded an examination of *The Politics of Partnership* on a more realistic note: 'The crux of the matter, then, is getting land and air forces into Southern Rhodesia ... It is the only instrument which will make outside political intervention practical.'[9] Without this, the prospects for majority rule were poor, indeed. Yet for the Conservative government, motivated in its colonial policy by a desire to stabilize foreign trade and investment, military intervention in Southern Rhodesia was not a serious policy option. The government was prepared to intervene militarily when, as in Malaysia, emergent nationalist movements challenged the hegemony of foreign capital. In Southern Rhodesia in the 1950s there was no such challenge. Military intervention would have threatened Britain's extensive interests throughout Southern Africa and would certainly have been vehemently opposed by sectors of the Tory party who had close economic ties with Southern Africa.

In search of a solution

The policy which the Conservative government adopted in Southern Rhodesia was one of working with the white élite to construct a new political coalition which would ensure the protection of Britain's economic interests and political stability. The objective of this gradualist approach was to create a governing alliance between the emergent African middle class and the white bourgeoisie.

The politics of racial cooperation

The change in the economic base of Southern Rhodesia produced by the growth of the manufacturing sector, the boom in tobacco exports, and the rapid increase in the white population, was reflected in changing pressures within the political sphere. Agriculture, which had accounted for roughly 17 per cent of white employment in 1936, accounted for only 5 per cent by 1956. In the same period industry increased its share of white employment from a level just below that of agriculture to 32 per cent of total white employment. The share of the commercial, public and professional sectors in white employment also rose relatively rapidly. The share of the mining industry fell from nearly 15 per cent to around 4 per cent, largely reflecting an absolute decline in the number of small workers. The number of gold workings fell from 1,754 in 1935 to 301 by 1956; and in contrast to the earlier period, when small workers accounted for two thirds of total gold production, the industry was now dominated by a few large companies. The concentration of production in the mining sector was paralleled by a growing concentration of industrial output. In 1957 the 85 industrial units with a gross output of £250,000 or more a year accounted for 67·8 per cent of the total value of manufacturing production but only 9 per cent of the total units.[10]

This economic concentration strengthened the economic and political bargaining power of capital, which exercised a growing influence on the political direction of both the federal and territorial governments. The country's future came increasingly to be seen in terms of an expanding manufacturing sector which, unlike agriculture and small-scale mining, depended not on maintaining barriers against African advancement but on gradually removing them. Politically this was viewed as requiring the emergence of an African middle class with which eventually power could be shared; these Africans would, it was supposed, vote on class rather than on racial lines and so serve to protect the existing economic order.

The major problem in the implementation of this strategy was the electoral power of the white working class and farmers. John Rex has described similar dynamics in South Africa:

Capitalist interests in the country could, subject to certain guarantees about the continued availability of cheap, unskilled labour, fairly readily accommodate themselves to African rule and to the expulsion of those settlers whose presence was not strictly necessary from an economic point of view. But the white working class, fearing competition of cheap black labour, and farmers, unable to compete with industry in what it is prepared to pay African workers, have succeeded in organizing themselves in defence of their economic interests as they see them. Thus the so-called Nationalist Party in South Africa is as much as any party in the world a class-based party, and one which has become sufficiently strong in the grip which it has on the settler electorate to force local and absentee white capitalists to respect the rule of white supremacy.[11]

In Rhodesia the same class forces did not come into power until 1962. Before that time, the government reflected an uneasy coalition, the stability of which was greatly influenced by the prevailing economic climate and level of African militancy. But throughout the 1950s and early 1960s, the programme of reform and inter-racial cooperation was defeated by the strength of the white backlash.

The government which tried to implement the new policy of partnership in Southern Rhodesia was a direct successor to the Reform Party government, which had been elected in 1933 on the policy of separate development. Lord Malvern, the new Federal Prime Minister, was the Prime Minister of the 1933 Reform Party government and remained Southern Rhodesian Prime Minister until 1953 (after 1934, as leader of the United Party). His successor in the Southern Rhodesian premiership was Garfield Todd.

The United Party was, as we have argued, based on an inter-class alliance within which, as the campaign for Federation revealed, industry and commerce came to play a larger role. G. Arrighi, in an excellent Marxist analysis of Rhodesia's development, has argued that 'The white bourgeoisie and white workers . . . controlled the government'.[12] The statement contains an important element of truth, particularly as applied to the post-1933 period. But the relationship of the urban working class to the government was more complex than this suggests. Large sections of the working class continued to vote for opposition parties – initially for the Labour Party and, after the Second World War, for the Liberal Party and its successors. The white working-class voting-pattern was influenced by the prevailing economic climate. Opposition voting in the thirties reflected the general economic insecurity. Faced with this, the working class demanded improved social security and welfare measures, and restrictions on black competition. After the war, with a new mood of African working-class militancy, opposition found expression in support for the Liberal Party. The Liberal Party, which gained only one seat less than Huggins's United Party in the 1946 elections, would have proved a more serious threat to Huggins, if it had not been handicapped by its pro-Afrikaner image. This became of crucial importance with the victory of the Afrikaner-based Nationalist Party in South Africa in 1948. Huggins capitalized on the anti-Afrikaner prejudice of other white ethnic groups, and in the election of that year the Liberal Party representation in the legislature fell from twelve to five.

The boom conditions and optimism prevalent in the early period of the Federation led in 1954 to an overwhelming victory for the United Party, then running under the label of the United Rhodesia Party. The 1958 elections were fought against the very different background of an economic down-turn in the Federation, which 'brought to the surface once again the fear of white displacement by cheap African labour', and the birth of the mass nationalist movements.[13] In these circumstances, the government party, now running under the label of the United Federal Party, had great difficulty in retaining a majority and did so only because the number of second-preference votes it received enabled it to overcome the Dominion Party's advantage on the first count.

In 1962, with the Federation visibly collapsing, no sign of economic recovery and growing nationalist movements in all three territories, the white working class and farmers voted overwhelmingly for the Dominion Party. The resulting Dominion Party government, for the first time fully expressed the overriding interest of white workers and farmers in eliminating the threat of African competition.

The position of the government party in the late forties and fifties was secure only so long as there was full employment and no reason to fear a sudden deterioration in white security. In these circumstances it had some leeway in implementing its long-term strategy, but the potential strength of the opposition limited its ability to undertake the kind of thorough-going reform which offered the only possibility of success. This opposition found its expression not only in the official opposition parties but also, inevitably, in the governing party itself.

Capitalism in search of stability

The only consistent interest in a policy of systematically eliminating discrimination, and extending the size of the African middle class and the African market, was that of the larger manufacturing companies, many of them foreign-owned. While the extent of the penetration by foreign companies of Rhodesia was marked (over one third of the fifty largest British manufacturers had a direct interest in Rhodesia), this economic strength could not necessarily be translated into votes.[14]

One perspective of foreign capital was given in 1954 in the report of Sir Ronald Prain, Chairman of the largely American-owned Rhodesian (now Roan) Selection Trust:

The Africans are constantly pressing for a much greater share of political and economic power and there is no doubt in my mind that they will eventually achieve this. What is vital for the future of the territories is the means by which they obtain this goal. It is in my view of the utmost importance that they should do this with the goodwill of the European population.[15]

The Rhodesian Selection Trust, whose interests were mainly on the Northern Rhodesia Copperbelt, had in fact engaged in a prolonged confrontation with the white mine-workers over the question of African advance in the mining industry.

An American economist who analysed the Southern Rhodesian economy gave some indication of the way that foreign capital viewed the situation:

The careful steps taken to create a hospitable environment for foreign capital are in large measure negated by the unsound political conditions prevailing . . . The solution to the problem of the continuance of growth is tied to sustaining the flow of human and investment capital. A necessary prerequisite to this appears to be an accelerated programme for economic and social advancement which will satisfy the demands of the African leaders and people. Such a programme would require the acceptance of the possibility of ultimate African control of government, by the dominant European minority.[16]

The *Guardian* correspondent in the Federation wrote: 'By the beginning of 1963 an observable shift was taking place in British industry. Some of the copper companies were beginning to wonder if it would not be better to get Northern Rhodesia politically stable . . . by encouraging a strong African majority government on full adult suffrage and if necessary, cutting the Federal links as well.'[17] Another journalist reported: 'I have been told by the heads of two great trading companies that they would prefer the stable conditions which an independent Nyasaland would offer to the present situation [i.e., the instability that prevailed in the last years of the Federation].'

In dealing with the attitude of foreign-owned industries we are perhaps in danger of assuming that their prescription for Southern Rhodesia was necessarily the same as their prescription for Northern Rhodesia and Nyasaland. In fact, it is not clear that they had a clear-cut solution for the political future of Rhodesia at all. The largest company in Southern Rhodesia, the British South Africa Company (which should perhaps rather be called a Southern-Africa-based company), had a considerably less energetic policy towards African advancement than did the largely American-owned Rhodesian Selection Trust which was mainly active in Northern Rhodesia. The British South Africa

Company included among its directors those who had close personal links with the settler minority of Rhodesia. One of the directors was Lord Salisbury, a fervent opponent of any move which he construed to be a surrender to black nationalism, and a subsequent sympathizer with U D I. Lord Malvern, on his retirement as the Federal Prime Minister, also became a B S A C director. It is clear that those companies which were Southern-Africa-based, and whose top personnel were predominantly Southern African, provided a much closer reflection of prevailing settler views on race relations than did those companies directed from New York or London, whose top personnel were only temporary residents in Africa.

In practice, the only policy which large capital seemed able to agree upon was the gradual creation of an alliance with the emergent African middle class. Huggins's biographers note: 'Huggins, under the pressure of industrialization at home and the federation campaign abroad . . . now quite deliberately thought of power in terms of social class, and aimed at a working alliance between the European ruling strata and the more prosperous Africans . . . a common front in the political sphere, which as yet he believed to be compatible with social and territorial separation.'[18] His approach was, however, nothing if not gradualist. In May 1956 he said: 'We want to indicate to the Africans that provision is made for them to have a place in the sun, as things go along. But we have not the least intention of letting them control things until they have proved themselves, and perhaps not even then. That will depend on our grandchildren.'[19]

It was clear to leading businessmen in Southern Rhodesia that any solution would have to be acceptable to the white electorate, while their own influence on government was dependent on maintaining the United Rhodesia Party in office. Todd, the only Prime Minister who pursued African advancement with any credibility in African eyes, was rejected by his party, which feared the electoral consequences of his 'liberal' image. There is no evidence to suppose that he had the particular support of business, and one writer states that his decree in November 1957, raising the minimum African urban wage by 30 per cent, lost him 'much of his remaining mildly-liberal business support'.[20]

In search of a solution

Whitehead, Todd's successor as Southern Rhodesian Prime Minister, attempted to continue the strategy of building an alliance with the emergent black middle class. His policy was slowly to break down the racial barriers; and he even went so far as proposing, if re-elected in 1962, to abolish the Land Apportionment Act – a move which many felt to be akin to abolishing the Europeans' 'Magna Carta'.

The failure of constitutional reform

The strategy of building an inter-racial governing 'liberal' alliance, pursued both by Todd and Whitehead, found expression in constitutional changes. In 1948, the United Party had promised to close the common voters' roll to Africans; but in view of the criticism that this would have provoked from abroad during the campaign to achieve federation, Huggins in 1951 instead introduced an increase in the means and educational qualifications for the vote, explicitly to exclude further African enrolment. Huggins said that the changes achieved 'almost as much as closing the roll for 15 years'.[21] In fact, African enrolment continued to rise slowly, and by November 1956 had reached 560 voters out of a total registration of 62,184.[22]

It was clear that if the strategy of the governing party was to have any prospect of success, the rate of African integration into the political system would have to be increased. Augmented African enrolment was necessary to indicate that the government had serious intentions of reform and to begin building a permanent racial coalition which would keep the United Rhodesia Party in power.

In 1956 a Commission under Sir Robert Tredgold, Chief Justice of the Federation, was appointed to make recommendations on franchise reform in Southern Rhodesia. In its report, whose proposals would effectively enfranchise only the African élite, the Commission explicitly indicated the intention to produce a class rather than a racial alliance, an electorate 'divided by political divisions based on the policies and record of the government and opposition, and not confused by differences such as race or colour'.[23]

The Electoral Act, introduced in Southern Rhodesia in 1957, raised the qualifications for the ordinary electoral roll. Electors had to fulfil certain means and educational qualifications, such as a minimum annual income of £480 or the ownership of property worth at least £1,000, plus primary education. The real intent of the Act is revealed by two significant changes which were introduced. A 'special' roll was created with lower qualifications than those needed for the ordinary roll. This new roll was intended to enfranchise the African middle class and it was estimated that 8,000 Africans would be immediately eligible. The number of voters registered on the special roll, however, could never exceed 20 per cent of those registered on the ordinary roll. Secondly, a system of alternative voting was introduced, designed to favour moderate over extremist candidates, since it was expected that voters for more extreme white candidates or for African nationalist ones would cast their second-preference votes for a 'moderate' candidate.

The attempt to create an extended constituency for the kind of reforms that the URP envisaged was largely a failure. In the 1958 election, instead of the anticipated 1,500 African voters on the ordinary roll and the 8,000 voters on the special roll, there were little more than 1,500 African voters in all. The alternative vote did serve to maintain the United Federal Party in power, however, since voters for Todd's breakaway United Rhodesia Party* cast their second-preference votes for the United Federal Party, which accordingly overcame the Dominion Party's lead on the first ballot. On the other hand, the failure of the attempt to gain the support of the African middle class was indicated by the fact that many Africans appear to have expressed no second preference.[24]

This and the low African enrolment was the result of a number of factors, which in many ways illustrate the dilemma that the government faced in trying to retain the support of white voters while gaining credibility in African eyes. The removal of Todd from the premiership had increased African doubts about the

---

*Before Todd's removal from the premiership, the United Rhodesia Party and the United Federal Party had merged. Todd subsequently took the name United Rhodesia Party when he split from the UFP.

possibility of working through the white political system. In addition, many Africans had refused to register until after the Delimitation Commission had finished revising the boundaries, since it was feared – no doubt justifiably – that the Commission, in redrawing the electoral districts, would seek to ensure that the Africans did not have a decisive influence in any one constituency. (This could have defeated the intentions of the electoral reform, since Africans would then have been in a position to elect nationalist candidates, rather than having to cast their votes for the best candidates of the white parties.) In addition, the African National Congress was severely critical of the proposed reforms and made no effort to encourage registration.

In 1961 a second and more thorough attempt was made to integrate the African middle class into the existing political system. After a full constitutional conference between the British government and the Southern Rhodesian political parties (including the National Democratic Party, the successor to the African National Congress), a new constitution was introduced. This for the first time ensured the election of Africans to the Assembly. Two separate voters' rolls, the 'A' and the 'B', were established. The predominantly white 'A' roll, which demanded substantially higher means and educational qualifications, was to elect fifty representatives to the Assembly; while the predominantly African 'B' roll was to elect fifteen. Again the changes specifically sought to increase the strength of the 'centre', with cross-voting allowed between the 'A' roll constituencies and the 'B' roll districts. Each voter could vote twice, once in an 'A' roll constituency and once in a 'B' roll district, though the 'A' roll votes could not count for more than 25 per cent of the votes in a 'B' roll district and *vice versa*, with the total number of votes being devalued accordingly.

A second change, which was to be of crucial importance in future negotiations with Britain and in the political strategy of the Rhodesian Front, was that a blocking mechanism was introduced into the constitution. Ordinary amendments to the constitution required a two-thirds majority vote in the Legislative Assembly; but amendments to entrenched clauses, which covered among other things the Declaration of Rights and the franchise qualifications, required both a two-thirds majority and either the approval of the British government or a majority vote of the registered electorate from each race – European, Asian, African and Coloured – in a referendum. This was seen by many white voters as a capitulation to majority rule, since the rate of African enfranchisement could no longer be controlled by simply changing the franchise qualifications at will. After UDI, legislative changes were introduced so that any section of the constitution could be amended simply by a two-thirds majority in the legislature, a majority which the Rhodesian Front could guarantee.

The 1961 constitution reflected a desire to achieve a *modus vivendi* with the African middle class and to reduce British control over the colony. The British government itself claimed to view the new constitution as a way of achieving a stable transition to black majority rule which it was estimated – with very doubtful accuracy – would take fifteen years.[25]

In return for the franchise changes, the incorporation of a justiciable Declaration of Rights and the creation of an independent Constitutional Council to review legislation, the British government surrendered its power to reserve or disallow legislation emanating from the Southern Rhodesian parliament or to legislate directly for Southern Rhodesia on matters within the jurisdiction of the Southern Rhodesian parliament.

The constitutional proposals were attacked by the Dominion Party as a capitulation to majority rule, 'a sell-out of the heritage we must hand to our children'.[26] Ian Smith resigned from the UFP, which he represented in the federal parliament, to oppose the proposals. However, in the referendum on acceptance, the United Federal Party were able to capitalize on the withdrawal of Britain's reserve powers which the new constitution achieved. The UFP claimed that the new constitution brought Southern Rhodesia much closer to independence. In the vote on acceptance, largely boycotted by those Africans who were eligible to vote, the proposals were accepted by a majority of nearly two to one; but, as the 1962 elections demonstrated, what the electorate had voted for was not a gradual transition to majority rule but rapid independence from Britain. The Rhodesian Front, the

Dominion Party's successor, promised in the 1962 elections to amend the constitution if elected:

The Front recognizes that inherent in the new Constitution there is the intention to ensure the dominance by the African of the European before the former has acquired adequate knowledge and experience of democratic government. The Front believes that this must be avoided. It will, therefore, *inter alia* seek in consultation with other groups, amendments to the Constitution to avoid the situation arising.[17]

The reaction to the 1961 constitution illustrates the difficulties faced by the UFP. The proposals represented the maximum concessions to African advancement which could be made without losing white support. Indeed, the new constitution had to be sold to the white electorate in terms which minimized the speed of possible African enrolment and the African influence which would result. The UFP emphasized, on the other hand, the advantages gained from the removal of British influence. The same arguments could only increase African suspicions and negate the possibility of creating an alliance with the African middle class.

The National Democratic Party had attended the Constitutional Conference; and it appears that both Nkomo and Sithole had accepted the new constitutional proposals, though with some reservations. However, faced with widespread protest from other NDP leaders and from the rank-and-file, Nkomo came out in full opposition to the proposals, and the NDP organized its own referendum to oppose acceptance. In addition, it discouraged registration and urged to considerable effect, a boycott of the 1962 elections.

The number of Africans eligible for the 'B' roll in September 1961 was estimated at between 55,000 and 60,000; but actual enrolment on the 'B' roll had only reached 9,585 by August 1962 and 10,689 by January 1965 by which time the number of eligible voters should itself have significantly increased. Of the estimated 5,500 Africans eligible for 'A' roll votes, only 1,920 had registered by August 1962, and 2,330 by January 1965. In the 1962 elections less than a quarter of the 'B' roll voters who were registered exercised their vote, a figure which by the 1965 elections had declined to 13·7 per cent.[28] Hence, while the United

Federal Party had accurately predicted that the 'B' roll votes would strengthen their position – they won fourteen of the fifteen 'B' roll districts – the small number of 'B' roll voters eliminated any significant cross-voting which could have influenced the 'A' roll results. In addition, the strength of the nationalist boycott suggests that had the other African voters registered, they would have voted not with the UFP, but for nationalist candidates, and refrained from cross-voting.

The success of the boycott campaign should in large measure be attributed to the way in which the United Federal Party had associated the 1961 constitution with Southern Rhodesian independence. African voters were not eager to participate in a process which could legitimate the granting of independence to a predominantly white government. The nationalist leaders were aware, in its campaign for the granting of independence by Britain, that the government could claim African electoral participation as indicating a general acceptance of the new constitution.

This brief survey of the 1957 and 1961 constitutional changes illustrates both the strategy of the white ruling group and the crucial racial dynamics which destined that strategy to failure. As the nationalist movement grew, so did its demands. By 1961 little less than electoral parity would have been an acceptable compromise substitute for the nationalist demand of 'one man, one vote'. Furthermore, the increased demands of the African nationalists coincided with a renewed fear among the European community of African competition. The growth of the nationalist movements in Southern Rhodesia and the other two territories in the Federation had alarmed the white population, which demanded strong measures against African militants and an undertaking that there would be no political hand-over to African nationalists. The reforms which Whitehead had introduced to improve the Africans' position, which included the addition of over two million acres to the African reserves – known as the Tribal Trust Lands under the 1961 constitution – and permission for Africans to compete equally with Europeans in the purchase of ten million acres of unassigned European Crown Land, were offset by the vigorous suppression of the African nationalist movement.

The Rhodesian Front in power

If the solution envisaged by the Southern Rhodesian UFP government was one that involved suppressing the African nationalists on the one hand and forming an alliance with the African middle class on the other, the Rhodesian Front government which came to power in December 1962 had no such divided aims. Its policy was to maintain white supremacy and to take any and all actions consistent with that end. One of the most important of these was the final removal of the remaining British powers over Southern Rhodesia, powers which otherwise might be used to undermine white supremacy.

The Rhodesian Front had been formed in March 1962 from the union of the short-lived Rhodesian Reform Party of John Gaunt and Ian Smith, with the Dominion Party. It was led by Winston Field, former Federal Dominion Party leader. In the party's election campaign, there were several issues at hand with which to rouse the white voters. In Northern Rhodesia an African majority government had come to power; in Southern Rhodesia the nationalist campaign was in full swing; in the Congo a full-scale war was in process. The British government had agreed not to announce that Nyasaland had been granted permission to withdraw from the Federation, in order to assist Whitehead's campaign, but it was clear that the Federation's days were numbered. The UFP advocated an end to racial discrimination, the abolition of the Land Apportionment Act, and promised an African Minister in the next government. In contrast, the Rhodesian Front promised to amend the 1961 constitution so as to reduce African electoral influence and to maintain separate racial facilities. The final results gave the Rhodesian Front thirty-five of the 'A' roll seats to the UFP's fifteen, and the fourteen of the fifteen 'B' roll seats gained by the UFP were not enough to offset this majority.

For the next four years, the issue of independence dominated Southern Rhodesian politics. In March 1963 it became clear that not only Nyasaland but also Northern Rhodesia would be allowed to leave the Federation, and Southern Rhodesia made a formal application for independence. In the subsequent negotiations with Britain, no agreement acceptable to the two governments emerged or even seemed possible. The Rhodesian Front government was committed to amending the 1961 constitution so as to reduce African electoral influence and in particular to eliminate cross-voting between the 'A' and 'B' rolls. Britain was not prepared to grant independence unless the franchise was substantially broadened.[29]

The origins of UDI

The possibility of a UDI was always one of the options considered. In February 1964, Duncan Sandys, Secretary of State for Commonwealth Relations, warned Winston Field: 'A unilateral declaration of independence by Southern Rhodesia would not, of course, make Southern Rhodesia legally independent ... I fear that feeling in Britain and the rest of the Commonwealth would be so unfavourable that we should be pressed to regard Southern Rhodesia as being in a state of revolt and to have no official dealings with her government.'[30]

In fact, public discussion of a unilateral declaration of independence goes at least as far back as 1958, while indications that Rhodesia would resist British demands pre-date that. In 1956 Lord Malvern had commented: 'You cannot make people do things unless they wish to except by force. One of the curious things about our Constitution is that we have complete control of our defence forces. I can only hope we shall not have to use them as the North American colonies had to use theirs. Because we are dealing with a stupid government in the United Kingdom.'[31] In the event, the British government made concessions to the Federal government in the 1957 constitutional reforms. The proportionate influence of African representatives was reduced, and the powers of the British government over the Federal government were decreased, so promoting a temporary truce. In 1958 the Dominion Party in its federal campaign had promised that if independence was not granted at the Federal Constitutional Review in 1960, it would implement steps to declare UDI; a promise which, it is thought, lost the party some support at the time.[32] Welensky, while condemning these proposals as irresponsible, had himself said that if independence was not granted in 1960, it would be time 'to take stock and decide what other action is necessary. I personally could never be prepared to accept that the Rhodesians have less guts than the American colonists had.'[33] One of the fears of the Federal government was that the Labour government in Britain might overrule the white settlers and force the pace of African advance. Referring to the possibility of a Labour victory in 1959, Malvern reminded the British House of Lords: 'We have a little army of our own and a little air force.'[34]

In fact, the Federal government had considered UDI and drawn up contingency plans in February 1961 at the height of the dispute over African advancement in Northern Rhodesia and Nyasaland. The Salisbury *Evening Standard* wrote: 'It is no longer a secret that some actions at least considered by Welensky during the 1961 crisis were anything but constitutional.'[35]

Britain was ultimately able to dismantle the Federation without any armed conflict; but her success on this occasion made future success less likely. Southern Rhodesia's white settlers had seen that negotiations with Britain had led not to the Federation's independence but to its break-up, with the subsequent granting of independence to Zambia and Malawi. In the future, the white electorate would be much more sympathetic to unconstitutional action.

Britain, on the other hand, seemed to have learnt little from history. Far from making plans which would enable her to exercise any countervailing force on the Southern Rhodesian government, the British government handed control over the bulk of the Federation's armed forces and equipment to Southern Rhodesia. This move cannot have been lightly taken since, for the first time since Suez, Britain was forced to veto a UN Security Council resolution asking Britain 'not to transfer ... the armed forces and aircraft as envisaged by the Central African Conference of 1963'.

Perhaps Britain imagined that, as in the case of Northern Rhodesia and Nyasaland, she would still be able to achieve her ends by negotiation. In any event, she told the United Nations that the hand-over of the Federal Armed Forces was the price that had to be paid for the peaceful dissolution of the Federation.[36] It was a short-sighted policy and one which contrasted dangerously with the strategic thinking of the Rhodesian government. Winston Field commented: 'There are timorous ones who say: "But we cannot afford a worthwhile defence force." My only reply in this day and age in Africa is: "We have got to." '[37] Indeed, a UDI without an army would have been a rather empty gesture.

The explanation for Britain's agreement to hand over the military forces can only be found in the wider context of Britain's unwillingness to confront Southern Rhodesian demands in any manner likely to provoke a major conflict. In contrast, many Southern Rhodesian whites were prepared to go all the way for independence with a white minority government. In these circumstances, they could hardly lose.

Pressures for independence built up at the grass-roots level. In August 1964, Welensky himself, who was leading the new Rhodesia Party (which in effect represented the same forces as the old UFP), and Sidney Sawyers, also standing for the Rhodesia Party, were overwhelmingly defeated at by-elections. Earlier in the year, Winston Field had been compelled to surrender leadership of the Rhodesian Front to Ian Smith who, it was rightly thought, would lead a more forceful campaign for independence. The stage was now set for the final defeat of the white moderates.

6 UDI and the failure of British policy

I am confident that we shall have not only the support of this House, not only the support of the nations of the world, but we shall have the clear and decisive verdict of history – Harold Wilson, announcing to the House of Commons measures to be taken against UDI, 1965

If Smith succeeds, the seeds of a future race war in Southern Africa will be sown – Kenneth Kaunda, 1966

The increasingly vociferous demand in Rhodesia for independence, if necessary through UDI, posed serious problems for Britain. In this author's view, the failure of Britain's political response can only be understood as related to Britain's heavy economic involvement in Southern Africa. The size and importance of her trade and investment in the area meant that a British government which wished to impose majority rule in Rhodesia would have to be prepared to confront powerful sectors of British opinion. The Labour government which had come to power in 1964 was not such a government. For Wilson's government, as for previous Labour governments, the 'national interest' generally appeared to be synonymous with the interests of those who controlled the British economy.

The Rhodesian Front's electoral triumph

The election campaign of April and early May 1965 was fought primarily on the independence issue. Both the Rhodesia Party (the chief opposition) and the Rhodesian Front favoured independence. The Rhodesia Party's policy was 'to maintain the *status quo* and work for negotiated independence, the maintenance of law and order, standards and responsible government'.[1] On the racial issue, it back-tracked considerably from the 'liberal' position of the old UFP. It would not tamper with the Land Apportionment Act or introduce integrated education, and it assured voters that under the 1961 constitution, Africans could not 'obtain power for many years . . . If we stick resolutely to our Constitution . . . we are safe'.[2] In spite of its concessions to racism, however, the party was not strong enough to field candidates in more than twenty-five of the fifty 'A' roll seats, though it contested all fifteen of the 'B' roll districts. It clearly no longer expected to have any opportunity of forming a government but hoped at least to control a sufficient number of seats in the legislature to block any constitutional changes.

The Rhodesian Front stated that while the election was not intended to provide a mandate for UDI, the Front would not hesitate to seize independence, if 'the only thing we can see ahead of Rhodesia is to be handed over to extreme nationalists'.[3]

The Rhodesian Tobacco Association, the Institute of Directors and the Association of Rhodesian Industries all issued statements warning of the possible serious economic consequences which would follow UDI. The Southern Rhodesian government, on the other hand, claimed in a White Paper that the imposition of economic sanctions was unlikely, in view of the West's economic and strategic interests in Rhodesia.

The final election results gave all fifty 'A' roll seats to the Rhodesian Front, while the Rhodesia Party gained ten of the 'B' roll seats. Ian Smith had effectively eliminated the opposition and assured himself that any UDI would carry overwhelming support.

European politics in Southern Rhodesia had now entered into its penultimate phase. Big capital and 'enlightened' liberals had failed to secure a commitment to gradual African advance. The white petty bourgeoisie and working class, anxious to prevent competition in farming or in the labour market, had put into power a government which they hoped would entrench white privileges for all time. They had shown that they would not accept a government which temporized or showed any sign of compromise on the racial issue.

Though there are few signs that the British government ever understood this, it was in fact negotiating with the direct spokesman for those sectors of white Rhodesian society which regarded concession as suicide. Large-scale industry can deal with black or white governments, black or white workers; profits continue and may well increase with a cheaper labour-force and a wider market. In contrast, for the white worker with only his labour to sell, his standard of living is crucially dependent on preventing black competition. In these circumstances, it is difficult to know what kind of 'compromise' was possible. Rhodesian society is based on white supremacy, and the high standard of living of its white inhabitants is a direct consequence of this. The position of the whites is legitimated – in their own eyes – by an ideology of racial superiority. The importance of this ideology in providing a 'moral' basis gives this position real strength and makes any acceptance of African rule impossible, even if the economic consequences were acceptable. For the majority of white Rhodesians, the question of majority rule at any time in the literally fore-seeable future was not negotiable. All that could be negotiated was the form which independence took; the window-dressing, but never the real content. To imagine that Smith could change this was to confuse the power of an individual with the strength of the social movement of which he was the spokesman. But such were the fond hopes of British statesmen.

Wilson even took upon himself the job of advising Smith not to allow himself to be 'pushed around by the right-wing, almost Fascist, element in his Cabinet. It would [thought Wilson] be the easiest thing in the world for him to move to the centre and ditch some of his extreme supporters.'[4] Speaking to the House of Commons just after U D I, Arthur Bottomley said: 'One thing I did judge during the talks with the [Rhodesian] Cabinet was that Mr Smith himself stood out as a man of character and integrity.'[5]

Even if Smith had been the 'reasonable' man that the Labour government so desperately wanted to think him, he could have done no more than temporarily delay events before being displaced by a more reliable representative of white interests. It would seem, from Bottomley's speech, that the Rhodesian Front's popular support came to the Labour leadership as something of a surprise: 'We had to sadly recognize that the broad masses of the people supported the Rhodesian Front government and the policy of a unilateral declaration of independence.'[6] In fact, as any reading of Smith's career should have shown, he stood not at some malleable centre but at the rational extreme of Rhodesian racism.

It is facile to represent racism as merely the product of prejudice and ignorance and to ignore its ability to provide an ideological rationalization for real sectional interests. Smith represented those interests, and history will show that he did so with a much clearer short-term vision than the social democrats of Westminster displayed. Our analysis of the negotiations indicates that the Rhodesian Front never at any time wavered from its commitment to minority rule. The negotiations were, rather, a series of alternative face-saving formulae which Smith was prepared to allow the British so as to help them sell his cause to the world. Perhaps the only limitation on Smith's effectiveness was his dependence on a white electorate which might have mistaken a feint in the direction of racial liberalism for the real thing and ditched him.

Britain's bargaining position

For British policy to be effective, Britain needed to exercise a very strong countervailing power. It is difficult to persuade a man to act against his interests as he sees them. In order to change his outlook, it is necessary to re-define those interests, generally by changing the real situation. It can be argued that a dramatic shock would have forced the white Rhodesians into realizing that they were sitting on a powder keg and that only concessions could assure their long-term survival. Mass movements of the right, however, have generally been concerned with an immediate crisis rather than with the long-term historical perspective. If Rhodesia could declare U D I without any adverse reaction from abroad which would significantly effect Rhodesia, then clearly U D I, with its real and symbolic effect of entrenching white supremacy, had much to commend it. The Rhodesian government consistently played down the consequences of U D I; and in this, it received the assistance of the British government.

On 24 October 1964, just after his election, Mr Wilson, in a statement handed to Mr Smith by the British High Commissioner and subsequently released by Britain to the Rhodesian news media, said:

A Declaration of Independence would be an open act of defiance and rebellion and it would be treasonable to take steps to give effect to it ... The economic effects would be disastrous to the prosperity and prospects of the people of Southern Rhodesia ... in short, an illegal Declaration of Independence in Southern Rhodesia would bring to an end relationships between her and Britain, would cut her off from the rest of the Commonwealth, from most foreign governments and international organizations; would inflict disastrous economic damage on her; would leave her isolated and virtually friendless in a largely hostile continent.[7]

One commentator has credited this statement with possibly delaying U D I for a year.[8] Wilson himself states that the publication of the message was prompted by information that Smith intended to declare U D I in a parliamentary debate on the 27th. In any event, Wilson's subsequent performance must have done much to reassure the Rhodesians on the more vital issue of the use of military force.

Wilson and his ministers were anxious to establish at the outset that military intervention was not a possibility. Few politicians can have been so ready to reveal and even proclaim their ultimate weakness at the bargaining table. As the Commonwealth Secretary told the House: 'In all his talks with the Africans, the Prime Minister made three things clear beyond all doubt. There could be no question of the use of armed force by Britain to impose a solution. Majority rule, to which the British government were committed, could not be expected today or tomorrow, it could be expected only when *achievement warranted it.*' [My emphasis.] And in continuing his speech, this latter-day representative of the government which had given Zimbabwe to Cecil Rhodes, then went on to explain to the House how he had lectured the Africans on democracy: 'We spoke very plainly to the Africans [at a meeting with nationalist leaders in February 1965]. I told them they should work the 1961 Constitution ... Unlike other African leaders, the African nationalists in Rhodesia have never fought an election and have never tried to show their ability to govern.'[9]

At the Commonwealth Conference in June 1965, Wilson again rejected the possible use of force, which 'could plunge Africa into armed conflict going far beyond the borders of Rhodesia'.[10] We shall have cause to return to Wilson's far-from-casual interest in what lay beyond the borders of Rhodesia – much of it British-owned. Two weeks before U D I, Wilson told the African leaders: 'If there are those who are thinking in terms of a thunderbolt hurtling from the sky and destroying their enemy, a thunderbolt in the shape of the Royal Air Force, let me say that the thunderbolt will not be forthcoming, and to continue in this illusion wastes valuable time and misdirects valuable energies.'[11] In any case, for Wilson the use of force 'was never on'.[12] (This statement is accurate as an ideological reflection of how remote such a possibility was from the thinking of the Prime Minister rather than as an indication that the use of military force was not formally considered.) So eager was Wilson to reassure Rhodesians that in his statement in Rhodesia on 29 October, after meeting Smith in Salisbury, he explicitly excluded the use of force yet again.[13] Since, by this time, U D I was obviously imminent, one can only wonder at his diplomacy.

Since force 'was never on', in order to create a situation in which most white Rhodesians could not see their interests as being best served by U D I, the British government had to produce an alternative threat. The alternative was to be economic sanctions. But this is not to suggest that the government consistently saw the situation in such unambiguous terms. Clearly it did not, or the negotiations would not have taken the course that they did, and the myths of Smith as an honourable man, a prisoner of 'the extreme right', would not have arisen.[14]*

The supposed strength of economic sanctions was based on the fact that Britain was Rhodesia's major trading partner, providing some 30 per cent of Rhodesia's imports and taking some 28 per cent of her exports. While these proportions were signi-

*Wilson revealed similar skill as a judge of Rhodesian character in the 'full confidence' he placed in the Rhodesian Chief Justice, Sir Hugh Beadle (C M N D 2807, p. 140). Beadle was to have the singular distinction of being the highest legal authority to support the patently illegal U D I.

ficant in terms of the Rhodesian economy, they were not crucial to the British economy. In 1964, Britain exported £33·4m. of goods to Rhodesia and imported £31·2m.[15] Rhodesia's second major trading partner was Zambia, buying £41·7m. of exports from Rhodesia and supplying £5·4m. of imports. South Africa ranked third, buying £26·6m. of exports from Rhodesia and selling £12·2m.[16] It was the trade with South Africa and the ability of Rhodesia to use South Africa and to a lesser extent the Portuguese colonies as a conduit for trade with the rest of the world, that proved crucial to Rhodesia's weathering of sanctions. Perhaps in anticipation of this escape route, or perhaps because, as the Rhodesian government declared in a White Paper, 'There is no sentiment attached to money . . . countries will continue to trade',[17] the threat of sanctions failed to provide a sufficient deterrent.

The pattern of negotiations

Since the British government had discounted the use of force, and the Rhodesian government was prepared to risk the imposition of sanctions, Britain's negotiating position was weak. Indeed, it appears to have been based on trying to find a solution acceptable to the Rhodesian Front which would not create too much uproar in the UN, the Commonwealth and among anti-racialists at home. The policy of NIBMAR (No Independence Before Majority Rule) rapidly gave way to the search for devices whereby independence would be given under some formula which would allow gradual progression to majority rule.* The Conservative government had formalized five principles which had

*On 2 October 1964, Wilson wrote to Dr E. Mutasa, a member of the Committee Against European Independence, in Salisbury: 'The Labour Party is totally opposed to granting independence to Southern Rhodesia as long as the country remains under the control of a white minority. We have repeatedly urged the British government to negotiate a new Constitution with all the African and European parties represented, in order to achieve a peaceful transition to majority rule.' (Quoted in Anne Darnborough, *Labour's Record on Southern Africa*, p. 3.) When the letter was released in Rhodesia, Smith demanded, as a condition for resuming discussions, an assurance that this was not government policy. Wilson replied: 'We have an open mind on the timing of independence in relation to progress towards majority rule.' (CMND 2807, pp. 47–8.) Hence, within eleven days of taking office, a major plank in Labour's Rhodesia policy had been demolished.

to be adhered to before independence could be given; and, ostensibly at least, these have served as a basis for all subsequent negotiations:

1. The principle and intention of unimpeded progress to majority rule, already enshrined in the 1961 constitution, would have to be maintained and guaranteed.
2. There would also have to be guarantees against retrogressive amendments to the constitution.
3. There would have to be immediate improvement in the political status of the African population.
4. There would have to be progress towards ending racial discrimination.
5. The British government would need to be satisfied that any basis proposed for independence was acceptable to the people of Rhodesia as a whole.

Subsequently, a sixth principle was added: 'It would be necessary to ensure that, regardless of race, there was no oppression of majority by a minority or a minority by a majority.'[18] The sixth principle was little more than a capitulation to European racism. George Thomson said: 'The sixth reflects our obligation to guarantee the future of the European minority.'[19] The only justification for such a guarantee lay in a breach of faith by a future African government. The principle was subsequently dropped by the Conservative government, whose own proposals offered little prospect of such a government ever coming to power.

In fact, no substantive progress was made in the negotiations, on any of the principles. As Rhodesia indicated her growing determination to obtain independence by any means, the Labour government made further concessions. By October 1965, the debate centred only on the second and fifth principles. By November even the second principle had faded into the background. On the eve of UDI, Wilson intimated that Britain might be prepared to grant independence on the basis of the 1961 constitution given the unanimous recommendation that it was acceptable to Rhodesians.* This recommendation would come from a

---

*In a debate on the 1961 Southern Rhodesian Bill, John Dugdale, speaking from the Labour benches, said: 'I believe, and I weigh my words very carefully, that this constitution is not only bad, but that it is positively a fraud . . . It had one aim and one

three-man Royal Commission headed, at Wilson's suggestion, by Sir Hugh Beadle, the Chief Justice of Rhodesia, and including one nominee from Britain and one from Rhodesia.[20]

The government was prepared to accept the 1961 constitution, which had been rejected by the African nationalists and by the Labour opposition in Britain, as setting a suitable pace for African advance. However, while the British government lowered its criteria, the Rhodesian government did not: it insisted on the right of the Rhodesian government to amend the 1961 constitution, 'if it appeared at a future election that an African government was probable and the Rhodesian government felt . . . that this would still be premature'.[21] In effect, the pre-UDI negotiations, therefore, became concerned not with securing further African advance in return for UDI, but with guarding against erosion, after independence, of an electoral situation already considered unacceptable by African leaders.*

The argument against military intervention

The Rhodesian government said: 'If they [the Europeans] did not obtain independence, they would have to leave Rhodesia. They would rather fight it out than go voluntarily.'[22] Nevertheless, it is by no means clear that, if the British government had

---

aim only, to remove the reserve powers now exercised by Her Majesty's Government. Anything given in this constitution, is given as a *quid pro quo* for that.' Marquand, on behalf of the Labour Party, moved to reject proposals, 'formulated without their [the Africans'] consent and which fail to provide for them a representation sufficient to their civil liberties'. (*Hansard*, 22 June 1961.) The 1962 Labour Party conference demanded of the Conservative government a new constitution for Rhodesia and 'no further surrender of her [Britain's] constitutional rights until genuine representative government exists in the territory' (*Talking Points*, II, Labour Party, 1963). An indication of the change can be given by contrasting this with the terms issued by the British government for a settlement with Rhodesia in October 1966: 'They [the British government] accept that the pace of the political advancement of the Africans should continue to be governed by achievements and merit, i.e. through the acquisition of the economic and educational qualifications prescribed under the 1961 constitution.' (CMND 3171, p. 21.)

*In the meeting with Smith in Salisbury on 29 October, Wilson stated: 'This one question of the entrenched clauses was the main outstanding issue.' (CMND 2807, p. 128.) This referred to Britain's demand that a mechanism be found to ensure that the Rhodesian government could not, by changing the number of 'A' Roll seats or eliminating the 'B' Roll seats, delay African advance.

consistently stated its resolve forcibly to prevent U D I, the Rhodesians would have gone ahead. They had no assurance of any outside support, and in comparison with Britain, their military power and even their potential was slight. However, without the threat of military intervention, the British had few bargaining cards.

The use of force was favoured by much of the Third World, including many African members of the Commonwealth. A United Nations General Assembly resolution of 5 November 1965 called on Britain to use all means including force to achieve majority rule in Rhodesia. As usual, Britain abstained, since it viewed Rhodesia as an internal affair.[23] The U N Security Council had previously (on 6 May) called on Britain to take 'all necessary action' to prevent U D I.[24] On 11 November the General Assembly adopted, by a vote of 107 to 2, a resolution calling on Britain to 'take all necessary steps to put an end to the rebellion by the unlawful authorities in Salisbury'.[25] Tanzania and Zambia, for both geographical and political reasons, particularly concerned with any extension or reinforcement of white supremacy in Africa, were energetic in demanding the use of force and did so at the June 1965 Commonwealth Prime Ministers' Conference. Wilson, however, was able to record with satisfaction that the final conference communiqué did not envisage the use of force.[26]*

The British government's argument against military intervention was nowhere clearly stated, but rested in part on logistical arguments and in part on political ones. The logistic situation from the British viewpoint was that Rhodesia was a land-locked country with powerful military forces, inherited from the Central African Federation; 500 miles from the sea; and largely surrounded by sympathetic governments.[27] British troops were at that time heavily extended in Europe and Malaysia, and an operation on the scale demanded was therefore beyond them. An imponderable element was the position of South Africa. In November 1968, George Thomson told Z A N U leaders: 'I have no doubts that they [South Africa] would fight. I have had several meetings with South African officials and I am left in no

*Demands for the use of force mounted after U D I.

doubt that South Africa would fight.'[28] Whether or not that was, indeed, the position in 1968, it had certainly not been generally accepted in 1965. Both the Commonwealth Secretary, Arthur Bottomley, and the Minister of State at the Commonwealth Office, Cledwyn Hughes, interviewed in March 1972, believed that immediate military intervention would not have brought South African involvement. In fact, there is some evidence to suggest that South Africa adopted a wait-and-see policy. Verwoerd announced that South Africa would make no intervention or comments on negotiations between Rhodesia and Britain – on the grounds that it was an internal affair – and that South Africa would not support any boycott or sanctions. South African banks did, however, freeze currency transactions between South Africa and Rhodesia from 11 to 18 November, an indication that they had not decided to tie their fortunes to Rhodesia, irrespective of the consequences of UDI. This suggests that if Britain had adopted a more vigorous response, South Africa might well have been more cautious.

Further military arguments related to the possibility that Rhodesia might take reprisals against Zambia by bombing-raids, by cutting off power from the Kariba Dam, or even by dynamiting the dam. The concern for Zambia should, however, be put in perspective; for the concern was, above all, with the Zambian copper mines regarded as vital to the British economy. This was the reason why Wilson subsequently sent a small force of RAF planes into Zambia and indicated that, in the event of Rhodesia's taking action against the Kariba Dam and hence Britain's copper supplies, military intervention would follow.[29] In any case, too much weight should not be attached to Britain's fears for the safety of Zambia, since the Zambian government itself consistently demanded military intervention against Rhodesia and offered the use of Zambian territory for this purpose.

One of the most publicized arguments against the use of force was that of 'kith and kin'. Briefly summarized, this held that British forces would not fight against fellow, English-speaking white men, especially since the Rhodesians had supported Britain in the last war. As might be expected, the fact that the majority of the Rhodesian troops in the Second World War had been African was rarely mentioned. In any case, the argument was not seriously credible. Indeed, the Commonwealth Secretary had been told by both the leaders of the Rhodesian Air Force and the Army that they would not support U D I;[30] though, had they refused to carry out orders, they could no doubt have been replaced. The Smith government was sufficiently unsure of its own military to obtain the resignation of Major-General J. Andersen, the General Officer Commanding Rhodesia, who had indicated that he could not support any unconstitutional action. And many of the officers in the Rhodesian army were British rather than Rhodesian citizens.

On the other hand, there is no real evidence that within the British army there would have been any resistance to armed intervention. John Rex, who spoke at a Northern Command meeting on Rhodesia at that time, found no evidence of any potential refusal in the army to carry out orders to restore constitutional rule in Rhodesia; indeed, many officers found the suggestion of such a refusal offensive. In any case, kith and kin, if this sentiment existed, was presumably a reciprocal feeling. Had Britain indicated that it was prepared to use force, not only might Smith, in spite of his speeches, have reconsidered any U D I, but loyalty problems would have been at least mutual. In the immediate post-U D I period, Rhodesia, small, isolated, with a hostile African population and a crisis atmosphere, was hardly in the stronger position to rely on the loyalty of its troops, when for some – including former Prime Ministers, the Governor-General and for a time the Chief Justice – loyalty was still to the Queen and therefore to Westminster. As late as 1968 two judges, Mr Justice Fieldsend and Mr Justice Dendy Young, resigned in protest against the failure of the Appeal Court to recognize the Privy Council as the highest court of appeal.

This writer is not competent to comment on the strategic factors. But it should be noted that Britain was at that time the third-ranking world military power, spending significantly more of its budget on defence than any other European power, with the exception of the U S S R. If it could not take on the military might of 250,000 Europeans, sitting on top of $4\frac{1}{2}$ million hostile

Africans, one is inclined to wonder why. David Owen, a junior Defence Minister from 1968 to 1970, wrote: 'There is little doubt, however, that these military difficulties were exaggerated in consequence of a combination of prejudiced military advice and the political reluctance of the Labour government to risk civilian casualties, which would have exaggerated the already strong 'kith and kin' arguments espoused by a largely hostile press.'[31]

The final arguments against military intervention were of a more explicitly political nature and can be summarized under two headings: the spectre of an African bloodbath; and the possible domestic consequences of the use of force. Journalists and politicians were ready in those years to brandish the spectre of the Congo, not in the hope that from it we might learn something of imperialism's victims in Africa, but rather to conjure up images of nuns butchered by rampaging African savages. Suffice it to say that no sane person relishes the prospect of bloodshed; but it is clear, from any reasonable reading of Southern African developments, that one day bloodshed will indeed envelop the region. A minimization of the bloodshed is likely to come only by matching vastly superior organized force against the military hardware of the white supremacists. A further argument presented to the author by Labour spokesmen on the left and the right was that the Labour Party has a 'natural antipathy'[32] to violence and military involvement. It is an argument, however, which seemed somehow more powerful in connection with Rhodesia than with Malaysia, Aden, Ireland or even Anguilla.

In Britain, Labour was concerned both with its slim overall majority in Parliament, and the danger that the Conservative Party would break with the bi-partisan policy on Rhodesia.* These arguments, however, were generally presented as additional rather than crucial. As one left-wing M P told this writer, the decision would have been the same with a majority of a thousand. Owen has commented that, with the much increased majority of March 1966, 'The opportunity existed ... to en-

*In his memoirs Wilson writes: 'It is true of course, that had we decided to intervene by force of arms he [Heath] would have led a united party and almost certainly won majority support in the country.' (*The Labour Government* 1964–70, p. 181.) On the other hand Wilson could have counted on some Liberal support in Parliament.

force a genuine solution compatible with the only defensible policy of not granting independence before majority rule. Moral outrage in 1972 should not be used as the cover for the failure of political will to match the problem with a credible solution in 1966.'[33]

No doubt, had Labour decided to use force, the pro-Rhodesian lobby of the Conservative Party would have initiated a major campaign of opposition. But had the Labour Party indicated its intention of using force all along, instead of repeatedly denying it, the opposition case would have been weak. It is, in any case, possible that the Conservative Party had itself considered the use or at least the threat of force. One pro-Smith writer claims that in 1964, after Field's resignation, Home had placed British troops in Aden on the alert.[34] However, since Labour had long eschewed the use of force, the Tory backwoodsmen could the more convincingly encourage ministerial spokesmen after UDI to repeat their commitment not to do so. In fact, on the day of UDI, Wilson immediately rejected force, 'unless, of course, our troops are asked for to preserve law and order and to avert tragic action, subversion, murder, and so on'.[35] This led some to speculate that troops were more likely to be used to preserve white supremacy than to overthrow it. Indeed, since law and order had been unequivocally attacked with UDI, it is difficult to know what other interpretation is possible.

Added to the fear of the Tory opposition – or perhaps at the root of that fear – was Labour's feeling that Rhodesia, like immigration, was an issue which should be handled with care. A progressive policy on race was not likely to gain Labour any support. Indeed, Richard Crossman, when being lobbied by Labour backbenchers against the 1966 *Fearless* proposals, ushered the lobbyists out of his office, telling them that they were sabotaging a perfectly good settlement and that Rhodesia was an issue which could certainly not help the party.[36]

It is worthwhile briefly to elaborate Labour's record in the area of race. In the autumn of 1961, Hugh Gaitskell led the Parliamentary Labour Party in total opposition to the introduction of a bill to control immigration from the Commonwealth. In 1963, when the Commonwealth Immigration Act came up for renewal, the new leader of the party, Harold Wilson, had already shifted the debate from the fundamental rejection of any control to argument about the best means. The Labour Party entered the 1964 elections committed to limiting the numbers of Commonwealth immigrants allowed into Britain. In 1968 Labour Home Secretary James Callaghan introduced the Immigration Bill to restrict the entry into Britain of British passport-holders from the Commonwealth and colonies. The move, which will surely be recorded as one of the most sordid moments in the modern history of the British Labour Party certainly ended any claim that the party might have had to being principled on issues of race.

John Rex, one of Britain's foremost race relations experts, wrote after four years of Labour government:

When Ministers did speak [in response to anti-immigrant campaigns] however, their utterances were disastrous. Judith Hart led the way by pointing out that voluntary repatriation was already available through the assistance board, while Wilson got in quickly to agree that there were some areas already saturated with immigrants which should be subsidized at the expense of the immigrant-free areas. The way was open for still further demands, for compulsory repatriation, for internal segregation in Britain, for camps, perhaps for the 'final solution'. Little wonder that in Washington, Paris or Moscow as well as in Dar-es-Salaam, New Delhi or Peking, Britain began to be seen as the world's most commitedly racialist country.[37]

Little wonder, too, that the government was not enthusiastic about appearing before the country as the defender of black Rhodesians against white kith and kin. Yet, none of this was to cause Wilson to be any less indignant when it was suggested at the 1966 Commonwealth Conference that he was a racialist.[38]

Andrew Faulds, in announcing that he would resign from the Labour Party if the *Fearless* proposals were accepted, placed the proposals in this wider perspective: 'The government need to remember that their record on matters affecting race relations is pretty tattered. On too many occasions, they have retreated before popular prejudice. They retreated on immigration controls, and on the status of Kenyan Asians. Now, from all appearances, they are in the process of retreating before Smith and his stand for white supremacy.'[39]

Clearly Britain is a racist country. But in the case of Rhodesia, there was a contradictory factor at work. Ian Smith had pulled the Lion's tail, and there were many in Britain who felt that the Lion still had teeth.* A Gallup poll published in June 1968 found that 41 per cent of those questioned felt Britain had not dealt strongly enough with Rhodesia, compared with 16 per cent who felt that action had been unduly harsh and 16 per cent who felt it had been 'about right' (Johannesburg *Star*, 29 June 1968). In the debate on the *Tiger* proposals, John Lee, Labour MP for Reading, had argued: 'I advocated military intervention at every meeting in my election campaign and we still swung my constituency more than the national average.'[40]

In addition, there were those, including the Archbishop of Canterbury, who felt that morality demanded the use of force to protect the African majority. The possible domestic unpopularity of a stronger policy against Rhodesia can of course only explain, not justify, the government's policy. In fact, Labour's constant concessions to racial prejudice, as Rex suggests, merely fed the flames.

Though Wilson said that the use of force 'was never on', it was in fact considered by the government. An interesting light on the quality of this consideration is thrown by the fact that the government sought the advice of the British military attaché in Rhodesia. Irrespective of any other qualifications, the attaché might reasonably have been supposed to be on close personal terms with senior Southern Rhodesian army personnel and hence, against any violent confrontation; as, indeed, he was. No doubt the government was also cautioned against the use of military force by senior civil servants and military officials whose background would again dispose them to caution where fundamental imperial interests were not at stake.

In the final analysis, we shall argue that the rejection of the use of military force was essentially not the consequence of these

*Frank Judd, MP for Portsmouth, stated in an interview in March 1972 that during the *Fearless* negotiations he had found a great deal of opposition to any sell-out in his constituency precisely on these grounds.

factors. It was not a consequence of Britain's military weakness or the small size of the Labour majority or indeed even the possible reaction of public opinion to military involvement. It was, rather, related to the strategic interests of Britain and British capital, as seen by the Labour government. Before developing this argument, however, we shall briefly examine the line of action which Britain adopted, a line which was destined to fail because it was rooted in the same factors which gave rise to the rejection of military intervention.

UDI and the imposition of sanctions

The British government, Conservative and Labour, had repeatedly warned Rhodesia of the economic consequences of UDI. On 11 November 1965, when UDI was declared, Wilson announced that Rhodesia had been removed from the sterling area, British capital exports to Rhodesia were banned, the purchase of Rhodesian tobacco was halted, and it was intended to take similar action on Rhodesian sugar. Rhodesia was denied access to the London capital market and suspended from the Commonwealth preference area. On 16 November, the Southern Rhodesian Act outlawed most trade with Rhodesia. In urging its support, Wilson referred to the danger of a Chinese or Soviet military intervention in Rhodesia.[41] Apparently, even as white supremacy strengthened its hold on the continent, Wilson could not forget that the real war was the Cold War. On 20 November the UN Security Council adopted a resolution urging all states to end economic relations with Rhodesia. Britain both submitted a draft resolution and voted for the final form. Rhodesia was no longer an 'internal' affair.

Perhaps thinking that this economic rap on the knuckles combined with Wilson's 'Churchillian' speeches would suffice to bring Rhodesia to heel, an oil embargo was not introduced until 17 December. Indeed there was much talk of the need not to offend loyal Rhodesians. The Conservative Party issued a statement attacking Britain's support for the UN Security Council resolution, which 'would have the effect of alienating loyal elements in Rhodesia'.[42] While it is true that a number of prominent Rhodesians opposed UDI, the size of the opposition was small and likely to remain so, or decline – as it did – when it became clear that Rhodesia would get away with it.* The loyal elements in any case must have been somewhat confused by Wilson's rhetorical flourishes, which made up in drama what they lacked in content. On 11 November Wilson told the House of Commons: 'It is the duty of everyone owing allegiance to the Crown, in Rhodesia or elsewhere, to refrain from all acts which would assist the illegal régime to continue in their rebellion against the Crown.' Later in the same speech, he said: 'It is the duty of public servants to carry on their jobs, to help to maintain law and order, certainly the judges and the police, at this critical time, but they themselves must be the judges of any possible action which they might be asked to take which would be illegal in itself or illegal in the sense of furthering this rebellious act.'[44] Attempting to clarify the position on the next day, Wilson distinguished between a legal order, such as ordering surgical dressings in the Ministry of Health, and an illegal order such as shooting all the occupants of a detention camp on instructions from the Ministry of the Interior. Certainly those police who arrested more than fifty Africans around Bulawayo, broke up numerous African demonstrations and invaded the dormitories of university college in Salisbury, could – if they had been concerned – have found little in Mr Wilson's statement to indicate that they were doing other than their job. Mr Wilson's obsessional concern for law and order appeared to exceed his concern with whose law and order was to be preserved.

The British government expected that the imposition of the oil embargo would be sufficient to bring the régime into line. What kind of scenario of events was anticipated is unclear: negotiations with Smith; a palace revolt in Salisbury; popular white reaction produced by the growing economic difficulties; a general upheaval? Many members of the government and backbenchers appear to have seized on sanctions as a policy, but never considered its implications. Arthur Bottomley, Secretary of State for Commonwealth Relations at the time, subsequently said that

*Kenneth Young claims that only 36 of Rhodesia's 12,000 civil servants resigned after UDI.[43]

he thought sanctions would produce chaos and the army would have to go in to re-establish order.[45] Wilson, on the other hand, appeared to believe that Smith himself would be brought to heel and forced to concede British demands. He told the January Commonwealth Conference on Rhodesia, held in Nigeria, that the oil embargo would bring the rebellion to an end 'in weeks not months'.[46] Wilson said that he had 'good reason to believe that Portugal would not challenge the determination of the U N nor seek to encourage sanction-breaking'.[47] Cledwyn Hughes, Minister of State at the Commonwealth Relations Office and Chairman of the Cabinet Rhodesia Committee, took a similar stand. He later argued that the crossing of the South African border post at Beit Bridge by oil tankers had been crucial in saving Rhodesia. Reliable daily reports had indicated that oil supplies were reaching a critical level.[48]

The government appears to have been either lamentably ignorant of the politics of the situation – and to have taken no account of South Africa's repeated declarations that she would not adhere to sanctions – or to have been pursuing an elaborate charade with no real hope of having any effect. In any case, Verwoerd was moving into an election; even had he wanted to avoid entanglement in Rhodesia, he could hardly risk taking action against the 'friends of Rhodesia' group and others who were supplying oil to the territory. The opposition United Party had already called on Verwoerd to accord a *de facto* recognition to the régime. Portugal, heavily involved in its own colonies, might have been susceptible to strong pressures economically or through N A T O; but, with the exception of the attempt to close the port of Beira in Portuguese Mozambique to Rhodesian-bound oil, that was no part of British policy. In fact, a strong argument can be made that Portugal and South Africa, like some Rhodesian whites, were waiting to see whether Smith could get away with U D I.* Britain's policy of caution and gradualism, far from weakening Smith, showed in fact that he could.

In spite of Verwoerd's statement to the South African Parlia-

---

*Colin Legum has argued: 'A hard knock at the beginning, especially if it had been keenly backed by the U N, would almost certainly have been decisive in limiting South Africa's role.'[49]

ment, on 25 January, that his government would not hinder oil shipments to Rhodesia, Britain continued to rely on this tactic, concentrating on at least preventing supplies from reaching the port of Beira. Indeed, in this, the British showed a rare determination. In April, British frigates were used with U N approval to block oil carriers destined for Beira. Spectacular as the gesture was, it was too late; for, by this time, Rhodesia was estimated to be receiving 145,000 gallons of oil per day, against its estimated need under rationing of 83,000 gallons.[50] More effective action would have been to invoke penalties against the parent companies, Shell and B P, whose South African subsidiaries were supplying much of the oil.

Despite the failure of the oil embargo, Britain did not seek mandatory sanctions from the U N Security Council until December of 1966, when the *Tiger* talks appeared to have temporarily persuaded Wilson that Rhodesia was not prepared to compromise. And even at this late date, only 'selective mandatory sanctions' were invoked.

The failure to invoke immediate mandatory sanctions, and the open sanction-breaking operations of South Africa and Portugal, meant that according to one expert estimate, 'the policy of economic sanctions had only a limited effect on the Rhodesian economy during the first year of U D I'. While British imports from Rhodesia fell to 15 per cent of their 1965 level, U S imports only declined to 67 per cent, and Federal Germany's to 87 per cent. Germany's exports to Rhodesia actually increased to 103 per cent of their 1965 total.[51] One writer estimated that 'in 1965, about 26 per cent of Rhodesia's exports were to South Africa and Mozambique. In 1966, about 35 per cent of Rhodesia's exports went either to or through South Africa and Mozambique. In 1967 (after the invoking of selective mandatory sanctions by the U N), this proportion had risen to 65 per cent.'[52] Subsequently the proportion going to or through South Africa was to rise further. These figures serve to indicate the formal adherence of other countries to the boycott and South Africa's and Portugal's effectiveness in breaking it.

David Owen argues: 'The greatest error was never seriously to consider threatening a maritime blockade of any countries which had connived at sanction-breaking.'[53] Undoubtedly, had this policy been vigorously pursued, sanctions would have had a devastating effect on the Rhodesian economy. What Owen does not explore are the very sound reasons why such a blockade was never seriously considered. Indeed, like virtually all exponents of sanctions, he fails to deal with the crucial question: If they had been effective, if Rhodesia had been economically crippled, what then? The key failure of any sanctions policy was that it included no strategy for taking power out of the hands of the white settlers; ultimately that could only be done by military intervention, or as a result of a successful rising by the African population within Rhodesia.

Even if sanctions had crippled the Rhodesian economy – which was only possible if supplies from and sales through the Portuguese colonies and South Africa were stopped – Rhodesian whites would not have been prepared to concede majority rule. Some of those involved in formulating policy have subsequently suggested that they expected the effects of sanctions to create internal disorders which would justify military intervention. This appears to be little more than a retrospective rationalization for an ill-conceived, poorly enforced policy, which did little more than afford a face-saving device for Britain and limit Rhodesia's economic growth. Certainly no preparations were ever made for military intervention, which, in any case, would have been much easier immediately after U D I, when the Smith régime was still stabilizing the situation.

South Africa played a crucial role in breaking sanctions, but Britain resisted any move to extend sanctions to South Africa. In opposition, Wilson had opposed sanctions against South Africa on the grounds that 'if it [an international trade embargo] was effective, it would harm the people we are most concerned about, the Africans and those whites fighting to maintain some standards of decency',[54] an argument which might have sounded a little thin after a policy of economic sanctions became the chosen method of dealing with Rhodesia.* In any case, now in govern-

---

*Ian Smith had, in fact, told Wilson that, with sanctions, 'Europeans could pull in their belts, but Africans would lose their livelihood and might even be without food'.[55]

ment, Labour had a more powerful reason. Britain stated frankly at the U N that the interdependence of the economies of South Africa and Britain prevented the extension of sanctions to South Africa. Such an extension would cause widespread unemployment in Britain and worsen the balance of payments position by about £300m. a year.[56] On 27 March 1968, Wilson told the British House of Commons: 'Rejecting the use of force as I do ... I have warned my Commonwealth colleagues and all at the United Nations that we cannot accept unwise proposals which involve a head-on confrontation with South Africa, which would escalate in a manner which would do irreparable harm.' Wilson went on to reject 'proposals ... for the extension of sanctions beyond Rhodesia'.

It is worthwhile briefly exploring the ties between Britain and South Africa and their development under the Labour government. For it was this heavy involvement of British interests in South Africa which was to be crucial in the weakness and failure of Britain's Rhodesia policy.

Britain and South Africa

The Labour Party entered power with a commitment to end the arms trade with South Africa firmly entrenched in its election manifesto. This pledge was formally kept on 7 November 1964, when an arms embargo was legislatively imposed. In practice, however, the embargo was qualified and failed to meet the specifics of the United Nations resolution.* Wilson undertook to fulfil existing contracts and provide spares for 'certain equipment'. The government approved the shipment of sixteen Buccaneer aircraft to South Africa, aircraft well suited for internal security work. Barbara Castle, speaking for the National Executive Committee at the 1963 Labour Party Conference, had said that a Labour government would cancel the project. If Wilson could plead that Britain had to stand by her contractual obligations in the delivery of the Buccaneer

*Paragraph 3 of Resolution 181 (1963) of the Security Council called on all states 'to cease forthwith the shipment of arms, ammunition of all types and military vehicles to South Africa'.

aircraft, the granting of a permit in June 1965 to Vauxhall Motors to sell £400,000 of four-wheel-drive motor chassis to the South African army was a little harder to justify. Both the United States and Canada had refused to issue licences to firms previously approached with a similar order.

The arms deal was merely the tip of the iceberg. Under the Labour government, as under previous Conservative ones, military relationships with South Africa were closely cemented by the Simonstown agreement, the continued arms trade, and the active assistance that companies such as ICI were giving to the development of South Africa's domestic arms industry.[57]

In spite of South Africa's departure from the Commonwealth in 1961, she continued to benefit from Commonwealth trading preferences. In opposition Labour had attacked the maintenance of the Commonwealth preferences; in power, they anxiously sought to increase South African trade. At the 1963 Party Conference, in the speech cited above, Barbara Castle delivered a warning to British investors in South Africa: 'If they choose to build their future in a slave state, they should not call for help when the powder barrel blows up beneath them.'[58] On 11 February 1965, Lord Rhodes, Parliamentary Secretary to the Board of Trade, was able to tell the House of Lords: 'We are proud to trade with South Africa, make no mistake about that.'[59] Between 1965 and 1969, Britain's imports from South Africa increased from £181m. (c.i.f. – charged in full) to £302m. (c.i.f.) while her exports rose from £265m. (f.o.b. – free on board) to £293m. (f.o.b.). From 1965 to 1968 exports to South Africa rose, as a proportion of total British exports, from 3·1 per cent to 3·4 per cent.[60] The Southern Africa Committee was set up by the British National Export Council to foster increased trade and work in conjunction with the independent, pro-South Africa, United Kingdom–South Africa Trade Association. Mr W. E. Lukes was the Chairman of both the Southern Africa Committee and the United Kingdom–South Africa Trade Association from 1965 to 1968. He was also a Trustee of the South Africa Foundation, an influential organization based in the South African business community, which seeks to counteract information and activities hostile to apartheid and South Africa's international image.

Investment in South Africa, which represents some 10 per cent of Britain's total overseas investments, also increased. Observing a Labour government in action, one could be excused for thinking that the tail was wagging the dog. Barbara Rogers has argued that even in the area of trading relationships, South Africa has been much more aggressive than Britain and has forced many advantageous changes in the terms.[61] Certainly, as the Rhodesia crisis developed, South Africa appears to have shown much less concern for the fate of a third of its exports than Britain did with a mere 3·1 per cent of her own. Perhaps this was because South Africa had been assured that the UK government would take no action which would jeopardize their economic relations. Anthony Crosland, President of the Board of Trade, told the United Kingdom–South Africa Trade Association in October 1968; 'We have made it clear that we cannot contemplate any economic confrontation.'[62]

When, in 1967, South African troops were used in the Zambesi Valley to combat the first ANC–ZAPU guerilla offensive, it was South Africa and not Britain that warned against outside intervention. Writing on South Africa's Defence Strategy, Abdul Minty commented: 'The failure of any meaningful response from Britain to this blatant intervention in the British colony gave South Africa increased self-confidence.'[63] A speech by Prime Minister Vorster in September 1967 in which he warned that South Africa would not allow any outside interference with the stability of Southern Africa was interpreted by a pro-government South African newspaper as a warning to Britain that South Africa would not allow any move in Rhodesia which would upset South Africa's interests in the region.[64] By this stage, South Africa had established that, when pushed, Britain would retreat. The prospect of any conceivable military conflict with South Africa clearly did not enter into British thinking. Three months after this speech, the British Cabinet was closely divided on the issue of selling a reported £200m. worth of arms to South Africa. It has been argued that it was only prevented from doing so by prior publication of the impending deal by the British Anti-Apartheid Movement and the consequent uproar.[65]

Britain could, theoretically, still have applied sanctions more vigorously without directly extending them to South Africa. Yet little attempt appears to have been made to uncover sanction-breakers in England who regularly traded with Rhodesia through South African firms, nor did Britain make any attempt to close down the operations of British subsidiaries in Rhodesia. Firms which, when convenient, were apt to claim that they had no control over their Rhodesian subsidiaries, were allowed to continue moving personnel to and from Rhodesia. The agencies of surveillance which showed themselves so competent in uncovering the communists in the National Union of Seamen were far less successful in exposing city businesses who deliberately broke sanctions. (There were, of course, some prosecutions; but the massive scale of continued sanction-breaking was common knowledge in import–export circles.)

The government in fact, having imposed sanctions, seemed to regard its job as finished. Arthur Bottomley inferred that when he left the Commonwealth Relations Office (in August 1966) the rigour and the enforcement of sanctions might have declined.[66] Subsequent suggestions for the reinforcement of sanctions were generally rejected. Civil servants dealing with Rhodesia found their proposals criticized by those whose job it was to foster good relations with Portugal and South Africa. A suggestion in 1968 from Transport House, backed by the National Executive Committee of the Labour Party, that all products destined for Rhodesia be barred from entry to Beira and Lourenço Marques in Mozambique, was rejected, though this was militarily feasible. Such a move would have imposed crippling shipping costs on Rhodesia, since all goods would have had to be sent through South Africa. The author of this proposal, a researcher in the International Department of the Labour Party, resigned in disgust.

As we shall subsequently argue, sanctions did indeed have a strong effect on the Rhodesian economy, but one which could be borne, at least in the short-term. At no time did they succeed in bringing the economy to a halt, or anything like it. Since they did not, they were therefore ineffective in ending UDI. Rhodesia's successful weathering of the sanctions certainly strengthened Smith. Sir Edgar Whitehead, the former Rhodesian Prime Minister, wrote: 'As far as the Smith government is concerned, sanctions have rallied the moderate Europeans behind it, and it will not fall until there has been an economic collapse.'[67] It could also be strongly argued that the imposition of sanctions forced Rhodesia into an even closer relationship with Portugal and South Africa. Rhodesia was crucially dependent on the relationships with these countries to help her break the sanctions.

The British government's fear of antagonizing Portugal and South Africa, the eagerness of firms, both British and foreign, for trade wherever possible; and the failure of Britain and other governments to take firmer action to prevent violations, inhibited the policy from the outset. The British government was firmly resolved to avoid confrontation with South Africa. And to interfere with the affairs of the companies holding £1,200m. worth of investment in South Africa was clearly to begin confronting the South African government.

The African response

African countries, as we have said earlier, had demanded a vigorous policy against Rhodesia, but their own efforts were characterized more by thunder than by lightning. On 11 November, President Kaunda declared a state of emergency in Zambia and moved troops up to the Rhodesian border. On the 14th, the Presidents of Senegal, Mali, Guinea and Mauritania, at a meeting in Nouakchott, Mauritania, proposed the establishment of an African Liberation Committee and the sending of African troops to Rhodesia. The UAR announced that it would seize all cargoes moving through the Suez Canal on the way to Rhodesia. Meeting in Ethiopia in December 1965, the Council of Ministers of the OAU adopted a series of measures against Rhodesia including an economic blockade, the severance of all communication links, and the establishment of a committee to plan future military moves against Rhodesia if the rebellion were not ended. The council warned that member states would terminate diplomatic relations with Britain by 15 December 1965, if the rebellion had not been ended by then. In the event, nine members did so but only two of the Commonwealth states – Ghana and Tanzania. Kenya declined to terminate relations, since Kenyatta declared himself convinced that Britain would eventually use force to pave the way for the establishment of majority rule. Kenyatta also did not press his proposal to the U N Security Council for mandatory sanctions: on the grounds, he declared on 14 December, that Britain was 'not at the moment in a position to take part in the debate centred around Chapter VII'.[68]*

In retrospect, it may well be argued that the politically divided and militarily weak African states were in no position to confront Rhodesia, particularly since isolated African action would inevitably have resulted in South Africa's giving military assistance to Rhodesia. In any case, as history has shown, a number of African countries were moving, not to want confrontation with the white supremacist governments, but to want collaboration.

The Labour Party and the anti-colonial struggle

In our description of the Labour government's policy towards Rhodesia, we have frequently contrasted the statements made in opposition with the policies followed in power. In doing this, we have sought to expose the hypocrisy of the Labour government, the divorce between what the party apparently felt were correct principles and what the party in power was prepared to put into practice.

The Labour Party has been in opposition for much of the twentieth century. It has, therefore, frequently been in a position to attack Conservative colonial policy, as it did over the creation of the Central African Federation and the promulgation of the 1961 constitution for Rhodesia. The vocal left wing

*Chapter VII refers to 'action with respect to threats to the peace, breaches of the peace, and acts of aggression'. Under Chapter VII the Security Council can impose mandatory sanctions and initiate military intervention.

of the party have associated it with groups such as the Movement for Colonial Freedom and the Anti-Apartheid Movement. In short, the party has had an apparently credible image as an anticolonialist and anti-racialist party. In our analysis of the party's actions in power, we have been concerned to show that the image has no substance, that the differences in practice between a Conservative government and a Labour one are slight. The Labour Party may have had 100 backbenchers who were prepared, in the post-UDI period, to sign motions warning against any sell-out of African interests, while, in contrast, the Conservative Party had the pro-Rhodesia lobby and the Monday Club. It is, however, doubtful if the policy pursued by a Conservative government would have been substantially different from the Labour government's. In the actual exercise of British power, the range of options must be limited, unless a government is prepared decisively to re-orient British politics.

In his memoirs, Wilson appears to give support to the above view. He argues that there were four elements to be considered in dealing with Rhodesia: the opinions of the Rhodesians; the opinions of the British people; the opinions of the Commonwealth; and the opinions of the UN. Wilson states that even had the Conservatives discounted the importance of foreign opinion, they 'would have had to count the economic cost of appeasement. And the principal key ... was Zambia.'[69] In this analysis, the role of principle is secondary to the demands of statesmanship; demands which are, of course, shaped by the current organization of the British state.*

Labour's failure to put its proclaimed principles into action

*Wilson's policies have also been criticized for lack of statesmanship. Peter Calvocoressi wrote of the failure to end UDI: 'Great Britain's standing and capacity in the world have been mutilated because Great Britain has seemed to be careless about its obligations and feeble in action although manifestly not feeble in potential.'[70] Labour politicians, interviewed in March 1972, were unable to understand why the question of Rhodesia was the first preoccupation of all African visitors to Transport House. The case we are making, however, is that this failure cannot be comprehended without understanding the very real *forces* acting on the Labour government which operate against taking any effective action over Rhodesia. In the final analysis, British capitalism can survive with the disapproval of a section of the Third World countries that are in any case too weak to take effective retaliatory measures against Britain.

was not confined to the field of foreign policy. In introducing a series of essays dealing with the domestic record of the last Labour government, Professor Peter Townsend wrote: 'Democratic socialism did not fail in the 1960s, it was not tried.'[71] In his analysis of the Labour Party, Ralph Miliband commented: 'The Labour Party is [also] a party whose leaders have always sought to escape from the implication of its class character by pursuing what they deem to be 'national' policies: these policies have regularly turned to the detriment of the working classes and to the advantage of Conservatism.'[72]

Any government which wished to take effective steps, economically or militarily, against Rhodesia, would in one way or another have to confront South Africa. And it could not confront South Africa without confronting British business. A confrontation either at the military or the economic level would not only have had an immediate impact on businesses which were involved in the area, but would have indicated to the economic decision-makers in Britain that the government was more concerned with principles than with Britain's 'economic interest'. To commit British troops to defend areas in which Britain has substantial economic interests or related strategic ones is a very different matter from committing troops to be used against a government that vigorously defends private enterprise, and where the political outcome of any intervention is uncertain, but may well be more damaging to British economic interests than the *status quo*.

In this sense, one can argue that the failure successfully to end U D I and gain majority rule in Rhodesia cannot be divorced from other aspects of British politics. A government which is not, for example, prepared to confront the City by introducing measures which would effectively redistribute income in Britain in favour of lower-paid workers, is much less likely to confront business over an issue far removed from the concerns of many British electors and where, therefore, there is even less countervailing political influence.

This relationship between domestic and foreign policies has been remarked by other writers. Ralph Miliband and John Saville argued in 1964:

It would clearly be a mistake to expect the next Labour government to reach out for deep structural changes in Britain, or to embark on new foreign policies. These are not, in any case, two separate spheres of policy, independent of each other: without a radical re-casting of foreign policy, involving a drastic cut-back in defence spending, the domestic programme of the government would be that much more modest in scope.[73]

Perry Anderson, also writing before the advent of the Labour government, argued:

Labour's foreign policy, finally, needs to be considered in the light of its home policy. For the continuity between the two is very close. There is the same iridescent *mélange* of radicalism and conformity; the same *ambience* of equivocation and ambiguity. The context however, is altogether graver and heavier with consequences. In it, the same qualities acquire a new significance. What is caution and moderation at home can easily become, by a logic characteristic of social-democracy, complicity and brutality abroad: temporization with capitalism, collusion with imperialism.[74]

In opposition, the Labour Party again returned to a position apparently sympathetic to anti-colonialist movements. Amilcar Cabral, leader of the PAIGC of Guinea Bissau was received by the Labour Party on his visit to Britain in October 1971. The Labour Party National Executive Committee has undertaken to raise money for the liberation struggles in the Portuguese colonies. Yet we should note that in power, the Labour Party took no action at all to jeopardize its close alliance with Portugal through NATO. This alliance was not even shaken when, in 1968, five Labour backbenchers who visited Zambia testified that NATO equipment had been used by Portugal against Zambia (as well as in the Portuguese colonies).[75]

In office, the Labour Party adhered to the Southern African idea that freedom-fighters are terrorists. On 25 June, 1968, replying to a question from John Biggs-Davison, a right-wing Conservative MP, on the issuing of British passports to alleged 'terrorists', Wilson said: 'It is our policy to deny [passports] to known terrorists, and any information subsequently about known terrorists would lead to a failure to renew passports which, in any case, are only issued for six months.' In contrast, known white subversives who supported an illegal régime which had usurped power in a British colony had less difficulty. Sir Hugh Beadle, after his findings that the Smith régime had *de jure* legal powers, managed to get his British passport renewed for a further ten years.

The 1971 settlement terms negotiated between Sir Alec Douglas Home and Smith were vigorously attacked by the Labour Party, yet they were not qualitatively different from the proposals put forward by the Wilson government in its own attempts to reach a settlement. The British Labour Party did not and cannot be expected to produce a government which is prepared to engage in the restructuring of the British economic and political system needed effectively to combat racism in Southern Africa. To argue, as David Owen does, 'a fundamental change in political attitudes to South Africa which followed the return of a Conservative government in June 1970'[76] is to confuse the Labour Party's rhetoric in opposition with its shoddy and disreputable performance once in power.

Conference decisions by the Labour Party are no guide to its performance in office, whether the policy covers South Africa or any other issue. In October 1968, the Party Conference

welcomed the government's declaration in December 1966 that they would not 'submit to the British Parliament any settlement which involves independence before majority rule' ... Conference calls upon the National Executive Committee to urge the government to implement the part of Paragraph 13 of the British-sponsored United Nations resolution on sanctions against Rhodesia which asks for 'moral and practical assistance' to those people struggling for freedom.

The British Labour government continued to pursue a settlement based on minority rule, and within two weeks of the motion the *Fearless* proposals had been made. No move to give any assistance to people whom the Labour Prime Minister was apt to call 'terrorists' was ever made.* In the light of this, it is difficult to take the Labour Party's recent decisions to support liberation movements with any degree of seriousness. The

*Not such a revolutionary principle, after all. The Social Democrat government of Sweden officially gives financial support to the African guerrilla movements against Portuguese rule.

Labour Party's performance in office between 1964 and 1970 was a clear indication to the African liberation movements that they have little to expect from any British government except opposition. In the words of Labour Defence Secretary Denis Healey: 'There is no such thing as a Socialist foreign policy. There is only a British foreign policy.'[77]

7 The makings of a sell-out

Because, after all, we must resign ourselves to the inevitable and say to ourselves, once for all, that the bourgeoisie is condemned to become every day more snarling, more openly ferocious, more shameless, more summarily barbarous; that it is an implacable law that every decadent class finds itself turned into a receptacle into which there flow all the dirty waters of history; that it is a universal law that before it disappears, every class must first disgrace itself completely, on all fronts, and that it is with their heads buried in the dunghill that dying societies utter their swan songs –
Aimé Césaire, *Discourse on Colonialism*

The need for a settlement

We have argued that in the late 1950s and early 1960s, the British government and the large international corporations had adopted a policy in Africa of granting independence, concerned only to ensure that the new governments would not take a hostile view of existing trade and investment patterns. It is important to emphasize that the motivation for this was not a sudden conversion to democratic values, but rather the realization that stability and economic expansion in Africa were best served by this policy. A policy of resisting African demands would have required a costly military involvement, which would have created domestic problems for the imperial governments and would have prolonged conditions of economic and political uncertainty.

Southern Rhodesia was not a typical colony, however, and its dominant settler community rejected compromise. The Rhodesian Front victory served to block what international investors saw as essential reforms and exacerbated the economic uncertainty caused by the break-up of Federation. Indeed, U D I and the resulting imposition of sanctions created great problems for companies with investment and trading links in the area. The restoration of legality was imperative for profitable economic activity, though that in itself could not resolve the underlying contradiction. Nevertheless, as the Smith régime survived sanctions and showed every sign of maintaining control, the pressure for a settlement with the rebel régime increased. If international capital was to be denied its preferred solution of a gradual transition to an inter-racial bourgeois government, then it must deal with Smith. The continued conflict with Southern Rhodesia was, in any case, a destabilizing element in Southern Africa and consequently jeopardized other trade and investment interests.

The pressure to settle was particularly strong in Britain, where companies with South African interests are a powerful political force. But a settlement had to take into account the British government's need to maintain a vestige of international credibility and avoid economic reprisals by independent African and Asian states. The issue that has, therefore, essentially agitated successive British governments has been: What kind of concessions would the Smith régime make to provide an adequate window-display for the legal hand-over of power to a white minority government? How could sanctions be removed and normal economic relations be restored? The last question was of particular importance to British industry, which before the imposition of sanctions had possessed a major share of the trade with, and investment in, Rhodesia. Sanctions had allowed competitors from other countries, whose governments were even less scrupulous in pursuing sanctions, to move in and capture the market.

One of the reasons for the somewhat more vigorous enforcement of sanctions by the British government was that, with the rejection of military intervention, sanctions were the only means of imposing British policy. In addition, sanctions had been the minimum response necessary to preserve the Commonwealth, while enabling Britain to reject demands for military intervention. Yet sanctions, as we have argued, could not achieve the ends set for them. Even if the Southern Rhodesian government had been prepared to make the fairly minimal constitutional compromises required of it, it would have been toppled by its own Rhodesian Front party members. In fact, the proposed terms of the 1969 constitution in Rhodesia, which we discuss below, and which were far from liberal, resulted in the resignation of William Harper, a Cabinet Minister. The opposition demanded the complete exclusion of Africans from parliament, and the new constitution only passed the Rhodesian Front Party Conference by eleven votes.

It was not only the Rhodesian government which was in a situation where little compromise was possible. If the British government had accepted either the *Tiger* or more especially the *Fearless* proposals, it would have had to face serious international criticism, including perhaps the kind of economic retaliation which Nigeria took when Heath decided to renew arms sales to South Africa. (Nigeria represents a valuable export market and supplies some 10 per cent of British oil needs, a figure expected to rise to 20 per cent by 1980.) President Kaunda of Zambia and President Nyerere of Tanzania both privately told the British government at the January 1969 Commonwealth Conference that they would leave the Commonwealth if anything like the *Fearless* proposals were accepted.[1] In addition, acceptance of the *Fearless* proposals would have produced a backbench revolt and the certain resignation of at least one minister – Lord Caradon, British representative to the United Nations. Forty-nine Labour MPs voted against the government in a debate on Rhodesia on 23 October 1968, to demonstrate their opposition to the *Fearless* proposals.

Nevertheless, sanctions did have an effect on the Rhodesian economy, an effect which was more serious in its long-term than in its short-term consequences. Rhodesia was denied access to foreign capital markets, and this created a scarcity of foreign exchange and a consequent decline in the economc infrastructure of Rhodesia, particularly in the transport section, which was already over-extended because of the need to re-route exports and imports to evade sanctions.[2] It became clear that the place of sanctions in British thinking, after Wilson's initial and absurd comments about bringing the rebellion to an end in 'weeks rather than months', was as a lever on the Smith government to come to some agreement which would enable Britain to extricate itself from the Rhodesian situation.

Indeed, though it is generally now agreed that the effect of sanctions has been more serious in the long than in the short term, an examination of the negotiations between Britain and Rhodesia in 1966, 1968, and in 1971 might lead an observer to the conclusion either that the reverse were true, or that it was Britain that was suffering the sanctions. There is no more telling criticism of the strategy and technical implementation of sanctions than the fact that, as the years passed by, it was Britain and not Rhodesia which made the substantive concessions.

The pattern of negotiations

The major preoccupation of the British government in the negotiations prior to U D I was to ensure 'the special entrenchment of Chapter III of the Constitution ... Without special entrenchment, it would be possible for a two-thirds majority to amend the clauses governing the number of 'A' or 'B' roll seats.'[3] In other words, the government was concerned to ensure that the Rhodesian government could not reduce African representation by decreasing the number of 'B' roll seats through a two-thirds vote in the Legislative Assembly. Instead, it required that any amendment to specially entrenched clauses would require approval by a referendum of all voters, including all African taxpayers, who would be eligible for the 'B' roll, or the support of a three-quarters majority in the Legislative Assembly, in which the African 'B' roll seats would have to be increased from 15 to 17, so as to provide a blocking quarter.

The Rhodesian government was insistent upon retaining the authority 'to delay the transfer of power to people who were simply not capable of using it responsibly'.[4] It was on this point that negotiations broke down.

The Rhodesians did, however, secure an early victory when Wilson stated that 'in his view, Rhodesia was not yet ready for majority rule'[5] – a concession which is hard to explain except as a consequence of Wilson's capitulation to racism. If Rhodesia, which had one of the highest gross domestic products of all

Britain's colonies, and a more advanced educational system, was not ready for majority rule eight years after Ghana had secured independence, one is inclined to ask why.

The proposals put forward by Britain on *H.M.S. Tiger* in December 1966 were substantially the same as those discussed before U D I. But a significant addition, designed to fulfil the Sixth Principle, that 'there be no oppression of majority by minority or a minority by a majority', was that 17 'A' roll seats were to be reserved for Europeans.

The new proposals also gave the chiefs a role in the government. A senate would be established with 12 European and 14 African members; and with 6 of the African members elected by the Council of Chiefs. The Senate would have powers to review legislation, and some special legislative powers 'in respect of tribal land, law and custom'. It would vote together with the Legislative Assembly on amendments to entrenched clauses in the constitution. This entrenchment of the powers of the chiefs in the 1966 proposals could only be seen as a further capitulation by Britain to the philosophy of the Rhodesian Front.

The *Tiger* proposals were to be put into effect under the auspices of a 'broad-based interim government' appointed by the Governor, who would have legislative authority while the agreement was being implemented. The new government would be headed by Smith and would include 'in addition to representatives of existing political parties, independent members and Africans'.[6] This government would continue for no longer than four months, during which a Royal Commission would test the acceptability of the new constitutional proposals. An election would be held after the test of acceptability had been completed. If the result of the test was favourable, further elections would then take place under the new constitution either immediately before or immediately after the granting of independence to Rhodesia by Britain. Britain claimed the right to intervene militarily if the terms of the constitutional settlement were broken.[7] The *Tiger* proposals were rejected by the Smith régime, which said that the interim arrangements were unacceptable.

Wilson assured Smith that the *Tiger* talks were the last opportunity to reach a settlement. If no settlement were reached, 'the

British government were committed to withdraw all their previous proposals for settlement including those which had been under discussion during the present weekend, and to adopt a policy of 'no independence before majority rule'.[8] Wilson subsequently repeated this assurance in the British Parliament.

In October 1968, Wilson met Smith aboard *H.M.S. Fearless*. The *Tiger* proposals were basically unchanged. But now there was no demand for an interim government, which Wilson had argued at the time of the *Tiger* proposals was essential for any fair test of opinion. In addition, there was no safeguard providing for British military intervention if Rhodesia broke the agreement.

It will not have escaped the reader that the proposals envisaged did not imply majority rule before independence, or even, indeed, in the foreseeable future. Claire Palley, the foremost constitutional authority on Rhodesia, estimated that the earliest possible date at which majority rule could result would be thirty years later – in 1999.

The over-riding significance of these proposals is that the British government was prepared to grant independence on a basis which left political power in white hands, even after U D I; and although the legislative record of the Rhodesian Front had clearly indicated the repressive direction of white politics. The *Fearless* proposals, which would have left Smith in full control, were, in that sense, much worse than the *Tiger* formula. But again they were rejected by the Rhodesian government, which would not accept the proposed mechanisms for constitutional amendment.

The danger that even if the Rhodesian settler régime accepted the settlement it would subsequently back-track, was real. There was not only the influential precedent of white South Africa's constitutional retreats from supposedly safe guarantees. But Rhodesian settler politicians gave warning enough. John Howman, Rhodesian Minister of Foreign Affairs, declared in June 1969, referring to the earlier discussions with Britain: 'We made these offers always with this understanding, that we would change the constitution as we saw fit.'[9]

The proposals which Sir Alec Douglas Home presented in 1971, on behalf of the new Conservative government, were not qualitatively different from the earlier proposals. Like the proposals presented at the *Fearless* talks, they offered no possibility of majority rule in the foreseeable future. Claire Palley suggested 2035 as the earliest date, compared to 1999 for the *Fearless* proposals. Indeed, the negotiations on which they were based predated the Conservative government; and their chief architect, Lord Goodman, a friend of Harold Wilson's and his personal solicitor, first visited Salisbury in August 1968 with Sir Max Aitken, Chairman of Beaverbrook Newspapers, to try and negotiate a settlement between Wilson and Smith.

The 1969 republican constitution

As distinct from the previous proposals, the basis of the new settlement was to be not the 1961 constitution but the 'illegal' 1969 republican constitution, which had created a much more rigid racial division. This constitution set up racially separate rolls – a European roll which elected 50 members, and an African roll which elected 8. A further 9 members were to be elected by 8 tribal electoral colleges, containing chiefs, headmen and members of local councils. The number of African seats was to be determined by the proportion of the total national income tax paid by Africans. In 1969 this was less than 1 per cent; and not until Africans paid 24 per cent would any further seats be added. At no time would the number of African seats exceed 50. As one Rhodesian economist pointed out: 'The criterion of individual income tax patently neglects other sources of taxation revenue accruing to the government and . . . it helps to foster the creation of the illusion that those who finance the fiscus possess some inalienable (and presumably proportional) claim upon society at large and the rest of the national economy.'[10]

The likelihood that Africans in such a society will secure a larger share of the national income, and therefore pay a higher proportion of income tax, is slight. In South Africa, the ratio of white to black wages in the mining industry was 11·7 to 1 in 1911; 17·6 to 1 in 1966; and 20·3 to 1 in 1971. In manufacturing between 1957 and 1967, white wages increased by 61·4 per cent and African wages by 59 per cent; and between 1966 and 1971, the ratio of white to black wages had risen from 5·1 to 1 in May 1966, to 5·85 to 1 in March 1971.[11] As for Rhodesia itself, extrapolating from the income changes which had taken place in the first six years of the Federation – a time, it will be recalled, when African wages were rising relatively rapidly – an economist estimated that if those trends continued, it would take 60 years for African wages to reach one tenth of the level of European ones.[12] Hence not only did the 1969 constitution make no provision for majority rule at any time, but it is probable that, under its provisions, the number of directly elected African seats will never exceed 8 out of 66.

The 1969 constitution greatly extended the role of the chiefs, who had already shown themselves publicly servile, if ineffective and privately unreliable, supporters of the government which paid them. A chiefs' indaba in 1964 had supported the government claim for independence; and, in 1965, a meeting of the Chief's Council had come out in support of U D I. The chiefs were being paid either £420 or £240 a year, depending upon whether they had more or less than 500 followers, while those who were deemed of particular merit – in government eyes – were paid a bonus. Chiefs who opposed the government were deposed. Chief Nyandoro, uncle of George Nyandoro, was deposed for his opposition to government de-stocking, and Chief Mangwende, for his support of the African National Council.[13] In 1953, the Chief Native Commissioner had commented on the chiefs: 'A description of chiefs, particularly in Mashonaland, takes on the nature of a catalogue of the vices and virtues of an old men's home. So many are beer-ridden, old, blind, opposed to all new ideas, servile, swayed by an entourage of hangers-on, lethargic and chronic invalids, that they are of little use administratively.'[14]

It appears that these were, however, just the qualities the Rhodesian Front desired. Under the 1969 constitution, not only do the chiefs effectively control the election of 8 members of the Legislative Assembly, they also provide 10 members of the Senate, which has powers to delay and review legislation. We will have cause to return to the role of the chiefs in Rhodesian politics in the next chapter, when we review the Rhodesian Front's attempts to find a lasting racial arrangement in Rhodesia.

The 1971 settlement proposals merit perhaps a fuller examination than the earlier proposals, because they were accepted by both governments and actually put to the test of acceptance. Indeed, despite the overwhelming rejection recorded, they are still openly being canvassed as the basis for a settlement, if only some way can be found of circumventing the unexpected problems posed by Principle 5: 'The British government would need to be satisfied that any basis proposed for independence was acceptable to the people of Rhodesia as a whole.' When the proposals were originally made, few suspected that they would founder on this point. Julius Nyerere wrote: 'The Pearce Commission was expected to register the necessary acquiescence. Everything which was said and done by the British government, by British business and by the Smith régime after the "settlement" and before the Pearce Commission arrived in Rhodesia, makes clear the confidence with which a "yes" answer was expected.'[15]

The 1971 settlement proposals

The 1971 settlement proposals can be best examined in the light of the principles which supposedly informed them.

PRINCIPLE I: UNIMPEDED PROGRESS TO MAJORITY RULE

The principle of unimpeded progress to majority rule was presumed to have been satisfied through the proposed revision of the electoral laws agreed by Sir Alec and Ian Smith. Under these revisions, a new roll of African voters would be established in addition to the existing African lower roll: an African higher roll with the same qualifications as for the existing European one. This new roll would determine the rate of African political advance. Two seats would be added to the existing African allotment when the number of Africans registered on the higher roll reached 6 per cent of the number of Europeans registered on the European roll. A further 2 seats would be added when the number of Africans registered on the higher roll reached 12 per cent of those registered on the European roll. And this process would continue until 34 additional African seats had been created – at which point Africans would have attained parity with Europeans.

In order to qualify for the African higher roll, an African would need:

a) an income at the rate of R$1,800 per annum* during the two years preceding the date of claim for enrolment, or ownership of immovable property with a value of not less than R$3,600;

b) income at the rate of not less than R$1,200 per annum during the two years preceding the date of claim for enrolment, or ownership of property with a value of not less than R$2,400 – and four years secondary education of prescribed standard.

Since the African higher roll determines both the number of new seats to be created and the composition of the electorate for these seats, the African lower roll is clearly of less significance. It is sufficient to point out that while some relaxation in the qualifications has taken place, the vast majority of the African population would still be excluded from this roll, which would provide the electors for the existing 8 African lower-roll seats in the Salisbury Parliament.

In order to appreciate the significance of the qualifications for the African higher roll, let us recall that in 1971 the average annual income of the approximately 800,000 African employees was R$314. Average earnings for Europeans, Asians, and Coloureds were R$3,374.[16] Of the 800,000 Africans working in Rhodesia over 300,000 were non-indigenous, and therefore ineligible to vote. Nor were the property qualifications likely to result in any significant additions to the electoral rolls. In 1964, only 7 Africans owned immovable urban property with a gross value of R$2,000 or more.[17] In June 1971, of the 5,200,000 Africans in Rhodesia, 7,460 earned more than R$1,200, which, together with four years secondary schooling, constituted one of the qualifications for enrolment on the higher African roll. Suffice it to say, that of Rhodesia's 20,000 African teachers, perhaps 1,000 would qualify to vote on the 'A' roll.

Dr Claire Palley, on the rather optimistic assumption that those who received the requisite schooling would also earn the

*R $1 = US $1·4.

necessary income, forecast that under these procedures, the earliest year when majority rule could be achieved, would be 2035, and that it might well take over 100 years. Dr Palley noted, too, that 'it is, of course, wholly unrealistic to make projections of an expanding universe in African education (which these tentative figures are based on). The likely reality is revealed by recalling the Minister of Education's prediction in 1964 that, by the end of 1971, there would be over 40,000 Africans with four years of secondary schooling or its equivalent. In fact, there will not be more than 25,000.' She further commented that the constitution provided for a concomitant rise in income qualifications to match inflation; and that Africans registering on the higher roll would have to answer technical questions and be subject to an English test, a precedure which she characterized as a 'Mississippi-type method'. Dr Palley concluded that all these predictions assumed scrupulous honesty from Mr Smith and his successors.[18]

The whole concept of qualifications to vote is strikingly reminiscent of the methods used by the eighteenth- and nineteenth-century bourgeoisie to retain power over a (frequently radical) proletariat. The intention is no doubt to ensure that such Africans as do qualify to vote will be those with the greatest commitment to the *status quo*. We previously noted the failure of the UFP government to reach an effective alliance with the African middle class, but it would nevertheless be a mistake to assume a permanent identity of interest between the affluent minority of Africans and the impoverished masses. The Pearce Commission found a more favourable response to settlement proposals from Africans in the 'upper middle class brackets; for instance, nurses, teachers, executives, civil servants, clerks, sergeants of police, and skilled technicians'.[19]

A further divide-and-rule tactic incorporated into the 1969 constitution was the division of seats between Matabeleland and Mashonaland. While Matabeleland has only 31 per cent of the African population, and Mashonaland 69 per cent, they receive the same number of seats. In any revival of tribalism, this could, of course, serve to divide the African support for universal franchise.

Only one half of the new African seats will be elected by the African higher roll voters. The remainder will be indirectly elected by the tribal electoral college dominated by the chiefs. Lord Goodman, writing in defence of the settlement, said that 'he, the Rhodesian white, retains the loyalty of the tribal chiefs, who prefer to see their tribesmen peacefully cultivating the land than engaged in political upheavals'.[20] As the *Rhodesia Herald* commented: 'By the provisions for increase in indirectly elected Africans, parallel with the directly elected, the braking power of African conservative opinion is applied about as fully as it could be.'[21] Under the proposed settlement terms, when parity is obtained, a referendum would be held among all African voters from the higher and lower rolls to determine whether all African seats should be filled by direct election. But Parliament might make provision before the referendum for a quarter of the new seats to be African lower roll seats, and for a specific number of new seats to be in rural constituencies – an open invitation to gerrymandering. We should recall that, on this occasion, the Europeans would need the support of only one African member. If this amendment were not to be made, and the referendum favoured direct election, then all new seats would be African higher roll seats. Hence, 100 years or more from today, many Africans would – according to these plans – be denied the right to vote for even the majority of African seats. And even if the amendment should be passed, Africans on the lower roll would be unable to vote for more than 16 of the 50 African M Ps.

Also consequent on the obtaining of parity, the White Paper provided for the creation of 10 extra seats to be elected from a common roll which would comprise the higher African and the European rolls. These seats would then be elected on a country-wide constituency basis. This, however, as stated by Ian Smith, would be subject to the approval of Parliament, which might, upon the recommendation of the commission (to be established at the time that parity is reached, and appointed by the government of the day), make alternative recommendations, which would be treated as a constitutional amendment. And, once the commission had reported, the approval of the majority of both races would no longer be necessary for a constitutional amendment. (See below.) After that date, all that would be required would be a two-thirds majority of the 100 MPs. In effect, there-fore, any government proposal would need the support of only 17 African MPs, who might, by that date, all be directly elected, but who would, nevertheless, be predominantly from the higher African roll.

Finally, it should be remembered that the relevant percentage of Africans on the higher roll compared to the European roll would be crucially determined by the rate of white immigration. Indeed, after the proposals had been announced, Ian Smith deplored speculation on the possible date of majority rule as a frivolous exercise and referred to 'the increase in [European] immigration to which we can confidently look forward'.[22] New immigrants would add to the European voting strength and in-crease the number of eligible Africans required to justify an in-crease in African seats. At the same time, they would deny new employment opportunities to qualified Africans, hence prevent-ing Africans from meeting the financial qualifications. The Rho-desian government recently gave assisted passages to fifty-nine unskilled Irishmen, who are to receive government training to become train crews – and this at a time when thousands of Africans are unemployed, no doubt including some of the same Africans whom the government, since 1962, has deliberately fired from the railways to ensure that jobs there remained a white preserve.[23] In contrast to the eager search for white immigrants of any type, the government refused an entry visa to the Col-oured South African doctor who was the successful candidate for the post of Deputy Medical Officer in Salisbury.

In short, if we assume 'unimpeded progress to majority rule' to mean the presence of an equal number of black and white faces in the Salisbury Parliament in 100 years or more, the first principle has been met. If, on the other hand, it means a rapid extension of the vote to all, irrespective of colour, social class, or the power of direct election, then Alec Douglas Home was, in the words of Peter Jenkins of the *Guardian*, 'lying through his teeth',[24] when he declared this condition fulfilled.

Interviewed on British television, Ian Smith could confidently state that Africans would not be in power in ten years' time: 'At the moment, I don't believe they're fit to govern the country;

what the position will be in a hundred years' time isn't easy to predict.'[25]

PRINCIPLE 2: GUARANTEES AGAINST RETROGRESSIVE AMENDMENTS TO THE CONSTITUTION

The crux of the safeguard placed on any constitutional changes is that amendments to the entrenched provisions of the constitution, concerning the composition of the Assembly and aspects of the Electoral Act, would require the approval of a simple majority of the parliamentary representatives of each race voting separately. Any amendment, therefore, could be passed by a vote of all the indirectly elected African representatives plus one directly elected representative. Clauses in the constitution which are not entrenched could be changed simply by a two-thirds majority. Since the Rhodesian Front currently holds 50 of the 66 seats, this should present no problem.

White Rhodesians could block African constitutional amendments in Parliament and would have an additional blocking power in the Senate. The composition of the Senate would remain unchanged, consisting of 10 Europeans elected by the European lower house, 10 Africans elected by the Council of Chiefs and 3 Presidential appointees. Two thirds of the Senate's members had to approve any constitutional change. It should be noted that Africans would have no direct representation in the Senate.

In the past, Britain had sought in settlement proposals to have some external guarantee against retrogressive amendments to the constitution. But plans for such a guarantee had always run into Rhodesian opposition. Furthermore, since Britain had already failed to use force against U D I, no British guarantee would carry much credibility. In any event, of course, there is nothing in practice to prevent an independent Rhodesia from changing its constitution in any way that it wishes – as it did at U D I.

PRINCIPLE 3: IMMEDIATE IMPROVEMENT IN THE POLITICAL STATUS OF THE AFRICAN POPULATION

In the sense that requirements for enrolment on the African lower roll would be reduced, one could argue facilely as did the London *Sunday Times*: 'The third principle has certainly been met. The immediate lowering of the franchise qualifications for the lower African voting roll improves the African's political status.'[26] As we have seen above, however, the lower roll would elect a fixed number of 8 African seats and could not determine the nature of the resulting distribution of African seats when parity was finally achieved, except to play a part in deciding whether the M Ps would be elected by the higher roll or by the Council of Chiefs.

Much has been made of the protection which the African population would receive under the new Declaration of Rights, a declaration enforceable before courts established by the Rhodesian government. Yet under this Declaration, Africans would still have no right to trial by jury and no legal aid would be available. Moreover, as Ian Smith assured Rhodesia's whites, under Provision 9 of the Declaration, 'a court shall not declare any provision of an Act enacted or Statutory Instrument made to be inconsistent with any provision of the Declaration of Rights if the provision concerned has been enforced for a period of at least ten years'. Thus existing discriminatory legislation would not be jeopardized, if generally based on laws which have existed for over ten years, modified through such devices as Statutory Instruments.[27] Among the many existing practices therefore excluded is the Land Tenure Act, which is based on the Land Apportionment Act. The Municipal Act amended in 1967 allows local authorities to segregate such facilities as eating-houses, swimming-pools, hotel bars and cinemas. The African Education Act ensures that education, while compulsory for Europeans, is not compulsory for Africans. In any event, the Declaration gives blanket approval to any discrimination which is justifiable as providing an 'equitable protection' for one race or the other, or is 'in the interest of Rhodesia as a whole'.

To fulfil Principle 3 in any meaningful sense, it would have been necessary for the government to restore political freedom to the African population. Both the Zimbabwe African National Union and the Zimbabwe African People's Union remain banned and their leaders in jail. Joseph Godber, Minister of State at the British Foreign Office, was not even able to assure reporters that the Reverend Ndabaningi Sithole, leader of ZANU, would be able to speak to the Pearce Commission and saw fit to add that he was not a political prisoner but in jail for a criminal offence (the alleged incitement of Africans to the murder of Ian Smith). Hence, as concerns the fulfilment of Principle 3, Africans are denied the political movement of their choice and their leaders remain in jail, while they are asked to accept as assurance a document the worth of which is already questionable, and which will be adjudicated before Rhodesia's racist courts.

Amnesty International issued a statement when the terms were announced, pointing out that in spite of pressure on the British government, 'no releases of detainees resulted from the negotiations', notwithstanding the British Privy Council's decision in 1968 that detainees were illegally held.[28] The International Commission of Jurists stated that the exceptions in the Declaration of Rights were 'so widely drawn that they offered very limited protection to the traditional freedom to which it refers'.[29]

PRINCIPLE 4: PROGRESS TOWARDS ENDING RACIAL DISCRIMINATION

This principle is assumed to have been met by the clause in the White Paper that reads, in part: 'The Rhodesian government have intimated to the British government their firm intention, within the spirit of these proposals, to make progress towards ending racial discrimination ... an independent commission will be set up to examine the question of racial discrimination'.[30] This commission would review existing legislation and practices, including the notorious Land Tenure Act. Its membership of three, including one African, would be determined by the Rhodesian government in agreement with the British government.

The quarter of a million whites would apparently provide two of the three commission members. And the Rhodesian government would presumably experience no insurmountable difficulty in finding one safe black. Should this commission nevertheless prove unreliable, the Rhodesian government would retain the power to reject any proposals where there are 'considerations that any government would be obliged to regard as of an overriding character'. Since political survival would doubtless be one of these, and the Rhodesian Front relies for its support on white racism, that would appear to cover any significant changes proposed.

PRINCIPLE 5: ANY BASIS FOR INDEPENDENCE MUST BE ACCEPTABLE TO THE PEOPLE OF RHODESIA AS A WHOLE

In fact, of the five (original) principles this proved to be the most difficult to subvert. The other four principles were vague and subject to a variety of interpretations – though it was generally accepted that the 1971 settlement stretched them to the limits. Principle 5, it had generally been agreed – since before UDI – would be met by the appointment of a Royal Commission – a somewhat suspect device from the perspective of those who have less than complete faith in the impartiality and the integrity of the British establishment, but one with consequences that few anticipated. Clearly, the rational way to test opinion in societies modelled on Western democratic lines is by voting. However, since any proposals short of 'one man, one vote' were based on the philosophical assumption that most Africans were incapable of such an exacting task, this method was excluded. What was not generally appreciated was that any mechanism which sought African views would legitimate for the first time the general expression of African opinion. Neither was it appreciated, after the relative silence produced by the intense repression of recent years, that African sentiment would be so overwhelmingly against any settlement not based on majority rule, and so solidly and effectively insulated against the pressures of employers, district commissioners and policemen, as well as the blandishments of the British government. In the event, the Royal Commission, composed of men not noted for their radical sympathies,* had little choice but to return a 'No' verdict.

This conclusion of the Pearce Commission overshadowed some criticisms of the whole undertaking; but these remain, nonetheless, valid, and provided further evidence of British 'good faith'. The 'normal political activities' promised in the settlement proposals were never allowed.[31] The major nationalist leaders remained in prison, in detention, or in exile. The proposals had, in any case, given a monopoly of radio and TV time to proponents of the settlement: 'Radio and television time will be made available to political parties represented in the House of Assembly.'[32] The full range of repressive legislation remained in force throughout the test of acceptability. Indeed, the Smith régime subsequently conceded that 1,736 people had been arrested during the course of the test.[33] Permission to hold meetings to discuss the settlement was frequently refused. The ANC made over 200 applications to hold meetings in the Tribal Trust Lands, where the majority of the African population live, and every one was rejected. The Secretary for Internal Affairs commented 'this is not normal political activity in the Tribal Trust Lands'.[34]

A meeting called in Umtali to allow Africans to present the Pearce Commissioners with their views was cancelled by the Rhodesian authorities. The Africans who had gathered for the purpose refused to disperse, since they believed that it was a trick to enable only pro-settlement Africans to meet the Commissioners and speak in the name of all. The Police broke up the gathering with machine-guns, killing fifteen Africans.

Employers put pressure on African workers to return a 'Yes' verdict, providing forms on which they could do so, and in some instances insisting on a positive response. In the words of the

*The Commission Chairman, Lord Pearce, was 70. In 1968, as a Law Lord, he dissented from the view of four other Law Lords on the Privy Council and agreed with five Rhodesian High Court Judges in finding that the Smith régime's powers of detention were legal (*The Times* 24/1/68). As for the other Commission members, Sir Morris Dorman and Sir Glynn Jones both had long careers in the Colonial Service, and Lord Harlech was a former Conservative Minister and widely regarded as the key link between the Cabinet and the Commission. The Chairman, Deputy Chairman, and Commissioners, were, of course, all white.

ANC: 'In a period of high unemployment, an African employee faced with his employer asking him to sign a pro-forma letter in his presence could certainly be said to be intimidated.'[35]

The Pearce Commission's response during the hearings was ineffective, and its subsequent report vindicated government actions. With that well-known concern for law and order which Pearce had demonstrated when finding the Rhodesian government's powers of detention legal – on the grounds that it had the responsibility to uphold law and order – the final report commented: 'Bearing in mind the scale of rioting during January, the number of arrests made immediately after the disorders was not unreasonable.'[36] In investigating claims made by African employees that they had been victimized for expressing opposition to the settlement, the Commission was content to cite the contrary explanation of the employers; presumably on the grounds that if they had dismissed any Africans for political reasons, the employers would have admitted it![37] Yet the Commission unwittingly suggested an alternative possibility when it dealt with allegations of intimidation by Africans against Africans: 'There were many employees who expressed fear of intimidation, possibly as an excuse to their employers for not saying "Yes".'[38]

In spite of the weight of oppressive legislation that the Rhodesian state can invoke for the slightest cause, the Commission did not 'accept that the presence of district commissioners or police in the vicinity of our meetings had any intimidatory effects on those attending to give evidence'.[39] It was a view not shared by the Africans, who were presumably in a better position to judge.

In general, the Pearce argument was that since Africans said 'No' anyway, they could not have been intimidated. This revealed not only a rather simple-minded logic, but entirely ignored the responsibility held by the British in a process established at British initiative. Mervyn Jones cites the case of the Chiripanyanga family. Mr Chiripanyanga, an executive member of the African National Council, was arrested, ironically on a charge of intimidating people, after ANC pamphlets opposing the settlement had been distributed; his wife and two children were also arrested. Mr Chiripanyanga was acquitted, but went home to find that he had lost his home and his job.

Many chiefs and headmen rejected the settlement when they could do so without fear of government reprisals. The report noted that the 26-member Council of Chiefs had unanimously accepted the proposals at a meeting with the Commission in Salisbury. When the Commission met the members in their own chiefly areas, however, only 13 expressed their approval, and 8 indicated their opposition to the settlement, though 2 among these last still supported it in private.[40] Among the other chiefs who gave their opinions, 44 accepted the proposals and 87 rejected them. An analysis of the written evidence again strongly suggests that the weight of intimidation came not from the African tribesmen but from the government: only 6 chiefs wrote in favour of the proposals, 14 against. 12 chiefs and headmen who opposed the settlement were charged in April under the 1964 Law and Order Act for intimidating their followers into saying 'No'.[41] The Commission, nevertheless, could state: 'We do not believe that the Rhodesian government set out to intimidate anyone into accepting and this was confirmed at various times in discussions with officials.'[42]

Sir Alec Douglas Home was not content merely to acquit the Rhodesian government of any charge of intimidation. He told the House of Commons: 'Lord Pearce reports that no intimidation was used on behalf of the Rhodesian government, and that very extensive intimidation was used by various African organizations.'[43] Perhaps Sir Alec was privy to information which had not appeared in Lord Pearce's published statements. More probably, like Ian Smith himself, he was grasping at any straw which appeared to save his proposals from ignominious rejection. The Pearce Report, in fact, had concluded that the assessment by two special commissioners, assigned to look into African intimidation, was correct: 'The actual number of cases of intimidation were in their view, however, very small when one considers the size of the country and the five million or so African inhabitants.'[44]

The overwhelming rejection of the proposals has not dimmed the enthusiasm of the British government, whose spokesmen told Africans that their rejection of the proposals would not bring forth any new plans but rather result in a stalemate. Any stalemate, however, can hardly be laid at the door of the British government which has done all it can to continue pressing the rejected settlement proposals. Sir Alec Douglas Home told the House of Commons: 'I would ask them [the Africans] to look again very carefully at what they have rejected . . . The proposals are still available, because Mr Smith has not withdrawn or modified them.'[45] On 29 September 1972, Britain used no less than three security council vetoes to kill a resolution which would have barred independence for Rhodesia except on the basis of majority rule.

8 Rhodesia or Zimbabwe?

Every ruling minority needs to numb and, if possible, to kill the time sense of those whom it exploits by proposing a continuous present. This is the authoritarian secret of all methods of imprisonment. The barricades break that present – John Berger

It is not easy to foresee the future direction of Rhodesian politics. Both the African opposition and the white ruling group face an impasse. The nationalists have so far failed to establish a serious guerilla movement. The Rhodesian Front has stayed in power and survived sanctions, but presides over a government which is denied foreign recognition and over an economy which is stagnant.

The developing pattern of Rhodesian society

The Rhodesian Front has so far failed to develop a comprehensive ideology which can legitimate and institutionalize its rule. The government has extended racial segregation but has stopped short of apartheid. The new constitution prevents Africans from ever achieving majority rule but, unlike South Africa, blacks and whites still sit in the same legislature. Africans are prevented from drinking in white areas after seven o'clock in the evening, but segregation is not legally enforced during working hours. The government, through its programme of provincialization, has begun to develop its own version of the South African Bantustans, but has not felt secure enough to give the Rhodesian chiefs even the power granted to the Transkei and Kwa Zululand legislatures. In the new Senate, representatives elected by the traditional African leaders sit side by side with whites.

The Rhodesian Front is attacked by its own rank and file for not introducing thorough-going segregation at every level. The new opposition Rhodesia Party attacks 'petty apartheid' which needlessly alienates the African population at a time of renewed guerilla activity.

In an attempt to force neighbouring Zambia to back down, Smith sealed off the Rhodesian border. It was a move which revealed Rhodesia's weakness and the 'rogue' character of the Rhodesian Front government. In consequence, Rhodesia has lost further valuable exports and essential hard currency gained from transporting Zambian copper.* The move also served to remind international capital that the Smith régime is not to be trusted, for the closure disrupted important trade and investment in which the U S and Britain have a major stake. Portugal and South Africa, aware of their need for international support, conduct their own foreign policy with a scrupulous eye to legality and a close concern for the interests of foreign investors.

The dilemma which the Smith régime faces is real enough. The long-term stability and economic prosperity of Rhodesia remain dependent on foreign recognition and the consequent inflow of badly needed investment capital. The Rhodesian Front, however, remains a victim of the dynamics which first brought it to power. The Front's white electorate demand further protection from any possibility of African competition, and the permanent entrenchment of white supremacy. On the other hand, to obtain any settlement with Britain, at the very least some semblance of African agreement must be obtained. The Rhodesian Front faces the same dilemma as the previous Whitehead government, though arguably in more intense form. To gain African acceptance, it must adopt more conciliatory policies, yet it is not only ideologically opposed to any 'integrationalist' policies, it is also dependent on a white electorate which would never accept them. The Pearce Commission noted that in the African rejection of the settlement proposals, 'mistrust of the intentions and motives of the [Rhodesian] government transcended all other considerations'.[1]

Britain's flexibility in reaching a settlement with Rhodesia must be influenced by Rhodesia's international image. Since the election of the Rhodesian Front and the subsequent U D I,

*The annual loss to Rhodesia railways is estimated at £10m.

the Rhodesian government's reputation has clearly been that of an intransigent white supremacist régime. One of the arguments that British politicians have sought to use in justifying a settlement is that this would act as a moderating influence on the régime. But the credibility of this argument depends in part on the recent record of the Rhodesian régime. Thus it is in the interests of the Smith régime to restrain the tendency towards thorough-going apartheid policies, since such policies could easily be used by opponents of a settlement to demonstrate that in fact the Smith régime was fully committed to apartheid, and to argue that no concessions would reverse the process. The dilemma of the régime in this respect was amply demonstrated in March 1973 when, after a great deal of effort, it was able to produce 80,000 African signatures supporting the 1972 settlement terms only to find that any advantage it had secured from this was offset when the multiracial Centre Party withdrew support for the terms because of the recent batch of racist legislation. This included restrictions on African drinking in European areas, a tightening of the pass laws and provision for collective fines on Africans in areas where freedom-fighters are operating.

The second difficulty which the Rhodesian régime faces in implementing a comprehensive socio-economic framework and promoting a relevant ideology is of a more pragmatic nature. In South Africa, whites constitute some 20 per cent of the population. In Rhodesia they constitute less than 5 per cent. Viewed from another angle, there are nearly 4 million whites in South Africa, and only a quarter of a million whites in Rhodesia. The comprehensive development of separate facilities is a luxury that Rhodesia can ill afford.

The University of Rhodesia provides a good illustration of the dilemma. The university is situated in a European area, and the presence of a large number of Africans resident at the university provides an easy basis for complaint. There is constant pressure to segregate university education completely, or, at least, drastically to reduce the number of African students attending. In 1972, the Triennial Review Committee called for the preservation of a 'racial balance' at the university, where

Africans, who compose 95 per cent of the country's population make up 40 per cent of university enrolment. In the peculiar semantics of white Rhodesia, the Committee was not calling for an increase in African enrolment but rather warning against it. The university's Senate responded by stating that admission was 'decided solely on considerations of character and academic merit'.

To segregate university facilities would be enormously expensive. Total university enrolment is little over 1,000; and white students prefer, by a ratio of two to one, to study in South Africa. The university is just beginning to develop an Engineering Faculty, which is itself a heavy expense on the education budget. To develop a second faculty for African students would be impossible. A similar argument can be made in the case of Medicine. The second factor which has discouraged attempts to segregate the university is the effect this would have on the quality of education. Since UDI a number of lecturers, particularly in the Arts Faculty, have been deported or have left voluntarily. The standard of the replacements has given little cause for comfort. If the university ceased to be multi-racial, many of the remaining competent faculty would leave.

The university was established in the later years of the Federation, and its early reputation, particularly in History and the Social Sciences, was high. The segregation of its facilities would prove the final blow to its remaining international reputation, a factor which has encouraged white students to oppose demands from some of their more virulently racist colleagues, such as segregated eating, sleeping and toilet facilities. Finally, the protest which any move to segregate the university would stimulate would ensure that it received full international publicity. Segregation at this level could readily be presented by opponents of a settlement as conclusive proof that the Rhodesian Front was beyond the pale.

In the circumstances, the Rhodesian Front has had to fall back on a policy of containment. Financially, support for African students is severely limited. Rhodesian whites studying in Rhodesia and South Africa already outnumber Africans 4 to 1 which is to say that a white Rhodesian has a 400 to 1 advantage in university education. If the World University Service and the World Council of Churches had not given support in 1972, then hardly more than 200 African students would have been able to study at the university. In addition, the government has also, unsuccessfully, attempted to prevent the construction of new residential facilities at the university – which are largely used by Africans. The government has discouraged the expansion of African sixth forms and stopped Africans studying for A-levels at the Salisbury Polytechnic where a number of Africans had pursued A-level Science, a subject, that, unlike Arts courses, cannot be pursued by correspondence. This has reduced the number of Africans eligible for university entrance; as did also the closure of the special qualifying year by University Principal Miller.*

This *ad hoc* approach is not confined to the university. At every level the Rhodesian Front acts on a step-by-step basis. The white Nationalists in South Africa have an ostensible objective towards which they say they are heading and which they are prepared to defend. White Rhodesia is still groping for such an ideology.

The rediscovery of the Rhodesian chief

If a coherent thread of policy does emerge from the Rhodesian Front's ten years in power, it is the attempt to restore the authority of the chiefs in African society and to create a separate traditional system of African local self-government. In the process of restoring this authority, however, the government is in fact considerably changing the nature of the chief's role. The clear intention is to use the chiefs and other traditional leaders as a bulwark against African nationalism.

The desire to use the chiefs and establish institutions in the African community which will act as a rival pole of attraction to nationalist sentiment is not a new one. In 1931 'native boards' were established, composed equally of chiefs, sub-chiefs and elected members, to provide a 'legitimate' outlet for African

*Miller is now at North London Polytechnic, which, since his arrival, has seen an unprecedented increase in student and faculty discontent.

opinion at a time of nationalist activity in the urban areas. The growth of nationalist activity in the late 1940s and early 1950s prompted a considerable restructuring of the African chieftain-ships. The government reduced the number of chiefs and increased the salaries of those remaining in office. Provincial assemblies were established through which the chiefs could meet and express their views. A. K. Weinrich has argued: 'As nationalism spread in the rural areas, the policy was to fortify the position of chiefs.'[2]

In 1957 the African Councils Act (ACA) extended the scope and power of the councils established under the 1937 Act, which had modified the old 'native boards'. The new councils were viewed as a means of modernizing the rural African com-munities. Again, the councils were seen as a means of counter-acting nationalist opinion. The Howman Report, on which the new Act was based, had argued: 'It would be foolhardy not to ensure that local government remains local and is not mixed up in any way with a structure that permits political ferment to seep down.'[3]

The government had some success in securing the chiefs' support, though, on occasion, the improvements in pay and status proved insufficient. In 1958, Chief Mangwende, who supported the African National Congress and opposed the imp-lementation of the Land Husbandry Act, was deposed. The general success of the policy was reflected in 1959, when the chiefs petitioned the government to give them the power to prevent nationalist meetings from being held in their areas. The government responded by further increasing the power of the chiefs. Then, in 1962, the chiefs were given a national voice with the creation of the National Council of Chiefs. Ironically, in 1963, the first President of the Council was forced to resign by his fellow chiefs because of his support for African nationalism.

The influence of the nationalist movement was opposed by the United Federal Party because it ran counter to plans for an alliance with the African middle class. In this strategy, the African Councils Act was a piece of paternalistic legislation, designed to modernize the African rural areas and integrate them into the politicial system. Under the Rhodesian Front,

however, the Act was viewed not as a mechanism of moderniza-
tion and integration, but as a vehicle for restoring and strengthening traditional authority, and constructing a largely separate
political system for the African population.

The role of African councils envisaged by the 1957 Act was
fairly modest. They were to have limited powers of taxation,
and responsibilities for roads, bridges, water conservation and
primary education. After 1962, the role of the councils was
greatly expanded into an important aspect of the government's
policy of 'community development'. The UFP introduced the
idea of community development, but it was the Rhodesian
Front which carried it through. The number of African councils,
which stood at 43 in 1952, had only reached 55 by 1962. But
by the end of 1970, no less than 105 councils had been established, with considerably increased powers. The Rhodesian
Front's intention to create a separate structure for African
government is reflected in its decision to abolish the poll tax in
those areas where the African councils are judged sufficiently
competent to take over local tax raising.

The Rhodesian Front government encouraged the establishment of the councils by providing financial support for council-
initiated projects, but withholding support for development in
areas where no councils exist. The government gave a further
boost when, as from 1971, it prevented any expansion of mission
schools in the primary education field. In addition, the government reduced its support for teachers' salaries – initially to
95 per cent. This forced some missions to hand over their schools
either to the local council or, where there was none, to the
government, which in turn declared its intention of passing on
responsibility to African councils at the earliest possible date.
The government has also encouraged councils to establish their
own schools and to take the initiative in taking over mission
schools. In effect, therefore, the government has forced those
who opposed councils as an instrument of apartheid, to accept
them or see their area stagnate, with many of the children unable
to attend school.

The Rhodesian Front government has further increased the
powers of the chiefs. In 1966 they were 'promoted' from con-

stables to peace officers, a change more in status than in power. But the chiefs were also given 'a sufficient number of messengers' to help them keep order. The messengers have powers of arrest and are of course a useful weapon which can be used against the chiefs' nationalist opponents. In 1967, the Tribal Trust Land Act restored the chiefs' right to allocate land, a right they had lost under the earlier Land Husbandry Act. In 1969, the African Law and Tribal Courts Act gave the chiefs jurisdiction over most civil and some criminal cases, and this again strengthened the chiefs against their political opponents. The chiefs were also given the power to banish from their communities those regarded as undesirable elements. Finally, the political role of the chiefs, and their importance in Rhodesian Front thinking, was given full recognition in the 1969 constitution, which gave them representation in both the Parliament and the Senate – a demand which the chiefs had first raised in 1964, as a *quid pro quo* for their support of independence under the 1961 constitution.

Despite these increases in the power of the chiefs, however, a comment on the trend in Rhodesian Front policy, made by Holleman in 1968, remains accurate: 'In short, Government's policy would be to increase the power of the tribal authorities sufficiently to strengthen its own powers of control over the majority of black citizens, but not to the extent of creating a force that might challenge Government's own authority.'[4] The government's policy remains, nonetheless, a double-edged weapon. We noted in the previous chapter that even the loyalty of the chiefs could not be taken for granted; and while many of them see an alliance with the government as the best means of protecting traditional authority against the threat posed by modern nationalism, others are firm, if cautious, supporters of African rule. In part, the government can rely on its control of the purse-strings to ensure obedience; and the government has, on occasion, made payments to the chiefs dependent on their terminating nationalist activity in the area for which they are responsible. Where chiefs are not prepared to accede to government demands, they can, if the situation is sufficiently serious, be dismissed.

The African councils may, as they are intended, serve as a mechanism for involving educated and progressive Africans in local politics, in a way which is not antagonistic to the continuance of white rule at a national level. Clearly this is the belief of the Rhodesian government. In 1971, the Secretary for Internal Affairs noted that 'there is no doubt that community advisers have done a first-class job in spreading the gospel of community development and in doing so, have contributed to the vastly improved security position that exists throughout the country'.[5] On the other hand, the councils may legitimize the involvement of local nationalists in political activity and enable them to strengthen their local community base. The councils are elected by the local community, though the chiefs and headmen sometimes play an influential role. The councils are less directly dependent on the government and consequently less easily influenced than the chiefs. The white district commissioner can make life difficult for an uncooperative council, and deny government financial support for its development projects, but this then defeats the objective of the local councils altogether.

It would appear that some chiefs and many councils maintain a public posture of cooperation but in practice are sympathetic to nationalist objectives. This helps to explain the Rhodesian government's complete ignorance of rural opinion, which enabled it to anticipate a favourable reply from the Pearce Commission. Further evidence to support this view comes from the assistance which the freedom-fighters have been able to get and the pressure which the régime has found it necessary to exercise on the chiefs in the wake of the Pearce Commission, including demands for loyalty pledges and threats to withhold salaries.

No doubt, on balance, the chiefs and councils have, so far, served the Rhodesian Front well. The chiefs in particular have enabled the Rhodesian Front to claim African support and to rely on some African cooperation. Holleman goes as far as to argue: 'Rhodesia's self-declared independence was brought about not least because of the loyal support of tribal authorities.'[6] Certainly, the support that the Council of Chiefs gave to the demands for independence under the 1961 constitution enabled the Rhodesian Front to maintain the charade that it had African support – with the exception, to be sure, of a few agitators and malcontents.

It is clear that in the future, if the necessity of reaching a settlement with Britain no longer imposes constraints on the Rhodesian government, the existing system may well be developed more thoroughly along apartheid lines. The government already envisages a programme of 'provincialization' which has been compared to the Bantustan system of South Africa.[7] Like the Bantustan system, 'provincialization' would institutionalize tribal differences. There will be one assembly in Matabeleland and one in Mashonaland. The government envisages a prominent role for the chiefs and headmen in these assemblies. The provincial administration will be responsible for the day-to-day administration of a wide variety of activities including health, welfare, education and agriculture. Overall policy direction will, however, remain with the Salisbury government.

Rhodesia in the context of Southern Africa

In 1965 Rhodesia's U D I was undoubtedly opposed by Western policy-makers, who would have preferred to see a gradual transition to African rule.* In 1973 Rhodesia could not be viewed in isolation, but only in the context of the West's total strategy for Southern Africa.

Rhodesia is closely involved in the joint defensive strategy of Portugal and South Africa, which both regard a sympathetic government in Salisbury as absolutely essential. The defence strategy of the white supremacist powers is closely integrated. By 1970 according to a German military magazine, South Africa had one third of its army stationed outside the country. The South Africans have been providing personnel to assist the Rhodesians since 1967 and are reported to have at least two battalions stationed in the Tete province of Mozambique to

*The time-perspective which the West had in mind was a long one and even members of the Labour government who were regarded as sympathetic to the African case, could talk, in interviews with this writer, in terms of a 15-year transitional process.

protect the Cabora Bassa Dam project and fight the FRELIMO guerillas.[8] The Rhodesians have also been giving assistance to the Portuguese, particularly in the border area with Mozambique. The three powers meet regularly to coordinate their strategy; and in October 1972, Smith and Caetano met in Portugal in flagrant violation of the UN resolutions, which specifically bind UN members not to advance the cause of the rebel régime by enabling its members to travel abroad. Rhodesia is legally a British colony; Portugal is Britain's oldest ally. The British government took no action.

The linking of Rhodesia's defence to that of South Africa immeasurably strengthens the régime. South Africa has the most powerful army in Africa; defence expenditure has risen from £22m. in 1960–61 to over £150m. in 1970–71. In comparison, Zambia's defence budget is 5 per cent of the South African.[9] In a conventional war with South Africa, no conceivable alliance of African countries could hope to be successful.

In view of the close links between the Portuguese colonies, South Africa and Rhodesia, any consideration of future political developments in Rhodesia must encompass a consideration of developments in those areas. The connection between the areas exists at three levels: first, close liaison between the white governments of these countries; secondly, the links between the respective liberation movements and their strategies; and, finally, the fact that for Western governments the area is increasingly seen as a whole (a view which is no less correct from the perspective of imperialism than from the perspective of the liberation movements). A victory for a revolutionary movement in any of the countries will have a profound impact throughout Southern Africa. If the South Africa government were defeated by a revolutionary movement, the repercussions could carry much further. South Africa's economic base, now the engine of white supremacy, is uniquely equipped to become the engine of a continent-wide socialist transformation.

We have already discussed Britain's stake in Southern Africa. A clear demonstration of Britain's loyalties was provided in the 1973 celebration of the 600th anniversary of the Anglo-Portuguese alliance. In June of 1973 the Duke of Edinburgh celebrated the alliance by visiting Portugal; and, in July, President Caetano visited Britain. Like Britain's other alliances, this, too, is based on a firm economic foundation. Britain is Portugal's most important trading partner, and in 1968 Britain accounted for 25 per cent of all foreign investment in Portugal. British enterprises have significant investments in the Portuguese colonies: in Mozambique, for example, British companies play the major role in sugar production.[10]

If Britain's position were an anomaly, the problem faced by the African liberation movements would not be so severe. In fact, Portugal and South Africa can rely on the support of practically every Western power. France, in particular, has been assiduous in cultivating arms sales to South Africa, and in 1972 pulled off what could be regarded as something of a *coup*. In the face of UN resolutions demanding a complete end to arms sales to South Africa, the French cooperated with the South Africans in the development of a highly praised guided missile system. The development of the system, called 'Cactus', was completed in 1972. The story is given added lustre by the news that the United States is now thinking of purchasing the system.

The assistance that the West gives to Portugal comes in part through the provision of arms under NATO agreements. The myth that these are not used in the Portuguese colonies has already been adequately demolished.* The Secretary-General of NATO, Luns, holds the highest Portuguese honour, the Grand Cross of the Order of Christ. In 1971, Luns told a meeting of the Foreign Affairs Commission of the Dutch Parliament: 'It must be understood that Portugal is sacrificing her blood for our liberty.'

Luns was not as diplomatic as other Western politicians, most of whom maintain an elaborate pretence of opposing Portuguese colonialism while continuing to oil the wheels of war. The most spectacular example of this approach came from the United States, which has consistently stated that it gives no

*See, for example, W. Minter, *Portuguese Africa and the West*; and *Portugal and NATO*, Angola Comité, Amsterdam, 1969.

military assistance to Portugal for use in its colonies and that it favours peaceful progress to self-determination. In 1970, Portugal started to use defoliants in its colonies, and the USA quadrupled its exports of herbicides to Portugal. In the same year, the USA spent $88,000 giving specialist training to thirty-three Portuguese officers.[12] In 1971, in return for a renewal of the US right to use the Azores bases until 1974, Portugal was offered a loan credit of $436,500,000. Since the costs of the war have crippled the Portuguese economy, the importance of this assistance is readily apparent. Secretary of State Rogers wrote to the Portuguese Foreign Minister that the objective of the new agreement was to 'enhance our political, economic and cultural relations with Portugal'. Caetano welcomed the deal as a victory for Portugal and said: 'The treaty is a political act in which the solidarity of interests between the countries is recognized and it is in the name of that solidarity that we put an instrument of action at the disposal of our American friends, *who are also now allies*.'[13] [My emphasis.] $400m. of the total will be provided through the US Export/Import Bank and amounts to eight times the total amount received by Portugal from the Bank since 1946. Assistance of a different kind is provided in Angola by Gulf Oil, whose contribution to Portugal's revenue in oil-mining royalties offsets some 20 per cent of Portugal's expenditure in its colonial wars.

US corporate involvement is not limited to the Portuguese colonies. Union Carbide and Foote Mineral made the American stake in Rhodesia clear in their successful lobby to breach sanctions by importing chrome. In South Africa, US investment is rising fast, and US companies earn record profit rates. In 1966 these companies recorded an average profit rate of 20·6 per cent, double the average for US overseas investments (10·4 per cent in 1966) and a much higher rate of return than British investments in the Republic (usually between 12 per cent and 13 per cent).[14] Dollar-area investments rose from £238m. in 1964 to £435m. in 1969.[15]

Britain, France and the United States are the largest backers of white supremacy in Southern Africa but not the only ones. West Germany has substantial investments in the Cabora Bassa

Dam project, which is of key significance in the Portuguese strategy for developing a strong, permanent white settler society in South Africa and of great importance as a source of future energy supplies to the South African Republic. Holland, West Germany and Italy all provide arms which are used by the Portuguese in the colonial wars. Switzerland, a supposedly neutral country, is the second-largest foreign investor in South Africa, and in comparison to the size of the Swiss gross national product, proportionately the largest.

The supporters of the liberation movements

Faced with these powerful opposing forces, the liberation movements fighting in the Portuguese colonies, in Namibia (Southwest Africa) and Rhodesia can call on relatively slight countervailing international power. The Soviet bloc has given support to those liberation movements which have the Kremlin's seal of approval, but as was clear in the Vietnam war, Soviet support is neither limitless nor free of political strings. Following their *volte face* in international relations, the Chinese, too, are more cautious about their foreign involvement. In spite of assistance from China and the Soviet Union, the liberation movements are constantly short of supplies, which can only suggest that, for China and the Soviet bloc, the liberation of Africa is not a high priority. The aid that has been given is necessary to protect the remnants of the Soviet Union's anti-imperialist image, but bears no relationship to the ability of the movements to absorb more supplies. The Scandinavian countries, particularly Sweden, have provided material assistance to the movements fighting in the Portuguese territories.

In Africa, the movements can rely on support from the OAU and the OAU Liberation Committee, and on direct bilateral assistance from some of the more progressive African governments. A glance at the political situation in Africa indicates that these constitute a small minority. For many African governments Southern Africa provides a convenient rallying-point and serves to distract attention from the unresolved internal contradictions of their own societies. The military dictators of Uganda and Nigeria, to name but two, are fond of making sweeping calls for the final liberation of the continent but, in fact, devote more attention to the suppression of their domestic opponents than their external enemies. Nigeria's oil revenue has done more to create a vast system of internal corruption and conspicuous consumption than to assist the P A I G C in liberating near-by Guinea-Bissau.

The frequent demand for a selective boycott of the more clearly culpable international companies and for sanctions against trade and investment links with Portugal's Western backers have come to nothing. Faced with the possibility of fewer consumer goods and a break with Western business friends, the African bourgeoisie have generally been prepared to let liberation take second place.

The liberation movements can rely on the support of UN resolutions passed by the General Assembly; but any proposed activity can be blocked in the Security Council by Britain, France, or the United States. The UN has passed a great number of resolutions, established special committees, organized conferences, and put out publications. The effectiveness of the UN is, however, indicated by its complete failure to enforce sanctions against Rhodesia and to terminate South African control over Namibia – a UN Trust Territory.

The measure of foreign support which the movements can rely on is clearly insufficient to offset the assistance on which the white supremacist governments can draw – assistance which includes the counter-insurgency tactics and technology which America has developed in her other imperial ventures. This inequality at the international level seems unlikely to change without a revolutionary re-alignment of the political forces in the major Western countries. There are, however, a number of weak spots in the white domination of Southern Africa.

Weak links in Southern Africa

In Rhodesia, nearly 45 per cent of the white population have been in the country less than ten years. And they are there to enjoy substantially higher living standards than they could anywhere else in the world. Unlike those who were born in Southern Africa, they could return to their home countries, and no doubt many of them would do so if the freedom-fighters made a more significant impact and jeopardized the stability of Rhodesia.* The increased guerilla activity in the latter part of 1972 forced the government to extend national service from nine months to one year. This move was inevitably unpopular with young Rhodesians and may encourage some of the more highly trained and more liberal young whites to leave the country.

Portugal faces a great strain on both manpower and finances in fighting her African wars. Defence expenditure accounts for more than 40 per cent of the national budget. From a total population of only 9 million, Portugal has raised an army of 200,000 and has been forced to extend compulsory military service from eighteen months to four years. Resistance to serving in the army is reflected in desertions and illegal emigration, estimated to have reached over 18,000 a year. Portugal's Western allies have provided equipment and financial support, but mounting domestic opposition to support for Portuguese colonialism, and increased international pressure, means that the West must pay a growing political price. In the existing international context, none of the major powers can be expected to commit troops to the support of Portugal. Assistance could, though, come from Brazil, which, since the military *coup*, has strengthened her ties with Portugal, and has given the Portuguese consistent support in the United Nations. Portugal in turn has promoted the idea of a South Atlantic Defence Organization (known as SATO) which would include Portugal, her African colonies, Brazil, Argentina, and South Africa. Prominent Conservative MPs have urged British participation in any such alliance.

If the West felt that the defence of Portugal's colonies demanded actual troop support, Brazil, with her historic link to Portugal, a military dictatorship, and complete subservience to

---

*The government discourages emigration by restricting emigrants to taking no more than £150 when they leave the country.

US foreign policy, would be the obvious country from which such support could be sent. In any case, it is clear that the Portuguese, in spite of the crippling financial burden, intend to hold on to their colonies. It is possible that if a suitable African 'leader' could be found in Guinea-Bissau, they might be prepared to come to a separate arrangement there. In Angola, and Mozambique with a considerably larger settler population, rich mineral resources and strategic significance for the whole of Southern Africa, such an outcome is unlikely.

The general picture then in Southern Africa is one of a strong military alliance backed by the Western powers which in the present circumstances can be expected to resist the liberation movements for the foreseeable future. Only in Guinea-Bissau is there any chance of a liberation victory soon: a victory in part facilitated by Guinea-Bissau's geographical separation from the other white supremacist countries. In Southern Africa, the liberation movements must be prepared to wage a long war of attrition, a war which undoubtedly will gain increased publicity and increased support in the West. In the short term, this support will be reflected in attempts to legitimize the conflict by new institutional arrangements which leave unchallenged Western domination of the economy. In the long term, Western involvement in Southern Africa, like American involvement in Vietnam, can be expected to be an important radicalizing force in Western society. It is this possibility, coupled with the growing strength of the liberation movements in Mozambique and Angola, which offers the most optimistic current perspective.

The prospects for Rhodesia's African opposition

UDI, as we argued earlier, left the nationalist movement weak and divided, and without a viable strategy for liberation. The first major response to UDI came from ZANU. In April 1966, the ZANU Zimbabwe African National Liberation Army engaged Rhodesian troops at Sinoia, in what according to one writer was 'a determined bid to start a generalized revolutionary struggle'.[16] This move was condemned by ZAPU and, of course, by Great Britain – from whom a condemnation of subsequent South African military activity, in what remained legally a British colony, was strangely muted. In August 1967 a joint South African National Congress and ZAPU force entered Rhodesia; like the ZANU force their effect was limited.

Today, both ZANU and ZAPU are committed to armed struggle as the road to liberation, and their disillusionment with the role of international pressure is clear. Addressing the UN Security Council after the 1971 British settlement proposals, the ZANU representative said: 'There is only one thing we want: our country ... We shall have it, with or without another veto in this Council of any resolution on Zimbabwe. We shall have our country by the only means that developments have left us: armed struggle!' The ZAPU representative condemned the British government, which had 'remained totally insensitive to any international appeals on the Zimbabwe question, just as they were, in the past, to those of the people of Zimbabwe themselves'; and declared: 'We have taken up arms – this is the only way open to our freedom.'[17]

Nevertheless, the movements remain divided, though there are still no clear ideological differences between ZANU and ZAPU, nor is any attempt made to conduct a debate in political terms. The debate continues to be characterized by the exchange of invective. An attempt in 1971 to promote unity in the creation by former ZANU and ZAPU members of the Front for the Liberation of Zimbabwe (FROLIZI) has to date succeeded only in creating a third grouping. A joint ZANU–ZAPU military command formed in response to the creation of FROLIZI failed to promote effective unity. In early 1973, encouraged by the OAU and strong pressure from Zambia and Tanzania, a joint ZANU and ZAPU council was formed as a first step to total integration. It is not clear, as yet, whether this will finally be effective.

Ideologically, the movements have shifted from the reformist position reflected in earlier writings and policy statements to a public Marxist position. In 1965 a ZAPU publication had argued: 'There is no difference between the liberty for which Winston Churchill was struggling [in the Second World War] and that for which Zimbabwe struggles today.'[18] In part, this reflects the dependence of the movements on the Eastern bloc countries and China; in part on the influence of other liberation movements; and in part as a reaction to Western policy in Southern Africa. It is difficult to say to what extent Marxist rhetoric has been matched by the application of Marxist analysis or Marxist-Leninist practice.

In the Portuguese colonies the MPLA, FRELIMO and PAIGC have forged and are still forging a revolutionary ideology through experience. In the process there have been splits in the movements between reformists and revolutionaries; there have been those who, finding the movement going too fast, have betrayed it; and there has been a constant need to counteract any attempts to create tribal power bases. For the Zimbabwe movements there has been little such fire in which ideas could be tested, and refined or cast aside. Rhetoric has been unhampered by the need to apply it to reality.

In the eight years since UDI was declared, the nationalist movements have not advanced beyond the stage of sending occasional commando squads into Rhodesia. There are no liberated areas, and few which, from a Rhodesian security standpoint, are consistently unsafe. The nationalist movements often continue to behave as though the battle can be won with words, making exaggerated and unsubstantiated claims of enemy casualties and their own victories. In January 1970, after a relatively heavy military commitment, ZAPU claimed to have killed more than forty Rhodesian soldiers and wounded many others. The only casualties ZAPU reported was one courier killed and seven freedom-fighters captured.[19] During the December 1972 offensive, ZANU claimed that, between 21 and 23 December, they had killed seventy-one Rhodesian troops. They reported no ZANU casualties.[20] The scale of the claims makes it unlikely that, if true, the Rhodesians could have effectively concealed their losses. They ignore the advice of Cabral: 'Tell no lies ... mask no difficulties, mistakes, failures. Claim no easy victories.'[21]

The nationalist groups in exile have often seemed more concerned with building up their own patronage by effective fund-raising than with developing a viable strategy for liberation.

Competition between the movements means that in planning military activities, the movements may be tempted to sacrifice strategic considerations in order to maintain a militant image and not be outshone by a rival. Some critics have claimed that too many freedom-fighters have been needlessly sacrificed in strategically useless and militarily bungled campaigns. One ZANU leader was quoted as saying: 'Even the loss of our men is positive. Their parents and friends always know that they are killed or prisoners, and their attitude quickly passes from apathy to militancy.'[22] The rhetoric of the movements often draws to mind Amilcar Cabral's strictures: 'The ideological deficiency within the national liberation movements, not to say the total lack of ideology – reflecting as this does an ignorance of the historical reality which these movements claim to transform – makes for one of the greatest weaknesses in our struggle against imperialism, if not the greatest weakness of all.'[23]

In spite of the claimed Marxism of the movements, analysis often lacks either a theoretical grasp or an empirical base. Charles Chikerema, a well-known nationalist now in FROLIZI, has argued: 'The emergence of Smith is nothing but a reflection of systematic British imperialist steps in consolidating Rhodesia as a buffer state against the north for the protection of South Africa ... There have never been any differences between the settlers in Rhodesia and the British government, whether it is a Liberal government or a Conservative government or the Labour Party.'[24] He presents no evidence to support this view – while, in contrast, considerable evidence exists to suggest that Ian Smith's government, far from representing a triumph for British imperialist policy, represents a defeat. There is no evidence to suggest that South Africa would have regarded a black bourgeois government, as in Malawi or Kenya, as any less acceptable than an illegal white minority régime which brings an added element of instability to Southern Africa.

Other spokesmen offer a more coherent explanation, but little serious debate seems to have taken place on important strategic questions: the role of the urban workers as distinct from the rural tribesmen; the role of armed struggle in politicizing the rural masses; the coordination of industrial action in the cities with military activity in the countryside (a key factor in Cuba).

Rhodesia constitutes, in many ways, the weak link in Southern Africa. She can call on no assistance from a metropolitan power, as can the settlers in the Portuguese colonies; and she lacks the high proportion of whites and elaborate defence establishment of South Africa. Now there are signs that this weakness is beginning to be exploited by guerilla activity. The white Rhodesian mood of self-assurance is no longer quite what it was.

The African National Council

Perhaps the major legacy of the ill-fated settlement proposals and the subsequent Pearce Commission has so far been the African National Council (ANC). After UDI political de-moralization, the imprisonment of many nationalist leaders, the departure of many others into exile, and the comprehensive repression which the Smith government imposed, left the African population with no organized legal expression for its discontent. Some of the African MPs in the Salisbury Parliament attempted to oppose government policy, but they were hindered by the total control which the Rhodesian Front exercised over the parliamentary agenda and debates. In any case, the MPs had never had a mass base, and the moderate standpoint which they reflected was unrepresentative of African views (though since the creation of the ANC, MPs have been able to relate to a mass movement).

The Test of Acceptability gave former ZANU and ZAPU supporters, and others whose introduction to politics was more recent, the opportunity to come together in the ANC. The formation of the Council at any other time would no doubt have led to its immediate banning. But with world attention focused on Rhodesia during the Test, the ANC became a celebrated body, and its public suppression now would jeopardize any remaining chance of a settlement with Britain. This has given the nationalists a very limited degree of freedom to work inside Rhodesia. Though the government has not banned the Council, it has arrested some of its militants, prevented it from selling membership cards and receiving funds from abroad, forbidden its leaders to travel abroad and stopped them from visiting the rural areas.

It is difficult to analyse the political position of the Council. The large national executive reportedly contains a wide political spectrum, from revolutionary Marxists to those who see the possibility of making an accommodation between the Smith régime and the African middle class. The public announcements of the A N C are directed in part to Europeans in Rhodesia and to world opinion. Clearly, given the repressive climate, the Council is not likely to call for armed revolution; but, on the other hand, it has refused to attack the liberation movements, arguing rather that they are an inevitable consequence of white domination. Nevertheless, in the public pronouncements of Bishop Muzorewa, and in the Council's manifesto, greater weight is attached to God, whose name is invoked six times in the short manifesto, than to class struggle. The Council's social policy is vague: 'We believe that the rights and property of the minority should be protected; we do not, however, believe in the minority's amassing of social, political and economic privileges at the expense of the freedom of the majority.'[25]

Whatever criticisms can be made of the Council's political line, its major achievement has been to revitalize and focus internal opposition to white rule and to demonstrate nationally and internationally that the Rhodesian government survives by force alone.

Conclusion

As we argued earlier, Rhodesian whites face an impasse. Denied recognition, they have no hope of economic expansion; and unable to come to terms with the African population, they face a protracted military struggle.

It is clear that this dilemma has been recognized by Smith, who, in spite of opposition from rank-and-file Rhodesian Front members, has continued to pursue a settlement with Britain and conduct tentative negotiations with the A N C. The dilemma is also clear to a growing number of white electors, and was reflected in the formation of the Rhodesia Party in 1972 by Allan Savory, an M P who resigned from the Rhodesian Front. The Rhodesia Party opposes what it terms 'petty apartheid' and adopts a paternalistic approach to African advance similar to that of the old United Federal Party.

The absence of a settlement with Britain may polarize the electorate between those who see the need for further compromises and new leadership to achieve legality, and those who reject any compromise and demand more vigorous racial segregation. The past dynamics of Rhodesian politics would suggest a victory for the right.

If a 'moderate' white government were elected in those circumstances, a deal could certainly be made with a section of the African population. The resulting government would, however, be incapable of solving the crisis faced by the African rural population, without a structural revolution which it would have no mandate to undertake. On the other hand, if a 'moderate' government came to power before a liberation movement had thoroughly established itself in the country, it would certainly delay the creation of a united armed resistance. This middle 'solution', favoured by Western capital and acceptable to South Africa and Portugal, is unlikely to receive the support of the dominant groups in the Rhodesian electorate – the white working class and lower middle class.

The nature of the liberation struggle in Rhodesia will be very different from that in the Portuguese colonies, not least because of the much higher level of urbanization. The African urban population forms 12 per cent of the total population in Guinea-Bissau, 10 per cent in Angola, and around 8 per cent in Mozambique; but in Rhodesia the figure is 37 per cent, or roughly the same as that in South Africa. In none of the Portuguese colonies is the African working class a major force. Basil Davidson writes of Guinea-Bissau's urban Africans: 'It is a shifting, barely crystallized urban population, with nothing that resembles the working class, but for various small groups such as the dockers of Bissau.'[26] Amilcar Cabral spoke of the difficulties which are involved: 'We are a country of peasants . . .

[In Guinea] the peasantry is not a revolutionary force.' This necessitated the formation of a vanguard group, largely recruited from among urban wage earners, who could instil a revolutionary consciousness into the rural masses.[27]

The presence of a relatively large African working class in Rhodesia means that the social base of the Rhodesian nationalist movements is substantially different. In addition, the tactics of the liberation movement will have to take into account the numerical and economic significance of the urban workers. The situation in Rhodesia in this sense is closer to that in South Africa than to that in the Portuguese colonies. A further difference lies in the extent of European colonization and control in the rural areas. The creation of liberated areas will, in consequence, be a more difficult task.

The urban working class cannot themselves overthrow the white government, but they provide a ready source of cadres with a predisposition to a collective socialist consciousness as distinct from the individualistic traits of the peasantry. Unless the struggle is led by an armed revolutionary nationalist party, there is a danger that the African working class will turn to merely pragmatic material goals, fighting to improve their own status but not using their power to confront the whole system. With an active liberation movement organizing openly and militarily in the rural areas and clandestinely in the cities, the economic power of the African working class can be used both to demoralize and destabilize the white population and to strike at the prosperity of the white economy. The government of Rhodesia has rested on the force of arms since colonization. Until 1965, there was perhaps some excuse for a belief that reform was possible. Today, eight years after U D I, there is no longer any basis for such hope. What was stolen by colonial violence can only be restored by revolutionary violence.

As we have argued, the fight for Zimbabwe does not exist in a vacuum. It is rather a fight against the local consequences of an international system which rates profit above people. The fight neither starts nor stops in Southern Africa, and the most concrete expression of solidarity remains, as the American Left put it: 'Bring the war home.'

Amilcar Cabral speaking to an Italian audience in 1964, made the point precisely and eloquently:

> To end up with, I should just like to make one last point about solidarity between the international working-class movement and our national liberation struggle. There are two alternatives: either we admit that there really is a struggle against imperialism which interests everybody, or we deny it. If, as would seem from all the evidence, imperialism exists and is trying simultaneously to dominate the working class in all the advanced countries and smother the national liberation movements in all the underdeveloped countries, then there is only one enemy against whom we are fighting. If we are fighting together, then I think the main aspect of our solidarity is extremely simple: it is to fight – I don't think there is any need to discuss this very much. We are struggling in Guinea with guns in our hands, you must struggle in your countries as well – I don't say with guns in your hands. I'm not going to tell you how to struggle, that's your business; but you must find the best means and the best forms of fighting against our common enemy: this is the best form of solidarity.
>
> There are, of course, other secondary forms of solidarity: publishing material, sending medicine, etc.; I can guarantee you that if tomorrow we make a breakthrough and you are engaged in an armed struggle against imperialism in Europe, we will send you some medicine too.[28]

Postscript

Since this book was written there has been a *coup d'état* in Portugal which will probably prove to be of major significance for the future of Southern Africa. The overthrow of Caetano's dictatorship and its replacement by a civilian government headed by General Spinola and backed by the military has been generally attributed to dissatisfaction with the continued search for a military solution to the problem of the Portuguese colonies.

The new Portuguese Foreign Minister, Soares, a member of the Socialist Party, is committed to decolonization, and it is clear that at least in Guinea-Bissau this process will take place quite rapidly. In Mozambique and Angola, however, there are large numbers of white settlers who, while in many respects different from those in Rhodesia – particularly in the large number of poor whites – are generally opposed to African rule. Multinational corporations are worried that the rise to power of revolutionary governments headed by FRELIMO and MPLA would jeopardize their heavy investments in the area. Yet there is no possibility of a simple transfer of power to suitably conservative African governments which would maintain the privileges of foreign investors and perpetuate traditional trading patterns. In one crucial respect, however, Mozambique and Angola differ from Rhodesia: they have no independent national governments and no independent military forces.

In the confused situation which has arisen with Caetano's overthrow a number of possibilities exist. The white settlers and spokesmen for foreign and domestic capital are already organizing to maintain their privileges. In Mozambique the strength of FRELIMO gives cause for optimism about the outcome, but in Angola the liberation movements remain divided and there may well be a long struggle for power. What effect this will have in Portugal itself is unclear. Certainly until a new government is elected, and the military forced to withdraw from its current role of power broker, internal contradictions and external pressures make it difficult to predict Portugal's future attitude with any confidence.

In Rhodesia the possibility of independence in Mozambique and Angola creates further economic difficulties in that sanctions would clearly be tightened, while a victory by FRELIMO or MPLA would provide concrete support for the liberation movements fighting in Rhodesia. Nevertheless the dynamics of Rhodesian politics remain intact. The less extreme Rhodesia Party has made no headway against the Rhodesian Front. The increased insecurity on Rhodesia's borders and the growing successes of the Rhodesian liberation movements have not shifted the supremacist attitudes of the settler population.

Now, as in 1896, the majority of the settlers in Rhodesia have but one way to preserve their privileges, and that is by retaining a monopoly of political power. The chance of compromise or of an alliance with middle-class Africans further recedes; the determination of the settlers to hold on increases the more their prospects of success diminish. Rhodesia waits to reap the whirlwind sown by the policies of successive British governments. Harold Wilson will have 'the clear and decisive verdict of history', but it will not be to his liking.

AUGUST 1974

Bibliography

ADAM, HERIBERT, *Modernizing Racial Domination*, University of California Press, Berkeley, 1971.

ANDERSON, P., and BLACKBURN, R. (eds.), *Towards Socialism*, Collins, 1965.

ARNOLD, G., and BALDWIN, A., *Sanctions against Rhodesia, 1965 to 1972*, Africa Bureau, 1972.

ARNOLD, G., and BALDWIN, A., *Token Sanctions of Economic Warfare*, Africa Bureau, 1972.

ARRIGHI, GIOVANNI, *The Political Economy of Rhodesia*, Mouton, The Hague, 1967.

BARBER, JAMES, *Rhodesia: The Road to Rebellion*, Oxford University Press, 1967.

BARBER, WILLIAM J., *The Economy of British Central Africa*, Oxford University Press, 1961.

BROWN, KEN, *Land in Southern Rhodesia*, Africa Bureau, 1959.

BULL, THEODORE (ed.), *Rhodesian Perspective*, Michael Joseph, 1967.

CABRAL, AMILCAR, *Revolution in Guinea: An African People's Struggle*, Stage 1, 1969.

CHRISTIE, M. J., *The Simonstown Agreement*, Africa Bureau, 1970.

CLEGG, EDWARD, *Race and Politics: Partnership in the Federation of Rhodesia and Nyasaland*, Oxford University Press, 1960.

CREECH, A., and HINDEN, RITA, *Colonies and International Conscience*, Fabian Publications, 1945.

CREIGHTON, T. R. M., *The Anatomy of Partnership: Southern Rhodesia and the Central African Federation*, Faber & Faber, 1960.

DARNBOROUGH, A., *Labour's Record in Southern Africa*, Anti-Apartheid Movement, 1967.

DAVIDSON, BASIL, *In the Eye of the Storm*, Longman, 1972.

DAVIDSON, BASIL, *The Liberation of Guiné*, Penguin, 1969.

DAVIDSON, BASIL, *Report on Southern Africa*, Cape, 1952.

DAY, JOHN, *International Nationalism: The Extra-territorial Relations of Southern Rhodesian African Nationalists*, Routledge & Kegan Paul, 1968.

Bibliography

FANON, FRANTZ, *The Wretched of the Earth*, Grove Press, New York, 1965, and Penguin, 1967.

FANON, FRANTZ, *Toward the African Revolution*, Monthly Review Press, 1967, and Penguin, 1970.

FIRST, RUTH, STEELE, JONATHAN and GURNEY, CHRISTABEL, *The South African Connection: Western Investment in Apartheid*, Temple Smith, 1972, and Penguin, 1973.

FRANCK, THOMAS M., *Race and Nationalism: The Struggle for Power in Rhodesia-Nyasaland*, Fordham University Press, New York, 1960.

GANN, L. H., *A History of Southern Rhodesia*, Chatto & Windus, 1965.

GANN, L. H., and GELFAND, M., *Huggins of Rhodesia*, George Allen & Unwin, 1964.

GIBSON, RICHARD, *African Liberation Movements*, Oxford University Press, 1972.

GLASS, STAFFORD, *The Matabele War*, Longmans, 1968.

GRAY, RICHARD, *The Two Nations: Aspects of the Development of Race Relations in the Rhodesias and Nyasaland*, Oxford University Press, 1960.

HARRIS, J., *The Chartered Millions*, 1920.

HINDEN, RITA, *Common Sense and Colonial Development*, Fabian Society Colonial Bureau, 1949.

HINDESS, BARRY, *The Decline of Working Class Politics*, Paladin, 1971.

HOLLEMAN, J. F., *Chief, Council and Commissioner*, Oxford University Press, 1969.

JONES, M., *Rhodesia: The White Judges' Burden*, International Defence and Aid Fund, 1972.

KANZA, THOMAS, *Conflict in the Congo*, Penguin, 1972.

KEATLEY, PATRICK, *The Politics of Partnership*, Penguin, 1963.

LEYS, COLIN, *European Politics in Southern Rhodesia*, Oxford University Press, 1959.

LEYS, C., and PRATT, C., *A New Deal in Central Africa*, Heinemann, 1960.

LOCKHART, J. G., and WOODHOUSE, G. M., *Rhodes*, Hodder & Stoughton, 1962.

MASON, PHILIP, *The Birth of a Dilemma: The Conquest and Settlement of Rhodesia*, Oxford University Press, 1958.

MASON, PHILIP, *Year of Decision: Rhodesia and Nyasaland in 1960*, Oxford University Press, 1960.

MILIBAND, R., *Parliamentary Socialism: A Study in the Politics of Labour*, Merlin Press, 1971.

MILIBAND, R., *The State in Capitalist Society*, Weidenfeld & Nicolson, 1969.

MILIBAND, R., and SAVILLE, J., *Socialist Register*, Merlin Press.

MINTER, WILLIAM, *Portuguese Africa and the West*, Penguin, 1972.

MINTY, ABDUL S., *South Africa's Defence Strategy*, Anti-Apartheid Movement, 1969.

MLAMBO, ESHMAEL, *Rhodesia: The Struggle for a Birthright*, C. Hurst, London, 1972.

MLAMBO, ESHMAEL et al., *No Future Without Us*, E. Mlambo, London, 1972.

MONDLANE, EDUARDO, *The Struggle for Mozambique*, Penguin, 1969.

MPLA, *Revolution in Angola*, Merlin Press, 1972.

MURRAY, D. J., *The Governmental System in Southern Rhodesia*, Oxford University Press, 1970.

NUTTING, ANTHONY, *Scramble for Africa*, Constable, 1972.

OWEN, DAVID, *The Politics of Defence*, Jonathan Cape, 1972.

PALLEY, CLAIRE, *The Constitutional History of Law of Southern Rhodesia, 1888–1965*, Oxford University Press, 1966.

POMEROY, WILLIAM J., *Apartheid Axis: The United States and South Africa*, International Publishers, New York, 1971.

RANGER, T. O., *The African Voice in Southern Rhodesia (1898–1930)*, Heinemann Educational, 1970.

RANGER, T. O. (ed.), *Aspects of Central African History*, Heinemann Educational, 1968.

RANGER, T. O., *Revolt in Southern Rhodesia 1896–7*, Heinemann Educational, 1967.

RAYNER, WILLIAM, *The Tribe and its Successors: An Account of African Traditional Life and European Settlement in Southern Rhodesia*, Faber & Faber, 1962.

REX, JOHN, *Race Relations in Sociological Theory*, Weidenfeld & Nicolson, 1970.

ROBSON, P., and LURY, D. A., *The Economies of Africa*, Northwestern University Press, Evanston, Illinois, 1969.

RODNEY, WALTER, *How Europe Underdeveloped Africa*, Bogle-L'Ouverture Publications, London, 1972.

ROGERS, BARBARA, *South Africa's Stake in Britain*, Africa Bureau, 1971.

ROGERS, CYRIL A., and FRANTZ, C., *Racial Themes in Southern Rhodesia: The Attitudes and Behaviour of the White Population*, Yale University Press, New Haven, Connecticut, 1962.

Bibliography

SAMKANGE, STANLAKE, *Origins of Rhodesia*, Heinemann Educational, 1969.

SANGER, CLYDE, *Central African Emergency*, Heinemann, 1960.

SHAMUYARIRA, NATHAN M., *Crisis in Rhodesia*, André Deutsch, 1965.

SITHOLE, NDABANINGI, *African Nationalism*, Oxford University Press, 1968.

STOKES, E., and BROWN, RICHARD, *The Zambezian Past: Studies in Central African History*, Manchester University Press, 1966.

TAWES JOLLIE, E., *The Real Rhodesia*, Hutchinson, 1926.

THOMPSON, C. H., and WOODRUFF, H. W., *Economic Development in Rhodesia and Nyasaland*, Dennis Dobson, 1954.

TODD, JUDITH, *Rhodesia*, MacGibbon & Kee, 1966.

TODD, JUDITH, *The Right to Say No*, Sidgwick & Jackson, 1972.

TOW, L., *The Manufacturing Economy of Southern Rhodesia: Problems and Prospects*, National Academy of Sciences, National Research Council, Washington DC, 1960.

TOWNSEND, PETER, and BOSANQUET, NICHOLAS, *Labour and Inequality*, Fabian Society, 1972.

TREDGOLD, R. C., *The Rhodesia That Was My Life*, George Allen & Unwin, 1968.

VAMBE, LAWRENCE, *An Ill-Fated People: Zimbabwe before and after Rhodes*, Heinemann, 1972.

WARBEY, WILLIAM, *Ho Chi Minh and the Struggle for an Independent Vietnam*, Merlin Press, 1972.

WEBER, M., *The Protestant Ethic and the Spirit of Capitalism*, Allen & Unwin, 1967.

WEINRICH, A. K. H., *Chiefs and Councils in Rhodesia*, Heinemann Educational, 1971.

WELENSKY, SIR ROY, *Welensky's 4000 Days*, Collins, 1964.

WILSON, HAROLD, *The Labour Government 1964-70: A Personal Record*, Michael Joseph, 1971, and Penguin, 1974.

YUDELMAN, MONTAGUE, *Africans on the Land*, Harvard University Press, Cambridge, Massachusetts, 1964.

References

Introduction

1. Frantz Fanon, 'The Pitfalls of National Consciousness', in *The Wretched of the Earth*.
2. *Daily Times*, Nigeria, 31 August 1972.

Chapter 1 – Conquest

1. Stafford Glass, *The Matabele War*, p. 2.
2. Philip Mason, *The Birth of a Dilemma: The Conquest and Settlement of Rhodesia*, p. 22.
3. e.g., L. H. Gann, *History of Southern Rhodesia*, Glass, op. cit.; and Mason, op. cit.
4. T. O. Ranger, *Revolt in Southern Rhodesia*, pp. 28–9.
5. Glass, op.cit., pp. 5–6.
6. L. Vambe, *An Ill-fated People: Zimbabwe Before and After Rhodes*, p. 63.
7. T. O. Ranger, 'The Nineteenth Century in Southern Rhodesia', in *Aspects of Central African History*, ed. T. O. Ranger, p. 122.
8. Richard Brown, 'Aspects of the Scramble for Matabeleland', in *The Zambesian Past: Studies in Central African History*, ed. E. Stokes and Richard Brown, p. 66.
9. ibid.
10. Mason, op. cit., p. 107.
11. Vambe, op. cit.
12. Ranger, *Revolt in Southern Rhodesia*, op. cit., p. 181.
13. J. Blake-Thompson and R. Summers, 'Mlimo and Mwari: Notes on a Native Religion in Southern Rhodesia', quoted in Ranger, *Revolt in Southern Rhodesia*, op. cit., p. 22.
14. S. Samkange, *Origins of Rhodesia*, p. 34.
15. Vambe, op. cit., p. 48.
16. Gann, op. cit., p. 45.
17. Brown, op. cit., pp. 68–9.

18. ibid., p. 69.

19. Ranger, 'The Nineteenth Century in Southern Rhodesia', loc. cit., p. 142.

20. Samkange, op. cit., p. 55.

21. Brown, op. cit., p. 74.

22. Samkange, op. cit., p. 60.

23. J. G. Lockhart and C. M. Woodhouse, *Rhodes*, p. 69.

24. ibid., p. 93.

25. R. Robinson, 'The Imperialism of Free Trade', *Economic History Review*, Second Series, Vol. VI, No. 1 (1953), p. 13.

26. ibid.

27. Quoted in Samkange, op. cit., p. 58.

28. Brown, op. cit.

29. Vambe, op. cit., pp. 65–72.

30. Samkange, op. cit., p. 59.

31. Ranger, *Revolt in Southern Rhodesia*, op. cit., p. 56.

32. Samkange, op. cit., p. 156.

33. ibid., p. 160–63.

34. Ranger, 'The Nineteenth Century in Southern Rhodesia', loc. cit., pp. 135–6.

35. ibid., pp. 131–2.

36. Ranger, *Revolt in Southern Rhodesia*, op. cit., p. 93.

37. ibid., p. 101.

38. John Rex, *Race Relations in Sociological Theory*, pp. 43, 54.

39. Max Weber, *The Protestant Ethic and the Spirit of Capitalism*, p. 60.

40. R. C. Tredgold, *The Rhodesia That Was My Life*, p. 17.

41. Ranger, *Revolt in Southern Rhodesia*, op. cit., p. 114.

42. Mason, op. cit., p. 192.

43. ibid., p. 203.

44. Gann, op. cit., p. 216.

45. Eric Stokes, introduction to 'Aspects of the Scramble for Matabeleland', in Stokes and Brown, *The Zambesian Past*.

46. Ranger, 'African Politics in Twentieth-Century Southern Rhodesia', in *Aspects of Central African History*, op. cit., p. 211.

47. Ranger, *Revolt in Southern Rhodesia*, op. cit., p. 192.

Chapter 2 – The basis of white society

1. D. J. Murray, *The Governmental System in Southern Rhodesia*, p. 6.

2. G. Arrighi, 'Labour Supplies in Historical Perspective: A Study

of the Proletarianization of the African Peasantry in Rhodesia', in *Journal of Development Studies*, Vol. VI (1969–70), p. 210.

3. J. Harris, *The Chartered Millions*, p. 259.

4. William Rayner, *The Tribe and its Successors*, p. 180.

5. Harris, op. cit., p. 258.

6. ibid.

7. Arrighi, op. cit., pp. 214–15.

8. ibid., p. 215.

9. United Nations Economic Commission, 4/III (February 1973), p. 81.

10. R. Gray, *The Two Nations: Aspects of the Development of Race Relations in the Rhodesias and Nyasaland*, p. 57.

11. Murray, op. cit., p. 100.

12. L. H. Gann, *History of Southern Rhodesia*, p. 190.

13. W. J. Barber, *The Economy of British Central Africa*, p. 26.

14. Gann, op. cit., p. 274.

15. Barber, op. cit., p. 155.

16. N. Yudelman, *Africans on the Land*, p. 53.

17. *Africa South*, July/September 1959.

18. Ken Brown, *Land in Southern Rhodesia*, p. 16.

19. Barber, op. cit., p. 153.

20. Yudelman, op. cit., p. 123.

21. R. B. Sutcliffe, 'Stagnation and Inequality in Rhodesia, 1946–1968', *Bulletin of the Oxford Institute of Economics and Statistics*, Vol. XXXIII (1971).

22. *Monthly Digest of Statistics*, Salisbury, November 1972.

23. Sutcliffe, loc. cit., p. 43.

24. P. Keatley, *The Politics of Partnership*, p. 196.

25. T. M. Franck, *Race and Nationalism: The Struggle for Power in Rhodesia-Nyasaland*, p. 111.

26. Gray, op. cit., p. 230.

27. Report of a native compound inspector, quoted in Gann, op. cit., p. 175.

28. L. Tow, *The Manufacturing Economy of Southern Rhodesia: Problems and Prospects*, Foreign Field Research Programme, Office of Naval Research, Report No. 10, Publication 850, p. 97.

29. E. Mondlane, *The Struggle for Mozambique*, p. 31.

30. Gray, op. cit., p. 91.

31. E. Tawse Jollie, 'Britain's Youngest Colony', *National Review*, No. 489 (November 1923), p. 457.

32. Legislative Assembly debates, 30 November 1944, quoted in Basil Davidson, *Report on Southern Africa*.

33. *Southern Rhodesia Hansard*, Vol. XXV (6 June 1945), col. 1285.

34. Gray, op. cit., p. 229.

35. Quoted in Walter Rodney, *How Europe Underdeveloped Africa*, p. 223.

36. T. O. Ranger, *The African Voice in Southern Rhodesia*, p. 42.

37. Franck, op. cit., p. 118.

38. E. Tawse Jollie, *The Real Rhodesia*, p. 262.

39. Quoted in *Rhodesian Perspective*, ed. T. Bull, p. 70.

40. Quoted in C. Leys, *European Politics in Southern Rhodesia*, p. 161.

41. Keatley, op. cit., p. 190.

42. Gray, op. cit., p. 90.

43. Sutcliffe, loc. cit., p. 43.

44. Gray, op. cit., p. 280.

45. ibid., p. 288.

46. Barber, op. cit., p. 171.

47. Tow, op. cit., p. 97.

48. Arrighi, op. cit., p. 223.

49. Calculated from *Monthly Digest of Statistics*, Salisbury, November 1972.

50. Sutcliffe, loc. cit., p. 49.

51. ibid., p. 48.

52. *Monthly Digest of Statistics*, Salisbury, November 1972.

53. J. Saul and G. Arrighi, 'Nationalism and Revolution in Sub-Saharan Africa', in *Socialist Register*, 1969, ed. R. Miliband and J. Saville, p. 147.

54. Barber, op. cit., p. 28.

55. L. H. Gann and M. Gelfand, *Huggins of Rhodesia*, p. 160.

56. Murray, op. cit., p. 178.

57. Gray, op. cit., p. 100.

Chapter 3 – The development of white politics

1. Arghiri Emmanuel, 'White Settler Colonialism and the Myth of Investment Imperialism', *New Left Review*, No. 73, pp. 38, 39.

2. L. H. Gann and M. Gelfand, *Huggins of Rhodesia*, p. 46.

3. D. J. Murray, *The Governmental System in Southern Rhodesia*, p. 207.

4. T. O. Ranger, *The African Voice in Southern Rhodesia*, p. 153.

5. Gann and Gelfand, op. cit., p. 78.

6. ibid., p. 92.

7. ibid., p. 99.

8. Quoted in C. Leys, *European Politics in Southern Rhodesia*, p. 182.

9. ibid., pp. 170–71.

10. E. Clegg, *Race and Politics: Partnership in the Federation of Rhodesia and Nyasaland*, p. 68.

11. Gann and Gelfand, op. cit., p. 213.

12. C. Leys and C. Pratt, *A New Deal in Central Africa* p. 12.

13. Quoted by James Griffiths: *Hansard*, Vol 519, cols. 685–6.

14. A. Creech and Rita Hinden, *Colonies and International Conscience*, p. 16.

15. R. Welensky, *Welensky's 4000 Days*, p. 59.

16. Sir Stafford Cripps at the African Governors' Conference, November 1947, quoted in Rita Hinden, *Common Sense and Colonial Development*, pp. 9, 10.

17. ibid., p. 42.

18. Leys, op. cit., p. 259.

19. Leys and Pratt, op. cit., p. 50.

20. A. K. H. Weinrich, *Chiefs and Councils in Rhodesia*, pp. 11–12.

21. Murray, op. cit., pp. 193–5.

22. C. H. Thompson and H. W. Woodruff, *Economic Development in Rhodesia and Nyasaland*, p. 187.

23. Clegg, op. cit., pp. 151–3.

24. N. M. Shamuyarira, *Crisis in Rhodesia*, pp. 15, 16.

25. Leys and Pratt, op. cit., p. 86.

26. ibid., p. 83.

27. P. Robson and D. A. Lury, *The Economies of Africa*, p. 432.

Chapter 4 – African opposition

1. Frantz Fanon, *Toward the African Revolution*, p. 186.

2. T. O. Ranger, *The African Voice in Southern Rhodesia*, p. 210.

3. ibid., p. 201.

4. ibid., p. 225.

5. ibid., p. 162.

6. R. Gray, *The Two Nations: Aspects of the Development of Race Relations in the Rhodesias and Nyasaland*, p. 318.

7. ibid., p. 316.

8. N. Shamuyarira, *Crisis in Rhodesia*, p. 36.

9. Gray, op. cit., p. 291.

10. ibid., p. 294.

11. Clyde Sanger, *Central African Emergency*, p. 256.

12. Shamuyarira, op. cit., p. 177.

13. ibid., p. 75.

References

14. John Day, *International Nationalism: The Extra-Territorial Relations of Southern Rhodesian African Nationalists*, pp. 80, 101.

15. Shamuyarira, op. cit., p. 58.

16. ibid., p. 61.

17. ibid., p. 59.

18. T. Bull (ed.), *Rhodesian Perspective*, p. 120.

19. 'Forward to Freedom', quoted in Anthony Atmore and Nancy Weslake, 'A Liberal Dilemma: A Critique of the *Oxford History of South Africa*', *Race*, Vol. XIV, No. 2 (October 1972), pp. 124–5.

Chapter 5 – In search of a solution

1. *Britain Strong and Free* (Conservative Party Electoral Manifesto 1951).

2. A. Gamble, *The Retreat from Empire and Conservative Politics 1959–1966* (Cambridge University mimeograph, 1970), p. 130.

3. Arghiri Emmanuel, 'White Settler Colonialism and the Myth of Investment Imperialism', *New Left Review*, No. 73, p. 43.

4. R. Welensky, *Welensky's 4000 Days*, p. 297.

5. ibid., p. 111.

6. D. Horrowitz, 'Attitudes of British Conservatives towards Decolonization in Africa', *African Affairs*, Vol. LXIX (1970), p. 13.

7. Welensky, op. cit., p. 364.

8. P. Mason, *Year of Decision: Rhodesia and Nyasaland 1960*, pp. 253–4.

9. P. Keatley, *The Politics of Partnership*, p. 497.

10. L. Tow, *The Manufacturing Economy of Southern Rhodesia: Problems and Prospects*, p. 17; W. J. Barber, *The Economy of British Central Africa*, p. 119; and D. J. Murray, *The Governmental System in Southern Rhodesia*, p. 17.

11. John Rex, *Race Relations in Sociological Theory*, p. 73.

12. G. Arrighi, *The Political Economy of Rhodesia*, p. 41.

13. E. Clegg, *Race and Politics: Partnership in the Federation of Rhodesia and Nyasaland*, p. 230.

14. Arrighi, op. cit., p. 49.

15. Clyde Sanger, *Central African Emergency*, p. 317.

16. Tow, op. cit., pp. 128, 134.

17. Keatley, op. cit., p. 78.

18. L. H. Gann and N. Gelfand, *Huggins of Rhodesia*, pp. 224–5.

19. Keatley, op. cit., p. 224.

20. T. M. Franck, *Race and Nationalism: The Struggle for Power in Rhodesia-Nyasaland*.

21. R. Gray, *The Two Nations: Aspects of the Development of Race Relations in the Rhodesias and Nyasaland*, p. 309.

22. C. Leys, *European Politics in Southern Rhodesia*, p. 196.

23. ibid., p. 219.

24. ibid., p. 310.

25. This was Sir Edgar Whitehead's estimate, in C. Palley, *The Constitutional History and Law of Southern Rhodesia, 1886–1965*, p. 316; Duncan Sandys's estimate was twelve years: Barber, *The Economy of British Central Africa*, p. 85.

26. William Harper, leader of the Dominion Party, quoted in Barber, op. cit., p. 100.

27. Official party policy statement, quoted in Barber, op. cit., p.158.

28. Palley, op. cit., pp. 421, 799.

29. CMND 2073; CMND 2807.

30. CMND 2807, op. cit., p. 11.

31. Quoted in Sanger, op. cit., p. 247.

32. Clegg, op. cit., p. 233.

33. ibid.

34. Franck, op. cit., p. 307.

35. Keatley, op. cit., p. 394.

36. *A Principle in Torment* (United Nations, New York), 1969, p. 32.

37. Quoted in Barber, op. cit., p. 174.

Chapter 6 – UDI and the failure of British policy

1. *Rhodesias's Independence* (Facts on File, New York, 1971), p. 15.

2. ibid.

3. Ian Smith, quoted in James Barber, *Rhodesia: The Road to Rebellion*.

4. Harold Wilson, *The Labour Government 1964–70: A Personal Record*, p. 162.

5. *Hansard*, 12 November 1965.

6. ibid.

7. Wilson, op. cit., p. 25.

8. W. J. Barber, *The Economy of British Central Africa*, p. 265.

9. *Hansard*, 12 November 1965.

10. Wilson, op. cit., p. 116.

11. *Hansard*, 1 November 1965.

12. Wilson, op. cit., p. 181.

13. *Southern Rhodesia: Documents relating to the Negotiations between the United Kingdom and Southern Rhodesian Governments, November 1963–November 1965*, CMND 2807, p. 132.

14. Wilson, op. cit., p. 162.

15. UN A/6300/Add. I Part II (7 October 1966), App. 1, pp. 1089.

16. ibid., pp. 110–12.

17. *Economic Aspects of a Declaration of Independence*, CSR 15 (Salisbury Government Printer, 1965).

18. *Rhodesia – Documents relating to Proposals for a Settlement, 1966*, CMND 3171, p. 3.

19. *Hansard*, Vol. 770, col. 1097.

20. CMND 2807, p. 143.

21. ibid., p. 105.

22. ibid., p. 86.

23. Res. 2022/XX Africa Anno XXVI No. 1 (Rome, March 1971), Marion Mushkat, p. 38.

24. *A Principle in Torment* (New York: United Nations, 1969), UN Security Council Resolution 202 (1965), p. 36.

25. *A Principle in Torment*, op. cit., Resolution 20204/XX.

26. Wilson, op. cit., p. 119.

27. See Wilson, op. cit., p. 116. These views were also presented to the author in various interviews.

28. *Sunday Times*, 14 November 1971.

29. Wilson, op. cit., pp. 181–3.

30. Bottomley to author, March 1972.

31. D. Owen, *The Politics of Defence*, p. 115.

32. The phrase was used by Cledwyn Hughes, interviewed in March 1972.

33. Owen, op. cit., p. 216.

34. Kenneth Young, in *Rhodesia's Independence*, op. cit.

35. *Hansard*, 11 November 1965.

36. Interview, March 1972.

37. John Rex, 'The Race Relations Catastrophe', in *Matters of Principle: Labour's Last Chance* (Penguin, 1968), p. 82.

38. Wilson, op. cit., pp. 283–6.

39. *Hansard*, Vol. 770, col. 1151.

40. *Hansard*, Vol. 737, col. 1677.

41. *Hansard*, 12 November 1965.

42. *Rhodesia's Independence*, op. cit., p. 43.

43. Young, loc. cit., p. 319.

44. *Hansard*, 11 November 1965.

45. Interview with the author, February 1972.

46. Wilson, op. cit., p. 196.

47. ibid.

48. Interview, February 1972.

49. C. Legum, *The United Nations and Southern African ISIO monographs*, First Series, No. 3 (Institute for the Study of International Organisations, University of Sussex, 1970), p. 28.

50. *Why Minority Rule Survives* (International Defence and Aid Fund, 1969), p. 25.

51. Robert McKinnel, 'Sanctions and the Rhodesian Economy', *Journal of Modern African Studies*, Vol. VII, No. 4. (1969), pp. 562, 578.

52. R. B. Sutcliffe, 'The Political Economy of Rhodesian Sanctions', *Journal of Commonwealth Political Studies*, Vol. VII, No. 2.

53. Owen, op. cit., p. 115.

54. A. Darnborough, *Labour's Record in Southern Africa*, p. 2.

55. CMND 2807, p. 85.

56. *Objective: Justice*, Vol. I., No. 1. (United Nations, New York, 1967), p. 42.

57. Darnborough, op. cit. pp. 9–12; and Abdul S. Minty, *South Africa's Defence Strategy*.

58. Darnborough, op. cit., p. 2.

59. ibid., p. 5.

60. Barbara Rogers, *South Africa's Stake in Britain*.

61. ibid.

62. Quoted in Minty, op. cit., p. 17.

63. ibid., p. 9.

64. ibid.

65. *The Life and Times of Private Eye* (Penguin, 1971), p. 169; Minty, op. cit., p. 3.

66. Interview, February 1972.

67. *Spectator*, 27 January 1966.

68. *Rhodesia's Independence*, op. cit., p. 49.

69. Wilson, op. cit., pp. 180–81.

70. 'Lost Purposes and Wrong Priorities: The Foreign Record', in *Matters of Principle*, op. cit., p. 48.

71. *Labour and Inequality*, ed. Peter Townsend and Nicholas Bosanquet.

72. R. Miliband, *Parliamentary Socialism: A Study in the Politics of Labour*, p. 348. For an analysis of the forces operating on reformist political parties in power, see also R. Miliband, *The State in Capitalist Society*. Barry Hindess has documented the increasing divorce of the party from the working class and the growth of a pragmatic, technocratic orientation within the party. See *The Decline of Working Class Politics*, particularly Chapter 4. Paul Foot has analysed the dynamics of the relationship of Wilson to the Labour left, dynamics which were

important in preventing the emergence of any consistent opposition to the government from a socialist position. The left frequently saw Wilson as one of them – Frank Allaun for instance saw Wilson as 'the best Labour leader since Keir Hardie', and the left invariably saw Wilson as preferable to any alternative leader. Many of the government's critics were quickly absorbed into the government in one capacity or another, only Eric Heffer refusing the offer of a position. ('Harold Wilson and the Labour Left', *International Socialism*, 33, Summer 1968, pp. 18–26.) See also Tom Nairn, 'The Nature of the Labour Party', in *Towards Socialism*, ed. P. Anderson and R. Blackburn.

73. R. Miliband and J. Saville, 'Labour Policy and the Labour Left', *The Socialist Register*, 1964, p. 154.

74. Perry Anderson, 'Critique of Wilsonism', *New Left Review* 27 (September/October 1964), p. 17.

75. Minty, op. cit., p. 11.

76. Owen, op. cit., p. 113.

77. Quoted in W. Warbey, *Ho Chi Minh and the Struggle for an Independent Vietnam* (London, 1972), p. 47.

Chapter 7 – The makings of a sell-out

1. *Sunday Times*, 19 January 1969.

2. G. Arnold and A. Baldwin, *Token Sanctions of Economic Warfare*; and G. Arnold and A. Baldwin, *Sanctions against Rhodesia, 1965 to 1972*.

3. CMND 2807, p. 142.

4. ibid., p. 125.

5. ibid., p. 132.

6. CMND 3171, p. 89.

7. ibid., p. 71, clause 19; p. 90.

8. ibid.

9. Judith Todd, *The Right to Say No*, p. 177.

10. D. G. Clarke, 'The Political Economy of the Republican Constitution of Rhodesia', *Rhodesian Journal of Economics*, Vol. IV, No. 3, p. 22.

11. R. First, J. Steele and C. Gurney, *The South African Connection: Western Investment in Apartheid*, pp. 64, 65.

12. Michael Faber, 'The Distribution of Income between Racial Groups in Southern Rhodesia', *Race*, Vol. II, No. 2 (1961), p. 42.

13. N. M. Shamuyarira, *Crisis in Rhodesia*, p. 35; and E. Mlambo, *Rhodesia: The Struggle for a Birthright*, p. 131.

14. Quoted in *Rhodesian Perspective*, ed. T. Bull, p. 64.

15. 'Rhodesia After Pearce', *Africa*, August 1972.

16. *Economic Survey of Rhodesia* (Salisbury, 1972), pp. 22–3.

17. *Guardian*, 31 January 1971.

18. *Sunday Times*, 28 November 1971; for clarification of the calculations, see also *Sunday Times*, 5 December 1971.

19. CMND 4964, para. 240.

20. *Observer*, 5 December 1971.

21. Editorial in *Rhodesia Herald*, 26 November 1971.

22. *International Herald Tribune*, 2 December 1971.

23. Mlambo, op. cit., p. 18; *Guardian*, 3 January 1972.

24. *Guardian*, 1 December 1971.

25. *Rhodesia Herald*, 3 December 1971.

26. Editorial in *Sunday Times*, 28 December 1971.

27. *Anglo-Rhodesian Relations: Proposals for a Settlement*, CMDRR 46 (1971); *Daily Telegraph*, 1 December 1971.

28. Press statement issued by Amnesty International, 26 November 1971.

29. *Guardian*, 20 January 1972.

30. *Proposals for a Settlement*, op. cit., pp. 6–7.

31. CMDRR 46 (Salisbury, 1971), p. 1.

32. ibid.

33. CMND 4964, p. 92.

34. E. Mlambo et al., *No Future Without Us*, p. 20.

35. ibid., p. 22.

36. CMND 4964, para. 351.

37. ibid., para. 361.

38. ibid., para. 390.

39. CMND 4906, para. 346.

40. CMND 4964, para. 101.

41. M. Jones, *Rhodesia: The White Judges' Burden*.

42. CMND 4964, para. 89.

43. *Hansard*, Vol. 837, col. 1232.

44. CMND 4964, para. 417.

45. *Hansard*, Vol. 838, col. 1758.

Chapter 8 – Rhodesia or Zimbabwe?

1. CMND 4964, para. 311.

2. A. K. H. Weinrich, *Chiefs and Councils in Rhodesia*, p. 13.

3. J. F. Holleman, *Chief, Council and Commissioner*, pp. 67, 68.

4. ibid., p. 316.

5. *Report of the Secretary for Internal Affairs for the Year* 1970, CMD RR 30 (Salisbury, 1971), p. 44.

6. Holleman, op. cit., p. 357.

7. U.N. Economic Commission, 4/III (February 1973), para. 293.

8. *Cabora Bassa and the Struggle for Southern Africa* (World Council of Churches, Geneva, 1971).

9. M. J. Christie, *The Simonstown Agreement – Britain's Defence and the Sale of Arms to South Africa.*

10. W. Minter, *Portuguese Africa and the West*, pp. 132–4.

11. *Afrique-Asie*, September 1972.

12. J. Davis, 'The US Supports White Rule in Southern Africa: Military and Strategic Aspects', *Southern Africa*, No. 6 (June/July 1972); D. Robinson, 'Alternatives to Nixon Policy on Southern Africa', *Southern Africa*, No. 7 (August/September 1972).

13. Robinson, op. cit.

14. W. J. Pomeroy, *Apartheid Axis: The United States and South Africa* (New York, 1971), p. 47.

15. R. First, J. Steele and C. Gurney, *The South African Connection: Western Investment in Apartheid*, p. 130.

16. R. Gibson, *African Liberation Movements. Contemporary Struggles Against White Minority Rule*, p. 178.

17. *Objective: Justice* (United Nations, New York, April/May/June 1972), p. 29.

18. *Zimbabwe Review*, Algeria (undated – 1965).

19. *Zimbabwe Review*, Vol. II, Nos. 3–4 (March/April 1970).

20. ZANU communiqué of 4 January 1973.

21. Amilcar Cabral, *Revolution in Guinea: An African People's Struggle*, ed. R. Handyside, p. 72.

22. 'La Difficile Naissance de la guerilla rhodesienne', (*Les Temps modernes*, No. 292, November 1970), p. 910.

23. Cabral, op. cit., p. 75.

24. *Zimbabwe, Babylon*, Vol. I, No. 4, New York (15 January 1972).

25. E. Mlambo et al., *No Future Without Us: The Story of the African National Council in Zimbabwe.*

26. B. Davidson, *The Liberation of Guiné: Aspects of an African Revolution*, p. 48.

27. Cabral, op. cit., pp. 46, 61.

28. ibid., p. 61.

Index

More about Penguins and Pelicans

Penguinews, which appears every month, contains details of all the new books issued by Penguins as they are published. From time to time it is supplemented by *Penguins in Print*, which is a complete list of all titles available. (There are some five thousand of these.)

A specimen copy of *Penguinews* will be sent to you free on request. For a year's issues (including the complete lists) please send 50p if you live in the British Isles, or 75p if you live elsewhere. Just write to Dept EP, Penguin Books Ltd, Harmondsworth, Middlesex, enclosing a cheque or postal order, and your name will be added to the mailing list.

In the U.S.A.: For a complete list of books available from Penguin in the United States write to Dept CS, Penguin Books Inc., 7110 Ambassador Road, Baltimore, Maryland 21207.

In Canada: For a complete list of books available from Penguin in Canada write to Penguin Books Canada Ltd, 41 Steelcase Road West, Markham, Ontario.

The Penguin African Library

Libya

The Elusive Revolution

Ruth First

'By God I am confused', exclaimed Colonel Gadafi at one Libyan popular conference. Where Libya is concerned, who isn't?

Ruth First's main emphasis falls on the causes and consequences of the 1969 revolution, in which a group of young officers ousted the monarchy. This thorough survey provides a wealth of information about the religious, economic and social springs of Libyan politics, the sudden explosion of oil revenues and the fanatical – often naïve – pursuit of Arab unity. She introduces the reader to a twentieth-century social revolution based on the Koran; to an oil-rich state determined not to copy Kuwait; to a new centre of pan-Arabism which has almost invited the hostility of other Arab states; and to a régime which exhorts the people to embrace its historic role but suffocates all independent action.

Nevertheless this nation of under two million inhabitants has struck giant postures in recent years. Its strengths and weaknesses become clearer in the light of Ruth First's able study.

The Penguin African Library